# Talking about Dying

## memoirs and essays

Gabriel Moran

ISBN: 1481850547
ISBN-13: 9781481850544
Library of Congress Control Number: 2012908641
CreateSpace Independent Publishing Platform
North Charleston, SC

# Contents

# INTRODUCTION

The title of this book, *Talking about Dying*, indicates the two themes that run throughout the chapters, namely, death and language. During the past forty years death has become a fashionable topic or at least there are more books about "death and dying," the phrase made popular by Elisabeth Kübler-Ross at the end of the 1960s. There is still a question whether we have made progress in honestly and clearly talking about dying. Euphemisms about death are inevitable and sometimes beneficial but at times they are a denial of the facts of life.

I began teaching a course on death at the end of the 1970s and I continued to do so until 2009. At least a thousand undergraduate students took the course. I was always surprised and a little worried that so many young people were interested in death. How to study death remained a puzzle to me. Unlike other courses I taught, I could never feel entirely comfortable in confronting the emotions at work in a course on death.

When I started teaching the course, I felt distinctly unqualified because of a lack of experience. My role at first was to participate in a team-taught course. My two colleagues worked full-time with the dying; one worked with children who were dying or whose parents had just died. Those two women were the experts on dying; I was just someone who had read books. Like many people today I had reached adulthood without death touching me directly. But by the time I finished teaching the course, I had experienced the death of both parents, the death of two of my closest friends, and finally the death of my wife. Although both of my original teaching partners were no longer present, I felt I now had at least a base of experience to work from.

The first and longest chapter in this book is a memoir about the sickness and death of my wife, Maria Harris. The piece was originally written as therapy for myself and as information for a few hundred people who knew her well. At the beginning of the essay, I write that I was hesitant about attempting such a memoir because I had never written anything similar. I had no idea how to organize the story or how long it would be. But once I sat down to write the essay it poured out of me almost non-stop. I published it in the small-circulation newsletter that I edit, and I did not intend to do anything further with it. However, when I learned that it had been used with a class in a New York medical school, I decided it might speak to a larger population, especially to people dealing with the difficult issue of dementia.

The second chapter is an attempt to capture the experience of dying from the side of the patient – myself. As it happens, I did not die so the essay lacks a dramatic finish. The essay was published in the same newsletter and it too found its way into a medical school classroom, this time in Philadelphia. The original essay, written six months after cancer surgery, is supplemented by some thoughts a year after that. Maybe when the final run does happen I will add the concluding note.

The seven chapters that follow these two memoirs are further reflections on dying and especially the language we use when we try to talk about dying. I doubt that anyone finds it easy to talk about dying, or perhaps I just distrust anyone who seems completely at ease with the death of someone they love and with their own mortality. I would not deny, however, that there are older people who seem to have "befriended" death and who do not seem to fear dying.

A concern in these chapters is education which should include the reality of death. How a young child first encounters death can have important consequences throughout his or her life. A young child can cope with death if the adults provide a calm atmosphere. All the details need not be loaded upon a child but lying to a child about death is decidedly unhealthy.

A child's questions force adults to confront their own fear, confusion and inarticulateness about death. Adults have to be careful about using a code language about death that can be misleading to children who take phrases literally. My colleague recounted the case of a child who was terrified when she was told she would view grandma's body in the funeral parlor. She thought that "body" meant that the head would be missing. It is debatable whether a child viewing a corpse is a good idea; but everyone could probably agree that viewing a headless corpse is not.

Old people are not the main culprits for the disingenuous language that affects talk about dying. The clash of generations is not usually between the young and the old; instead the young and the old are aligned against the middle. That is especially the case when it comes to thoughts and talk about mortality.

The very young and the very old share a sense of the cycle of life and death; but the middle-aged have temporarily put that knowledge out of mind.

The problem seems to be greater among men than women. Men are generally less comfortable with acknowledging the frailties of the human body. Perhaps women will catch up with the men as more women compete in the business, political and sports worlds. At present, however, the women are still overwhelmingly the people who care for the babies and the sick and the dying. Women seek medical care much more readily than men do; most women do not suddenly discover at the age of thirty-five or forty that they are mortal.

The flight from mortality among the middle-aged is the chief source of the twists of language that affect talk about dying. It has become common to say that someone "passed away" (or even just "passed") rather than that the person died. Perhaps that is simply a gentler way of stating the fact of death. However, it is part of a pattern in which dying is seldom spoken about directly, even by people who deal with dying all the time. Surveys show that most patients say that they wish to be told if they are dying; physicians insist that most people do not wish to be told. Neither side is lying. People do have a right to know if they are dying but they may not be ready for the blunt truth all at once. Physicians have to learn to avoid lying about dire situations while at the same time they gradually deliver the bad news.

One development that I note in these chapters is the rehabilitation of some terms to make them legally and morally acceptable. The clearest examples are "suicide" and "euthanasia." I express some skepticism about this attempt to provide a more positive meaning to these terms. I am not totally opposed to hastening death in some circumstances. I do object to equating suicide or some forms of euthanasia with the phrase "dying with dignity." There is subterfuge at work in calling a ballot initiative for suicide "the death with dignity act." Is there anyone lobbying for "death with indignity"?

The ambiguous word that shows up in almost every chapter of this book is nature/natural. The ambiguity of "natural" cannot be eliminated but many people do not seem to realize how ambiguous the word is. "Nature" has repeatedly shifted in meaning during the more than twenty-five hundred years of its use. Before the seventeenth century the most common meaning of nature referred to what a thing is. Every living being has a nature; that includes the human being, although the humans have a very peculiar kind of nature. Originally, nature applied only to living beings but eventually even nonliving beings were said to have a nature. The term could also mean a summation of those beings so that nature could refer to all of life or to the mother of us all.

The near reversal of "nature" in the seventeenth century made it the opposite of "man," and the object for man's conquest. The language of man versus nature was new even though the process of humans' controlling their physical environment as well as their own bodies has ancient roots. What was different in modern times was the accumulation of knowledge together with the development of instruments of power to such an extent that "man" could have the sense of being master of nature. The success of the scientific/technological revolution was dramatic and widespread. By the twentieth century the effects of the revolution had affected almost every region of the world.

Living beings are those that are born, grow, decline and die. To the extent that humans participate in nature, they too go through that cycle. Modern science and its applications improved both the length and the quality of human life. One intractable problem that remained was death; at least it was a problem for a human being who had drives and ambitions that seemed cruelly mocked by the voice within that kept reminding the individual that it all goes down to the dust again. Some scientists held out hope that the last enemy death could be conquered though probably not soon enough to benefit the present generation. For most people what seemed to be a more realistic strategy was to try to forget their mortality and live as if they would never die.

Just as modern science and technology were seemingly achieving their greatest success, a crisis of confidence suddenly appeared. The horrendous wars of the twentieth century caused some people to wonder whether the human race had lost control of its marvelous inventions. That could happen because the human race itself was not unified and, as a result, one group of people could misuse technological instruments in the service of war and terror instead of peace and harmony. Some people wondered if the human race has some fatal flaw so that it was preparing its own self-destruction?

The violent conflicts within the human race were signs of an even more fundamental war between "man and nature." The assumption until the second half of the twentieth century was that man was winning one battle after another over nature. In a way it was true that humans were winning battles but the war against nature was another story. C.S. Lewis in a prescient 1948 book, *The Abo-*

*lition of Man*, described man's war against nature this way: "All Nature's apparent reverses have been but tactical withdrawals. We thought we were beating her back when she was luring us on. What looked to us like hands held up in surrender was really the opening of arms to enfold us forever."

The human race is now engaged in reimagining, rethinking, and restating the relation of humans to what embraces them. It is unclear yet whether the human race has enough time, skill, and humility to re-establish a more friendly and sustainable relation with its nonhuman kin. If the whole human race were engaged in such a quest, it very likely could manage this new revolution. Unfortunately, the human race is still wracked with its own internal violence and wars. While groups hassle and kill one another to possess luxuries, the necessities of life, including clean air, potable water, moderate temperatures, and healthful food, are neglected or destroyed.

The chapters in this book may have only a distant relation to these world-shaking problems of politics, economics, and ecology. Nonetheless, every human being who walks the earth has to confront the question of what to make of his or her death. The severe problems of political, economic and environmental systems are driven in part by misplaced attempts to avoid dying. The solutions to these complicated problems will take a multiplicity of skills and widespread cooperation across every kind of boundary. There will be no solutions, however, unless humans can live calmly with their own acknowledged mortality and do not demand of earthly things what earth cannot provide.

Religion is a topic that appears in a number of chapters. Religion was mainly on the side of nature in the war between "man and nature." Until the second half of the twentieth century it was assumed in the enlightened world that religion was disappearing, being located on the losing side of the war. Then religions seemed to make a comeback although it was more a case of coming out of hiding. What reappeared was often not a religious tradition rich in symbols, philosophy, ritual, and moral stability but instead a vague mystical sense on one side and, on the other side, a rigid fundamentalism that attempts to fight the modern world while being thoroughly a part of it.

The last two chapters of this book are an attempt to look at what religion, especially the Christian religion, might helpfully say and do about death. Taken at face value much of what religion says seems childish or preposterous. Nonetheless, religion is still a powerful force in the world. Even Christianity, which has declined in Europe, has continued to expand in most parts of the world. My premise is that even to reject the Christian view of life and death one first has to understand it, at least to some degree. Much of what was taken literally in the Christian past may deserve to be studied now for its metaphorical meaning. Concepts such as sin and grace, heaven and hell, prayer and sacrament, are worthy of inquiry as possibly embodying some ancient wisdom.

I do not deny that religions are the source of superstition, violence, and misogyny. They can also be a discipline of life, a comfort to the suffering, a source of moral courage, and a hope for a transformed world. No one knows whether ancient religious traditions can shed some of their bellicosity from the past and become factors in the repair of the human race's relation to its environment and be voices for peace among the nations.

The first step is acknowledging the complexity of religion and the need to understand the peculiar language and logic in religions. Otherwise, we are likely to be afflicted with religious passions that do not have the restraint of long-standing traditions. Human death requires a context that provides some meaning to human life. Religion will probably continue to be the main source for that context. And the basic religious doctrine might be a line from Samuel Beckett's *Endgame*: "To think perhaps that it won't all have been for nothing."

# CHAPTER ONE: IN PRAISE OF MARIA: A MEMOIR

This essay is a witness to the life of Maria Harris, focused on the last four years of her life, her death, and the immediate aftermath of her death. I was with her during nearly every hour of the four years of her illness and at the moment of her death on February 1, 2005. Immediately following her death many people asked me if I was going to write about her illness and death. I said that I did not think so. However, after nine months of reflection, I have decided to write this memoir. I do so while still having some misgivings. My ambivalence has taken the form of the following debate.

Should this Document Exist: Con

There are two reasons why I have thought that this essay should not be written, one pertaining to her, and one to me. On her side, people have a right to privacy even after they have died. When they have suffered from a long, debilitating sickness, there are details of their life which in written form should not go beyond a hospital chart or a psychiatrist's notes. If someone wants to share intimate details of their own life with a reading public, that is their right. But it can be exploitative if someone whom they trusted publishes such details.

For myself, I am ambivalent about writing this essay because I am unskilled at this literary genre. I seldom read personal memoirs because I so often find them either boring or sensationalistic. The decision to write about these traumatic years may seem to imply that I have come to some new or profound insight about the experience. The truth is it was mostly confusion from which I cannot claim to have attained any shred of wisdom that requires being shared with the public.

Should this Document Exist: Pro

Whatever my personal misgivings, this narrative is about her not me. Maria had an amazingly wide circle of friends who would appreciate knowing more about the end of her life. I have told some of them some of this story but it seems appropriate to put the whole story in writing for all of her friends. This is an extended letter to Maria's friends, people who I hope will appreciate the spirit in which it is written. The material here is neither embarrassing nor secret. Obviously, there are details of a person's sickness that do not need to be in print. But as a whole, the story of how Maria dealt with her sickness and dying has a beauty to it that should be acknowledged. She approached death as she had lived her life with courage, candor and a gentle sense of humor.

On my side, I will simply recount the facts as I remember them without worrying about literary style. I should admit that I am writing this partly for myself, to put on paper the memories that flood my mind. This seems to be the right time to do it when the memories are still fresh but with some distance from the moment of death. After a year, one's memory functions differently; the remembrances do not disappear but it becomes harder to locate the details properly.

Joan Didion's book, *The Year of Magical Thinking*, helped to tip the balance for me. Didion describes the death of her husband, John Gregory Dunne on Dec. 30, 2003, and the year that followed. She is a brilliant writer who creates a coherent whole out of numerous precise details and a roaming memory. I identified with many of the details in the book. I am not the skilled writer that she is but I nonetheless got the feeling that I could do something similar on a smaller scale, that is, lay out the facts in one's memory and do so with a spare style that does not strive for literary effect.

In what follows, I have relied solely on my memory. There are probably errors of fact, especially in citing dates. Perhaps later I will check some sources and make corrections. There is a scarcity of personal names, sometimes because of a conscious choice to protect the privacy of people. But sometimes it is due to my inability to recall many names. The absence of the names of dozens of people who were extraordinarily helpful does not signal a lack of gratitude on my part.

Nearly the entire story takes place either in Montauk, Long Island, or in New York City. In Montauk, a tiny fishing and retirement village at the tip of the island, Maria with her usual outgoingness had developed a group of women friends in the town. They were anxious to do anything they could to help during Maria's illness. However, for medical reasons it was preferable to spend most of the time in New York's Greenwich Village where we lived in an apartment owned by New York University.

People outside of New York can find it difficult to believe me when I say that during this time we were overwhelmed with kindness and compassion. From physicians and social workers to cab drivers and subway riders, people were unfailingly kind and helpful. Some of that reaction was undoubtedly due to Maria's personality which seemed to bring out the best in people. Illness dimmed that light but only death extinguished the sparkle of her personality.

A single moment in Good Samaritan hospital toward the end of her life captures a central characteristic of her life. She was no longer able to do anything for herself and could not carry on a conversation. I would turn on music to which she did not react but which I felt sure that she liked. I would sit in silence next to the bed, not knowing what else to do. On this day I decided at noon time to go downstairs and get some lunch. I did not know if she would understand my words but I always spoke on the assumption that she could comprehend. I told her that I was leaving to go downstairs but I would be back very shortly. She looked up at me and said clear as a bell: "Is there anything I can do for you?" I almost fell over because at that point she could hardly get a word out. As far as I can recall, that was the last complete statement she made. Friends who heard the story agreed that it was a fitting sentiment as a last expression. The essential kindness and goodness of her person shone through until the end, despite the ravages of a terrible disease.

## Backdrop

A few details of Maria's life will be helpful to understanding the last years of illness. Maria had studied music and taught in elementary schools. As a member of the Sisters of Saint Joseph of Brentwood, Long Island, she had studied for sixteen summers to earn her B.A. After that, her academic career moved quickly. After getting a master's degree at Manhattan College in 1967, she went straight through for her doctorate at Teachers College, Columbia University, in 1972. While studying for her degree she began work in the diocesan office of Rockville Center. She did superb work with the emerging group of people known as parish directors of religious education. In fact, her *DRE Book* helped to establish the field and give a name to the role. Very quickly she was in demand across the country, and for the rest of her life she was held in high regard by educators in Catholic parishes.

Her next move broadened the base of those who looked to her for support. In 1975 she became a professor at Andover Newton Theological School, a seminary outside of Boston. I was skeptical, wanting to know how an Irish Catholic girl from Brooklyn could possibly fit in with New England Baptists and Congregationalists. To my surprise – though I should have known better – she immediately became good friends with faculty members and one of the most popular teachers in the school.

After a few years she was appointed to the Howard Chair of Religious Education. At her installation, I was one of several speakers ("representing the Catholic Church"). I reflected on the fact that Maria was the first Roman Catholic faculty member of the school. And it was a school founded in 1807 "to counteract the influence of Unitarians, Atheists and Papists." I said that perhaps the founders were rolling over in their graves but I suspected that they would recognize that her presence brought to the school only vitality, intelligence, and a profound religious sensibility. That this indeed proved to be the case is evidenced by numerous written testimonies from faculty and former students on the school's web site in 2005.

Maria left the place where she was respected and loved only because she missed being in New York. She thought that she would like to teach for a semester each year and free lance for the other semester. By this time she was in demand as much from Protestant audiences as Catholic and she liked traveling to places around the United States and beyond. Not knowing if such an arrangement was a realistic possibility, she consulted with Vincent Novak who headed the Fordham program where she had taught as an adjunct before going to Andover Newton. When Father Novak heard what she was looking for, his response was: Why not come to Fordham and do that. She was surprised at being able to arrange the deal so easily but Fordham knew that the luck was on their side.

Maria taught at Fordham for a semester a year until she decided to be self-employed in the mid 90's. She had more than enough to keep her busy. I did not fully appreciate how hard she worked until I went through her papers after she died. Most people who are regularly invited to speak on a few themes have a stock speech to which they give some local coloring. But what I found in Maria's materials is that she prepared each weekend workshop in meticulous detail, both the content of what she would say and how she would present it. She was a very engaging speaker from a lecture platform and she was even better in a classroom with a small group of students.

Maria always thought of herself as a writer by accident. She never set out to be an author of books. Her first books simply came along with her teaching. I think the book *Fashion Me a People* in 1989 was a breakthrough for her in her self-image as an author. Craig Dykstra gave her a lot of help in preparing that text and she got a better sense of what an author is. That book is still selling well, being used as a curriculum guide in Protestant seminaries and Catholic programs of religious education.

It nonetheless happened that when a literary agent pushed her to write a book on women and spirituality, she dashed off an outline for the purpose of getting rid of the agent. The agent went to Bantam Press and got a huge advance based on the outline. Writing *Dance of the Spirit* was perhaps the most difficult writing project she ever undertook. The result was a beautiful work that fully satisfied the Bantam editors and the book sold well. That experience led to a second book with Bantam. When Maria first proposed a book on older women and spirituality, Bantam was skeptical but she eventually persuaded them. This time Maria negotiated her own contract. After writing the book *Jubilee Time* for Bantam, she had some additional material that she thought might be made into a book for a church readership. She quickly put together a small volume, *Proclaim Jubilee!*

This book took note of the coming year 2000 which was about five years in the future. The year 2000 was a jubilee year in which debts are to be forgiven. For the years up to the new millennium she became a strong voice in the movement to forgive the debts of poor nations that were burdened with impossible interest payments. The New York newspaper, *Newsday*, did a Sunday feature on Maria's work in this area. She was invited to numerous parishes to speak on what individuals and parishes could do for the jubilee year. A few parishes bought copies of the book for each of its parishioners.

She had two other themes that especially interested her and drew invitations. She was invited to speak to many women's groups and to wrestle with the issues of the feminist movement. She was especially interested in the development of young girls and often spoke to women faculty of high schools and colleges. A further issue dear to her heart was Jewish-Christian relations. She often worked with the *Facing History* curriculum that deals with twentieth-century genocide. She became deeply committed to the appreciation of the Jewish people and their history. We once were attending a program of Jewish music in a German church. On noticing that Maria was weeping, a Dutch colleague asked me if Maria was Jewish. She had strong emotional reactions to works of art and music.

Maria's father had died when she was eight years old, a traumatic experience that affected her deeply. Her mother, Mary Harris, taught in the New York City school system to support Maria and her brother Tom. The family was a close knit unit. Maria got much of her winning personality and energetic drive from her mother. Mary Harris died in 1991 at the age of 93. She suffered from dementia in the last few years of her life (the majority of people over 85 years old have some degree of dementia). She was in a nursing home for about five years. I can picture Maria singing to her mother amid the cacophony in the nursing home. Her mother was seemingly at peace but not conscious of what was going on around her. But the sound of Maria's singing would light up her face.

Maria's brother Tom was a gentle and kind man. Maria thought the world of him and they remained close throughout their lives. Tom had been head of the pressman's union at the *New York Times.* He patiently dealt with the seemingly endless difficulties that his wife had. He had just retired at age 67 to take up some serious golf when he was struck down with dementia. One Sunday morning on returning from church he could not put the car in the garage. His decline was precipitous from that moment. It involved violent behavior, something utterly out of character for him, but a phenomenon not uncommon among men with dementia.

He had to be moved four times because the hospital or the nursing home could not handle his behavior. I remember one particularly harrowing experience when visiting him at Pilgrim State Hospital. I had the impression that each place that he went tried new drugs on him to control his behavior but the drugs quickly made things worse. When I went over his autopsy with a psychologist, I said that although it lists three causes of death I think what killed him were the drugs. She said "I think you are probably right."

At least the end was peaceful. I have a vivid memory of our visiting him in an ICU of the hospital where he died. A local priest known to both of us happened to be there at the same time. He said the Eucharist for the three of us at Tom's bed side. It was a religious moment that Maria always cherished. After Tom's death, Maria would say: "I don't want to hear people saying he is better off dead. That may be true but just don't say that to me now." She mourned deeply this last member of her immediate family.

She was also concerned that Tom had died of dementia and the disease appears to be at least partially genetic. Maria read that if a sibling dies of dementia, one's chances of having the disease increase by fifty percent. Maria was brilliant – except at math. I had to assure her that the statistic did not mean that she had a one in two chances of having the disease. I said that if five percent of people have dementia, then a fifty percent increase would mean that seven and a half percent of the population would get it. Her chances went from one in twenty to about one in fourteen. (I wasn't sure that the statistics meant that but I was sure her anxiety was exaggerated). The more important thing, I argued, was that she was a most unlikely candidate for the disease. It would not hit an active, healthy, intelligently creative person. I was dead wrong.

Maria and I met in 1966 at Manhattan College. Our first book was written in 1967 and caused some stir. We wrote together when opportunities presented themselves. We also team taught whenever we could. Our first attempts at team teaching were fairly disastrous. We each hit the students with all that we had. Eventually we learned to adjust to the rhythm of the other; our styles became complementary rather than additive.

At first I had more invitations and she came along as the junior partner. Rather quickly, she became the famous person and she would bring me along as part of the package. I learned a lot about teaching from her and still use some of her techniques in my classes. She was also the editor for everything that I wrote. She was excellent at editing and was inevitably right when she gently criticized my harsh tone or vague abstractions.

We were professional colleagues as well as loving partners. She used to tell people that we would spend two hours talking at breakfast. And then in the evening we would have the same conversation and get paid for it. That wasn't exactly how it worked but our last book, *Reshaping Religious Education*, actually did get written that way. In 1998 on the way back from teaching in Australia I suggested that we simply write down the table talk we had been having about our teaching.

In April of 2005 I was interviewed for an oral history of the 1960s catechetical movement. They wanted me to talk about Maria's part as well as my own. Maria's main influence had come later; mine was largely confined to the 1960's. I said in the interview that my voice in Catholic Church reform was effectively silenced by 1973 just as her voice began to be heard. I did feel that the things I cared about were not out of the picture. Maria and I collaborated on everything so that indirectly I still had some voice. She could say things in a way that did not alienate people. Even when she advocated fairly radical things, her opponents found it difficult to dislike her. Except when bans against me occasionally spilled over to her, she was always and everywhere in demand. In the 1970s she could playfully introduce herself as a priest of the diocese of Boston; no one missed the serious point she was making with a touch of humor.

She could charm most men right out of their socks. This included a fair number of bishops with whom she disagreed but who never banned her appearance in their dioceses. In her eulogy I told the story of one of the most conservative Cardinals in the U.S. church who took a shine to her. I don't think he had a clue as to what she was talking about. He called her aside and told her she could call him Father John. She received friendly notes afterward. I would often ask her what she and Father John were up to.

I think she was at her best in giving encouragement to young women that she met in the course of her travels. She had a talent for spotting bright young women who were on the shy side and just needed a little encouraging so as to let their light shine. She did not make a project of such people; it just seemed to happen. She would become friends quickly and deeply. To this day it puzzles me how she did that. Strong bonds of friendship take time to develop and require continual cultivation. I cannot figure out how she had enough time to sustain so many lasting friendships. When she was with anyone, she conveyed a sense that he or she was the most important person in her life; and for the present they were. At the funeral, several people said to me jokingly: "And I thought I was her best friend." I have a list of women in many U.S. states and several foreign countries who were her best friend.

The fifteen years before her illness was an idyllic time for us. We were about as happy as human beings can be. We were both doing what we loved to do and what we believed was important work. We traveled to many parts of the world and met wonderful people. When home we had the best of city life and our small piece of paradise at the ocean. I picture Maria sitting in the hot tub in Montauk on a cool, Fall evening. She has a glass of wine in her hand and is saying: "How could a couple of people like us possibly be so lucky?"

## Ominous Signs (Summer, 2000 to Summer, 2001)

If dementia is in fact genetic in origin, then no doubt there are telltale signs before its onset. Usually the signs are not obvious except in retrospect. The most extensive research project on dementia is being done on a congregation of six hundred nuns who have agreed to submit to annual tests and to have autopsies. One surprising finding has been that it was possible to identify from their teenage handwriting in the novitiate which woman would later have dementia. Certainly, early onset of Alzheimer's (people in their 40s and 50s) runs in families and is especially devastating.

I think Maria began to have problems in the middle of the year 2000 but at the time I thought any problem was minor and passing. Maria was amazingly free of health problems. I used to fill out for her those omnipresent forms on clip boards that every physician's office gives you. The form asks you for a complete medical history. I don't think they believed me when I would turn in the form with nothing checked. She had suffered no serious illnesses or surgery, with the exception of carpel tunnel syndrome acquired from typing at the computer.

The first noticeable problem came on a trip to Israel in July 2000. We were going to a meeting of an organization called ISREV (International Seminar on Religious Education and Values). Both of us had been members since 1980. Among the hundred or so members from about thirty countries, Maria was a bright light, livening up both the academic and social aspects of the meeting. Maria leading the group in singing on the last night of the conference was always a high point.

We had made our tickets through London because we planned to stop in London for a few days on our return. London was one of the places Maria most loved and we usually managed to get there once a year and spend a lot of time in museums. I knew the Tate Gallery better than any New York museum. The trip started badly; British Airways had problems with two toilets on the plane which delayed the flight four hours. We knew as we took off from Newark that we had missed the connecting flight to Tel Aviv. British Airways did have the decency to put us up in the Heathrow Hilton for a day and we watched the last day of the British Open as Tiger Woods wiped out the field.

I also spent that Sunday afternoon frantically trying to get through to the meeting's organizers in Jerusalem. Both Maria and I had duties on the first day of the conference and I had to inform them we were not going to be there. We finally did get there embarrassed to be twenty-four hours late. Maria seemed tired which was natural enough but it turned out she had an infection that required medical attention. At the time it just seemed a bother; she had developed a similar problem on the fifteen hour flight from Seoul a few years earlier. Maria was fascinated by the medical care she received from a Palestinian physician. Still, she was subdued for the whole conference. It proved to be the last conference she was able to attend.

When we got back to New York, she began talking about retirement. As I noted earlier, the year 2000 was her busiest time ever with invitations to speak on jubilee. I encouraged her to cut back on work, that we did not need the money, and that she was really free to do whatever she felt like doing. I did not think she would be happy if she just stopped. I tried to think along with her how she might take work close to home that did not require a plane ride and a motel stay. She did retreat work in two places that are an easy drive from Montauk. And there were plenty of places within a convenient train ride from New York. She had commitments until the end of the year but she stopped taking invitations beyond that.

She had some uneasy moments at presentations that Fall but I still thought it was just overwork and that she needed only rest. But she had an experience in Erie, Pennsylvania, in the late Fall that shocked her. She was doing a weekend workshop and on the Saturday afternoon her mind went completely blank. She was terribly embarrassed at having to cancel the remainder of the program, even though her hosts were only concerned for her health. This incident was indeed worrisome but one could still hope that the problem was a passing blip. For her that was the end of what she had been doing so well for twenty-five years. She feared having a repeat of the forgetting.

I tried to coax her into taking on a non-threatening situation. I said that the women at Cor Maria retreat center in Sag Harbor where she had a remaining commitment would understand if a problem developed. The director, Ann Marino, was a close friend and many of the women who attended were friends of Maria from Montauk. I quoted Rilke: "If tigers come into the temple, make that part of the ritual." But a shift of personality had begun. She had always been self-confident, assertive, and direct. Talking in public had never been fear-inducing. Over the next few years we had to have a near reversal of personalities. I had to take the lead in situations where she had always covered for my social ineptitude. She became dependent in ways that she had always avoided.

In the months that followed she became very jumpy. She used to refer to having the heeby-jeebys. Her primary care physician, who was a heart specialist, could not find anything wrong. She sent Maria to a psychiatrist. His first approach was to get Maria to draw on spiritual resources. He was taken by her background and personality. When meditation did not work he switched to medication. He tried a series of drugs, each of which produced a bad reaction. I think each of them was an anti-depressant but depression was not her problem. On one occasion in the Spring of 2001 I was in New York for my teaching duties and she was in Montauk. I got a frantic phone call at 4 AM. She was almost incoherent but said that she was calling the ambulance service to take her to Southampton Hospital. I did not know what to do. But she called back at 7 AM to say she was better. When the volunteer EMS team arrived she was embarrassed to tell them it was a false alarm. They assured her it was not a problem for them; they were glad for her that the ambulance was not needed.

The main problem at this point seemed to be the psychiatrist whose trial and error approach to drugs was not working. She left him but we did not have a ready replacement. We were hoping that with rest and without drugs she would regain her zip (her hairdresser in East Hampton insisted that was the remedy and Maria seemed to believe in her hairdresser's wisdom). When we visited my family in April, they noticed that Maria seemed tired and somewhat withdrawn, not the way she usually was at family gatherings. In April she also came to my class on Twentieth Century Philosophy. She was always a burst of energy when she came to my classes as a guest speaker. On this occasion she gave it her best but it was the first time ever that she did not make a strong impression.

In July, 2001, I went to teach in Brisbane, Australia. We had previously taught at the Catholic University of Australia and they had invited us back. They were more interested in her but I offered to do it alone and they agreed. As the time approached, I did not want to break the long standing commitment. But I should not have gone because I was a physical wreck. I had been suffering all year from undiagnosed lime disease. In March the lime disease brought on tinnitus (loud noise in the head that made hearing difficult) and led to unnecessary knee surgery in May. The lime disease was finally diagnosed the week when I was to travel but that meant starting on a regimen of strong antibiotics.

Because I did not want to leave Maria alone for a long period, I went to Brisbane and returned within a week, teaching a thirty hour graduate course while I was there. I can still picture Maria as I was leaving her at JFK; she looked confused and frightened. She who had been breezing through airports every week for many years was concerned about finding her way out to the street. I repeatedly explained where to go to get a taxi that would take her home. I called each night from the motel in Brisbane where I stayed. We talked at great length (the motel keeper thought there must have been a mistake on the phone bill until I told him that I had in fact made those calls). She seemed calm but very lonely.

For her birthday in August I gave her what would seem to an outsider a strange gift. I told her that I would renew my driver's license (after a 45 year hiatus). I would then be able to take over some of the driving if she wished me to do so. I was not sure how she would take the offer. Giving up the car keys is often one of the most difficult steps for someone in an early stage of dementia. Maria liked to drive. It was for her, as for many people, a chief sign of her independence. Since I have had a lifelong hatred of the automobile, I was happy to reverse the usual roles in which the man is assumed to be number one driver.

I was relieved that Maria accepted my offer enthusiastically. She did not sense any plot to take away her keys nor at that moment did I have any plan to do that. But I sensed that it might become necessary in the not too distant future so I had better start preparing the way. She did not seem to be having problems and she continued to do some of the driving. At the end there might have been some danger but fortunately she never had an accident. The last time I remember her driving was at the end of November when I had to go into Southampton Hospital for my lime disease. I was still uneasy driving through the Hamptons and I asked her to drive part of the way. She never lost her confidence driving but she later enjoyed being in the passenger seat.

In August, Maria's friend, Rosemary Crumlin from Melbourne, visited with us in Montauk. Rosemary always seemed to find a way to go through New York on the way to anywhere else. Maria had a great fondness for Rosemary. They had met in 1985 when Maria spent six weeks teaching at the National Pastoral Institute in Melbourne, where Rosemary was the director. Through phone calls and periodic visits they managed to keep in touch. I often said you know someone is a good friend if she travels 12,000 miles to visit you.

Rosemary was struck by Maria's change of appearance from the previous year. She was concerned about several things that Maria was doing, including driving. On two evenings, Maria had what later I came to call hallucinations. When we were sitting and talking in our apartment, Maria began to see a different person than Rosemary. Later, she dismissed the moment as a curious mistake. But on another evening she had a kind of vision. Rosemary awoke to find Maria standing over her and asking: "Are you an angel?" That was a more shocking experience, not unpleasant but definitely not a run of the mill event.

Rosemary is an unusually insightful, honest, and direct person. She took me aside and asked: "Has Maria been diagnosed yet?" I was taken aback by the question because I was still denying what was becoming obvious. I reluctantly had to admit that Rosemary was seeing the situation more clearly than I was. I appreciated her candor and concern.

The incident that pushed my thinking over the edge happened in New Hampshire later that month. We were visiting with my three sisters and my brother. Maria had the greatest affection for my siblings (and they, her). She had only her brother for family and now he was gone. My family had become her family. On Saturday evening the family sat around the dinner table, talking for hours as is our wont. Maria, however, was not in the conversation at all. I finally excused us and I went upstairs to the bedroom with her.

While we were getting ready for bed she suddenly asked: "Who was the woman in the red dress?" I was flabbergasted by the question. Maria had known my sister Louise for almost forty years. She then proceeded to ask about each of the people at the table, every one of whom she had known well for years. At that moment what crossed my mind was the thought: At some time in the future she is probably going to ask me: "And who are you?" I was right. The "some time in the future" was exactly a year later.

Diagnosis (Oct., 2001 to Nov., 2001)

At the end of the summer of 2001, it was apparent that Maria needed help but I did not know where to turn. Then, completely out of the blue, Maria received a phone call from a psychiatrist she had seen in Boston more than twenty years ago. She had not seen her since but Maria tended to leave a strong impression on the people she met. Apparently without any instigation, this woman called and asked Maria how she was. Perhaps sensing a problem from something conveyed in the conversation, the woman said that if Maria ever wanted to talk to a psychiatrist she had a friend she could recommend. This psychiatrist was in the East 70s, an easy trip from where we lived on East 8th street.

Maria took up the suggestion and made an appointment. But getting there turned out to be a problem. Maria was suddenly fearful and confused about using the subway. It was a simple trip as I explained over and over. She still managed to get lost on the train and confused about getting into the woman's building. The woman was very kind and much impressed by Maria; nonetheless, she did not seem to know where to begin. By the third visit it was clear that I would have to accompany her. And anyway the psychiatrist wanted to talk to us together. Maria did not see much point in what was going on and frankly I was frustrated, too. However, in early October the psychiatrist called me and said she was concerned that Maria had physical and mental problems which she could not treat. What she did was to get us an immediate appointment at the Neurological Institute of Columbia Presbyterian Hospital.

After meeting with a neurologist at the hospital we went back for a whole day of testing. Maria was exhausted by a battery of psychological tests that lasted about five hours. What little skill she had in math was now gone so the test was endlessly frustrating. After that day she went for various physical tests, including an MRI of the brain. Finally, after a wait of six weeks we were given an appointment to get the results. We met with the neurologist that we had initially seen.

Both Maria and I expressed our fear of Alzheimer's. The neurologist provided a relief by first saying that it was not Alzheimer's. She said she was fairly certain of what was the matter but one symptom was missing. She asked Maria if she had ever hallucinated. Maria told her about mistaking Rosemary for an angel. The neurologist said that confirms the diagnosis. "You have Lewy Bodies," she said. I asked her how to spell the word. I did not think I had ever encountered the term. Actually, I had seen it before on the autopsy report of Tom Harris, Maria's brother. At that time it had not registered in my memory. My second question was: "What is it?" Her response was: "Do you have a computer?" When I said I did, she said: "Look it up on the Internet." To put it mildly, I was surprised by her reply. I said: "Don't you have a pamphlet or something you can tell me?" She said no, she did not. She wrote a prescription for the drug Aricept and told us to come back in six months. When we protested that was too long, she said to come back in three months.

I left the meeting puzzled but with a ray of hope. We had a name for the disease and a possible treatment. I was unacquainted with Aricept, the standard drug for Alzheimer's. Maria was familiar with it, so she knew more than I did about what the prescription meant. Maria's concern was that she had read that Aricept is only effective for six months. That is not true but the effectiveness of Aricept is still a debatable issue.

When we got home I immediately went to the computer. When I called up the literature on Dementia with Lewy Bodies, the first sentence I read was: "This disease is progressive, completely destructive, and always fatal." The news did not get any better after that. I looked in vain for any glimmer of hope. The description of the disease said that people live with it an average of seven years. Averages in such a case tell you nothing about an individual. One person might live one year, another person ten or twenty years. With Maria's health record she was not in imminent risk of death. But living for years or decades with a destroyed mind was truly dreadful. I am sure there are worse things in the world but at that moment I could not think of anything worse than watching the person you love slowly losing her mind.

I was furious at the neurologist, much of it displaced anger. First thing Monday morning I called, hoping to learn something – anything – that would be helpful and positive. I was told that she returned phone calls only between 3 and 5 PM on Fridays. That added to my ire but I said I would be sitting by the phone from 3 to 5 on Friday. Come Friday I waited until it was after 5 PM. When I called her office, I was told that she had been busy. I concluded that she did not want to talk to me. At that point I didn't want to talk to her, either. I was disgusted at her handling of the situation. On reflection I guessed that she did not want to discuss the horror of the disease in front of Maria. But she could have taken me aside and said something human to human. She is supposedly a brilliant researcher but her interpersonal skills left room for improvement.

We went back in three months and received an additional drug. Maria was subjected to more long mental tests. She resisted doing the full line of testing; they obviously thought she was a good candidate for research and asked us to participate. I did urge Maria to keep going back because I thought that if any breakthrough in treatment occurred this Institute was a place that would know. Columbia Presbyterian is one of the four main research centers in New York for Alzheimer's. Later, I tried to switch to NYU Medical, one of the other four. I was told that they were interested only in people with Alzheimer's not Lewy Bodies.

Dementia with Lewy Bodies can most simply be described as a combination of Alzheimer's and Parkinson's. Maria had lately complained about stiffness in her left arm. I did not connect that to the other problem she was having but it was evidence of the "Parkinsonian dimension" of the Lewy Bodies. Alzheimer's is the main form of dementia so that many people equate the two words. Lewy Bodies is the second most common form of dementia but I found that many medical people had never heard of it.

Alzheimer's was first diagnosed in 1907 by Dr. Alois Alzheimer. For more than half a century, the disease given his name was thought to be a rare disease found among middle-aged people. Amazingly, no one made the connection between the "senility" of the elderly and this supposedly rare disease of people in their 40s and 50s. Hardly any research was done until 1980, a fact that I think is one of the great tragedies of twentieth-century medicine. Lewy Bodies was not diagnosed until the 1980s so that there is even less research on it than on Alzheimer's. The treatment of Lewy Bodies is difficult because of the physical and mental dimensions. The drugs for one side of the problem can interfere with drugs for the other side. The relation of the two treatments has to be carefully calibrated.

How much progress has been made in research on dementia is unclear. I had thought that a breakthrough might be just on the horizon. One constantly sees reports in the press of discoveries in the area. The only infallible test that a person has the disease is an autopsy. Despite the advances in studying the brain, researchers are still at the beginning in trying to track the growth of plaques in the brain that destroy short-term memory. At the 2003 meeting of the main researchers, there seemed to be little agreement on where we are. Some of the experts were skeptical that the present drugs had any effect at all.

I never told Maria the whole story of Lewy Bodies. By this time the computer was beyond her so she had to rely on my reports. When she would ask me what I had read, I never lied to her but I also did not share all that I knew. I think she was able to maintain the fiction that Lewy Bodies was not as bad as Alzheimer's though in fact it is worse. I do not know if she really believed that, but I was not about to correct her false belief.

I know that research is important and I wanted to be cooperative with the Neurological Institute. Nonetheless, my primary concern was getting clinical help. Going up to 170th street every six months was not going to be enough. Maria was attached to her primary care physician of many years. The woman was always kind and available to give what help she could. I did not think she was the right person to help us. I was still innocent of where to turn.

## Adjusting to the Horror (Dec., 2001 to August, 2002)

After an initial shock, human beings have a resilient tendency to adjust to whatever the situation is. Conditions of life that a few hours, days, or months previous would have seemed intolerable can become the "normal." One has to try to live with whatever has become the day to day experience. There is a blessing in not having to look into the abyss at every moment of the day. There can also be a disadvantage in shortening one's perception, thinking only of managing the immediate situation. Both of us started living in what the literature would probably call "denial" but denial is not all bad (as Kübler-Ross acknowledged while she placed it first in the stages of dying).

Maria sometimes would ask: "What is going to happen to me?" I would answer – truthfully – "I don't know; no one knows." Both of us knew that the long term prognosis was horrible. For the care giver, the later stages of dementia are the worst to observe. For the patient, the earlier stages must be the worst, when one is fully aware of what is happening. For my part, I would sometimes think: This is the worst experience of my life. But then I would also think: This may be the first time in my life that I am doing something that I am sure is good.

Hannah Arendt wrote that only really bad people have good consciences. That is, most of us most of the time, live with conflicts of conscience; we constantly submit our motives and actions to re-evaluation. In this case, however, I knew exactly where I had to be, what I was called to do, and why I was doing it. She would sometimes ask: Why are you doing this for me? That question had a very simple answer: I am doing for you exactly what I know you would do for me.

An extraordinary moment occurred in December, 2001. Maria's dearest friends invited her to a beautiful spot across from New York harbor called Breezy Point. I was not invited; it was a women-only event which I fully understood. A dozen or more of her friends wished to celebrate the greatness of her life while she was still able to join in the ritual. From what I gathered later, it was an event of profound joy and sorrow. As her obituary in *Newsday* noted, not many people would have the courage to take part in what was essentially a good bye to her life of sanity. Such an event could have been cruel but the women knew Maria well and the ritual supported the mix of emotions that was inevitable. Maria knew that day exactly what was at stake but her only feeling later was gratitude for the care shown by the women. They could have waited a little longer but they wanted to be sure that Maria could fully participate in the music, prayers, and conversations of the day.

In an effort to keep things normal, I went ahead with plans to use our time-share in Aruba. We owned week one in Divi Village where we had gone many times. I thought it would be a good break from the winter cold and a way to forget for a while. I was just coming off twenty-one days of intravenous antibiotics. The oral drugs had not been able to dislodge the deeply buried lime disease; my last hope was intravenous drugs. The treatment succeeded in killing off the spirochetes but it also knocked me around. Still, it seemed like a good idea to go to Aruba so as to sit on the beach and eat at our favorite restaurants.

The week did not go well. Maria came down ill after a few days; it was diagnosed as food poisoning. Although she was not very sick, they recommended she stay overnight in the hospital. When I left at the end of visiting hours, Maria had already made friends with the half dozen other women in the ward and they were pleased to have her with them. However, I got a call in the middle of the night that her behavior was disruptive and she was demanding to talk to me. On the phone she described terrible things happening in the hospital and claimed that people were trying to harm her. She had awakened in the night and being completely disoriented was frightened. I tried to calm her down and told her I would get her as soon as I was allowed into the hospital.

When I arrived, I found an exasperated hospital staff and patients in the ward who were upset at her behavior. It was several hours before I could get her released from the hospital. During that time she was not making much sense. However, as soon as we left the hospital, she seemed to return to a grasp of reality. Unfortunately, I got sick the next day which did not help the trip. But Maria was always at her best when she had to take care of me during sickness. We managed to make the journey home but I knew that was her last trip to Aruba.

As soon as we arrived back in New York, I set about with a more serious resolve to get some help. Her behavior in the Aruba hospital impressed upon me that her hold on reality was tenuous. I knew that the medical resources of New York City are almost limitless. I had good health insurance from the university. But it was a mystery to me how to start. I tried at first to get in touch with one of the nursing professors (NYU's nursing division has a palliative care unit). It was in between semesters and I was not able to reach the people who might give me advice.

I had the bright idea of calling the wife of one of my colleagues in the department. Cindy Hosay is a professor with a specialty in gerontology and was concerned about Maria. I knew she would at least sympathize with my plight and give me some advice but she did better than that. She put me in touch with a social worker. What I first needed was an assessment of the situation, someone who could oversee the problem as a whole and recommend specific steps.

This social worker, Kathy, proved to be an invaluable aide. She visited the apartment every other Monday. She would not only talk over things with Maria but she became the "gatekeeper" for other services we needed. She got us an appointment with a psychiatrist at Beth Israel Hospital who is an expert on Lewy Bodies. We began to see him on a regular basis and I finally had some confidence that the medicines were being carefully watched. On one occasion I made a separate appointment with him and he gave me a mini-course on the drugs involved. He was candid in admitting that there were no universal protocols; he had to feel his way with each patient.

The other big move in January was dumb luck on my part. In thinking about a primary care physician for Maria I went over to where I had found one for myself. NYU runs a health care center for students just a few blocks from us. There is a small faculty practice at this center, staffed at that time by two young women physicians. I spoke to the one who was available; she was willing to take on Maria but said that her colleague, who specialized in gerontology, was better suited for the job. I hoped that Maria would feel comfortable with this energetic young woman, Alexandra. She and Maria hit it off immediately and I had no difficulty in getting Maria to leave her primary care physician.

From that point on, Alexandra watched every aspect of Maria's health. After prescribing a B12 vitamin, she called and said it would be better if Maria came in every first of the month to receive a B12 shot. Each month when we came in, Maria would get a big hug and a generous amount of time for an examination of every aspect of her health. On two occasions, Alexandra phoned on a Saturday evening to recommend a change of treatment. On one of those occasions, she tracked us down in Montauk, called the pharmacy in Montauk which was closed, and finally found a pharmacy in East Hampton so that we could pick up the prescription first thing on Sunday morning.

One striking thing about many of the people we dealt with was they weren't just in the work for the money. Alexandra mentioned to me about six months into the shots that she had just discovered it was not covered by insurance. She did not like to ask – but would I pay for half of the expense already incurred. I said I would gladly pay the whole bill; she should not have to subsidize the cost of Maria's treatment. It was a similar case with Kathy, the social worker. She mentioned after about six months that she had not been paid yet. I was shocked, having assumed that she was receiving money from the insurance company. What really shocked me was that she would travel to the apartment, sit with Maria for an hour and supply me with useful information – while not getting paid. We fixed it up and got the proper papers filed. Filing health care claims and following up on delays and mistakes can be almost a full time job in itself.

With the social and medical aspects of Maria's illness being monitored by competent people, I could turn my attention to two other areas: nursing homes and legal affairs. I did not want to be suddenly forced into deciding about a nursing home in the midst of a future crisis. I wanted to get a sense of what the options were, even if all the possibilities were somewhat depressing. Maria was willing, if not enthusiastic, about taking a tour of a few nursing homes. I picked out two of the best in Manhattan. An inviting aspect was that each was within fifteen minutes of where we lived. However, both of us had bad vibes as soon as we walked into them.

I think that if you are not used to nursing homes the first impression is almost sure to be a shock. These two homes were clean, well-run, and equipped with numerous services for the patients. They still felt like warehouses. A lot of effort went into putting a happy face on sad and lonely lives. There were jarring elements, such as a loudspeaker system that would drive me crazy. The first place required documented proof that we had $100,000 in ready cash. The visits were worthwhile for us and on the whole not negative. But I hesitated before arranging visits to other places.

Maria would sometimes say: "Don't put me in a nursing home." I would reply: "I am not going to put you anywhere. Whatever is decided we will decide together." I was not sure I would be able to keep that promise but I would do so if at all possible. Some time during that year I received a message via a friend from the director of a nursing home in Brentwood, Long Island: "If ever and whenever Maria needs a nursing home, she should know that she has a place here." Nothing was more helpful to my sanity than receiving this message. I knew with Maria's history that no place would be as compatible as Brentwood. Through the next year and a half, having this available option was a great relief.

On the legal front, I gathered that I needed an elder care lawyer, someone knowledgeable in the increasingly complex legal world of the aged, sick and dying. My total experience with lawyers was making out a will in the early 1990s. We went to a lawyer we knew nothing about except that he came to the aid of a group of Buddhist nuns we knew. How does one find the right lawyer? I looked up elder care lawyer on the Internet and I was faced with one thousand names in Manhattan alone. I figured my best approach was to call Maria's cousin, Michael O'Brien, a lawyer on Long Island; it was the right move. Michael was particularly devoted to Maria and proved to be extraordinarily generous with his time and help during the subsequent three years. He said he knew just the right person that I needed.

I thought an hour's consultation to answer my questions would be enough but I was naive about lawyer work. It required many meetings and several months before we left with a dozen legal documents (wills, living wills, power of attorney, health care proxies...). Maria came to the first few meetings and could express her views. She did not understand much of the proceedings, but neither did I. Michael insisted on coming with us to make sure we understood all the legal talk (he would not hear of taking money for all the time he put in).

I was trying to avoid having Medicaid take over my life (sixty percent of people in nursing homes are on Medicaid). Of course, at the current New York area average price of $10,000 per month, everybody except the very rich would eventually run out of money. One of the first things the lawyer recommended was that I should get maximum coverage of long term care insurance for myself (we each had modest policies). I was surprised I could get it at my age but if you look at nursing homes you can see that not much insurance money is being paid out for men. The coverage for me was to protect her in case I went into a nursing home first. That did not seem implausible to me. At that time, I thought it was still likely that she would outlive me.

In the Spring of 2002 I considered quitting my job. Maria did not want me to do so and neither did I. If I were to quit work, I would have more time to attend to her but I feared that the world would close in on us. Having a job gave me perspective and periodic relief. Of course, I could not have kept most jobs but being a university professor has its advantages. My office and classrooms are about a three minute walk. During the Spring of 2002 I could still leave her alone for two hours at a time. She came to some of the classes, not as a visiting teacher but as an interested student.

An incident in April pointed to the difficulties of her traveling alone. I had gone to Montauk on the train; she was to follow on the bus. When the bus came in and she was not on it, I panicked. I got no answer when I called New York. I pictured her lying unconscious in the apartment or wandering the streets of Manhattan. Without thinking to leave a note, I took the next bus back to New York. Her bus had been delayed and detoured. When she arrived and I was not there she immediately called the police to report a missing person. Two cops from East Hampton took the information and calmed her down somewhat. As soon as I entered the apartment, I had a call from the police. The message: Your wife is looking for you. The department at NYU was curious as to why the East Hampton police were looking for me.

The next week I got two cell phones so that nothing similar would happen again. However, she was intimidated by anything technological and never became adjusted to the cell phone. I would show her repeatedly that she could reach me and some of her friends by pushing one button on the speed dial. It was still too complicated. The part of the brain that handles pushing even one button was no longer working.

In July, 2002, I went to Norway for the ISREV conference. I would be gone for just a week and Maria's longest and closest friend, Joanmarie Smith (a.k.a Dulcie) came to Montauk to stay the week with her. Dulcie and she had a history of fifty years; Dulcie could do things with her that I could not. Although Dulcie has lived in Ohio for more than twenty years, she and Maria remained as close as ever, talking on the phone almost daily. I had no misgivings leaving Maria with her dearest friend who could handle whatever came up. I called each day from Norway and found Maria to be lively and enthusiastic. The only peculiarity was that she kept referring to the nuns taking care of her and the two Dulcies who were there. That seemed like a minor slip of the tongue but it presaged another stage of development and confusion about me.

A Turn for the Worse (August, 2002 to Dec., 2002)

One of my most vivid memories is of a Sunday evening in late August, 2002. We had been watching the last round of the PGA tourney. Suddenly, with no provocation, Maria did not know who I was. I must have reacted strongly and tried to argue with her. That made things much worse. She said she wanted to leave and go home; I insisted she could not leave and that she was already home. At one point I called Dulcie in Ohio to see if she could talk her through this confusion. That helped a little but she still wanted to leave. When I would not let her, she asked me why I was keeping her a prisoner. It got so bad that she asked me if I was going to kill her. I don't know how we got through the night. I was hopeful that by the next morning she would have forgotten the whole incident.

Although she was calm in the morning, she still did not know who I was. The mother of a close friend had died that weekend so we went to the wake on Staten Island. On the ferry boat, at dinner, and in the funeral home she still did not know who I was. I said to my friend: "Something seems to have snapped; I think I have lost her." On the cab ride back home, she said it was amusing that all the people there thought I was Gabriel Moran. I suggested to her that perhaps they were right but that did nothing to convince her. The confusion continued until Wednesday when I went back to Staten Island for the funeral; she preferred to stay home. When the funeral took longer than I had anticipated, I called to let her know I would be late. She recognized my voice on the phone and said excitedly, "Where have you been for the last four days; I have been looking for you." The recognition carried through when I arrived in person.

That was the first of numerous occasions when I had to cope with her confusion of who I was. When I had first heard that hallucination was part of the disease, I assumed that I could be her bridge to reality. Instead, I was what she hallucinated about. The psychiatrist said it was fairly common, a form of hallucination called "reduplication." It is directed at the people who are closest. Only with me and Dulcie did this confusion seem to occur. Maria could recognize by name people she had not seen in twenty years. But sometimes in the blink of an eye she would not recognize me.

The fortunate thing was that she usually got along with all of us. After the first incident, I learned how to react and simply go with wherever she seemed to be. Neither reasoning nor facts made any penetration once she became convinced I was another person. The metaphysics of the brain constantly surprised me. We would seem to be having an ordinary conversation and she would suddenly say: "You never married did you?" I would calmly answer: "Yes, I did; I married you at the NYU Catholic Center." She would just smile and listen, wondering perhaps at my confusion. She asked me one morning at breakfast where I had slept the night before. When I said in the bed next to her, she said: "There were three of us in the bed?" I assured there were just two of us.

At times, she almost seemed to be on the inside of a playful joke. She told the psychiatrist that she could not use the toilet when she wanted because we had a public bathroom that she shared with ten men. I hastened to tell the psychiatrist that was not the case. In subsequent visits he would ask her how many men she was now living with. With seeming playfulness, she would say four or three. I had several names; her favorite was one that went through a couple of evolutions before ending as "Bonaventura." She always got along well with kindly Bonaventura. I sometimes had the feeling that she was seeing a younger version of me, someone she knew from thirty-five years ago. She told me one day about a nice young man who had taken her to the subway. When I told her that I was the one who had accompanied her, she said, "Oh, no; he was a young man."

One day she said to me: "How do you know I have this disease?" I replied: "I was with you when we received the diagnosis. She said: "No you weren't; I went with my mother." One's instinct might be to correct the person and say: "Don't be foolish; your mother has been dead for ten years." Such a response could cause the person great sorrow. It might be like hearing the news of her mother's death for the first time. Like others confronted by a person living in another time zone, I learned never to force my world on hers, wherever in the past she was.

Only on a few occasions did her confusion become a situation difficult to manage in public. I finally recognized that travel often brought about the confusion, and the psychiatrist recommended that we not go out to Montauk. What she needed was stability and a consistent environment. Although our house in Montauk was a place where she was at home, the travel to there caused confusion.

Once on the bus she became extremely agitated because she had left her husband behind. Why had I rushed her on to the bus without waiting for him? I had to physically restrain her from getting off the bus in Southampton. She wanted to ask if anyone had seen her husband. A few minutes later when the bus ride continued she went to the toilet at the back of the bus; on returning to her seat she recognized the back of my head. Where had I been, she wanted to know. All my talking to her had brought no conviction at all; one glance at the back of my head did the trick.

A particularly difficult incident happened in a hotel in Philadelphia. Maria had been active in a professional organization called the Association of Professors and Researchers in Religious Education. The meeting that year being an easy ninety minute train ride from New York, I suggested we go. Maria was happy to do so. I knew that the women in the group would be glad to see her and would give her affirmation. They did so beyond my expectation. The difficult part came in trying to check into the hotel. After the pleasant train ride, she suddenly did not know who I was during the five minute cab ride to the hotel. She refused to take a room with anybody except her husband. I was lost as to what to do. She finally relented enough to wait in the room until her husband arrived. Then she recognized me when I was speaking at the front of the hall and she was in the audience.

One of my most painful memories relates to Thanksgiving that year. My two sisters brought a complete turkey dinner with them down to Montauk. We had a wonderful meal and lively conversation. But after the meal, Maria took my sister Dotty aside and said: "Can you get a message to my husband; I don't think he loves me anymore and he seems to have abandoned me." Such moments were paralyzing for me. They were indicative of great suffering on her part. I was in some sense the cause of the suffering but I was utterly helpless to relieve it. The only recourse was patient waiting. By the next day she might have forgotten that she said that. For me, life became unending surprises and constant learning of how to respond to whatever might suddenly be the reality.

The Year of Living Dangerously (Jan. 2003, to Dec., 2003)

When I reflect back on the year 2003 I am most struck by the many possibilities for disaster that we avoided. That result was due in part to my watching out for terrible things but often it was just a matter of luck that disaster did not strike. What I feared was that Maria would have a crippling accident. As any parent or a care giver of a disabled person knows, one has to balance control and freedom. I did not want to hover over her every move but that meant allowing that something untoward might happen. Many Alzheimer's patients fall and break a bone, spend time in a hospital, and then are sent for rehab to whatever nursing home is available. The family's choice is limited once this process has begun. I was determined not to follow that route.

We were still able to go out to a movie or a restaurant. In January we went to a theater up on Broadway. I had an attack of vertigo coming out of the theater. I have no idea how we got home because I could not keep the pavement from moving under my feet and I was violently sick to my stomach. I had to lean on her to help me get home. We must have been a pretty picture making our way down those ten blocks of Broadway. But similar to what happened in June that year when I got seasick coming back from Block Island, Maria's instincts for taking care of me shifted back into operation.

I realize now that I was taking chances because I was lulled by what seemed to be normal behavior most of the time. The drugs she was taking were apparently successful in stabilizing the situation. That is, the decline was very gradual until the end of 2003. The danger in being so close to the situation is that one does not see – perhaps does not want to see – the small changes and the imperceptible descent that is occurring daily. Managing the drugs was a major task. From the start I had to watch over the ingestion of every pill she took, but that was just part of the daily routine.

A bigger problem was the apartment's layout and location. We were living just off a street bustling with buses, cars and crowds. The building was constructed in the 1840s. Some aspects of the apartment were very appealing (the high ceilings, the thick walls). But the major problems were the lack of an elevator and the design of the bathroom. I was constantly warned about the stairs, that as her condition worsened she was liable to fall. Remarkably, she never had the least problem or even hesitation with the stairs right up to the end.

The bathroom was another story. Without going into all the details, suffice it to say that eventually life revolves around the bathroom. I asked the contractor for the building if he could build in guard rails. He thought it would require smashing down the wall into the next apartment. He was reluctant to do anything for which he might be legally responsible if a fall occurred. I eventually fashioned my own safety devices, learning as I went along.

At present, sixty percent of Alzheimer's patients are being cared for at home. In most cases, a man is being cared for by his wife. I cannot imagine how they manage the physical part. Maria was barely a hundred pounds but I was often at my limit in trying to move her about. I also have increased respect for the twenty thousand home health care workers in New York City. They are not paid much over the minimum wage for work that is both physically demanding and mentally exhausting.

By 2003 it was apparent I could no longer leave her for the two hours I was in class. Kathy, the social worker, investigated the visiting nurse organizations in mid-town Manhattan. None could provide the flexibility I was looking for. Kathy put up a notice in St. Francis Xavier Church asking for help. That turned up a person who was perfect for what I needed. Delores was a retired woman who lived a few blocks away. She was the kind of help that no amount of money can buy. She was willing to come for whatever hours were needed. She and Maria immediately struck up a friendship and Maria felt completely at home with her. The two of them would sit quietly listening to music. Or they would go to Delores' apartment to visit with the two new dogs she had. It was great companionship, neither more than that nor less.

I had to make sure that Delores did not leave before I got back, especially if it was in the evening. A couple of times when I was delayed a few minutes, Maria was getting ready to go out looking for me. Fortunately, she was stopped each time by women in the building who waited with her.

One of my most frightening moments occurred in the middle of a Monday afternoon. We had hired a cleaning woman to come in every other Monday.

I thought it was safe to leave Maria because she had company. When I came back from school, Maria was not there. The cleaning woman was not at fault; I had not given her any warning or instructions. Given the amount and pace of traffic right outside the door, I was fearful of her being on the street.

I rushed up and down all the streets of the neighborhood but found no trace of her. I went over to the health center, thinking that was one place she might have headed for. Actually, that was where she was but I looked only in the waiting room and Alexandra had taken her inside. I went back to the apartment not knowing what to do next but she showed up just a few minutes after me. She was not upset in the least; she simply thought she was keeping an appointment. I was relieved that she could find her way over to the health center on Broadway and return to the apartment. I also felt guilty for neglecting to get an ID bracelet that many Alzheimer's patients wear.

The most remarkable thing Maria did that year was to take four trips to Delaware, Ohio to visit with her friend, Dulcie. Both I and Dulcie were amazed at her willingness to make the trip the first time and then casually to repeat it. We used the same flights on the same airline for stability sake. I would bring her to the door of the plane at LaGuardia and Dulcie would meet her at the door in Columbus. The airline people on board never had any problem. And I discovered that the airlines are very ready to provide wheel chair assistance. Just once when they did not have enough wheel chairs at the door, she took off on her own and I found her making her way through the labyrinth of LaGuardia Airport.

Dulcie and she would not do much except sit and talk; they could do that endlessly. Maria was content to go each time and content to return. I realized on the last trip that I should have got on the plane with her and that I could not let her go alone again. But another trip was never possible. Making those trips must have included some shaky moments for her, especially the ninety minutes in the air. Nevertheless, I think the travel gave her a boost and released some of the spunky self-confidence she had possessed when healthy.

The other big help to me during that year was that my sister, Mary (a.k.a. Madonna) took the train down from New Hampshire five times to stay with Maria over a weekend; I went out to Montauk and slept. Mary had headed an order of sisters for many years and is comfortable among the sick and aged. She is an unusually patient, kind, and understanding person. Not surprisingly, she and Maria became good friends. In addition to Dulcie, my sister was the only person I was confident could handle the situation. To stay with Maria for a couple of days was to ask too much from most people. My sister managed effortlessly and Maria loved having her company.

There was more to do in New York City than in Delaware, Ohio, so the two of them did a little exploring. Maria insisted each time that they have a pedicure from the Korean salon next door; Maria had the idea that a pedicure had roots in the New Testament. I think a pedicure was about the last thing my sister would have got for herself but she always graciously accepted Maria's gift. And occasionally Maria could still assert her native know how. Once they went downtown to visit the World Trade Center site, an area that was still a traffic muddle. When my sister asked a cop where they could get a cab, the cop said they would have to walk north for several blocks. But when my sister and the cop turned around, Maria was in the middle of the street with a cab she had just hailed.

In the Fall of 2003, Cindy Hosay, who had been helpful in getting me started, gave me the name of a music therapist on the upper East Side. The woman and her husband do wonderful work with people who are disabled, including people with dementia. Maria, as I noted earlier, was a musician, an expert pianist and singer. I had often read that music is one of the last things to go in people who are suffering from dementia. I thought that music therapy would be especially appropriate in Maria's case; and it was.

I bought a keyboard so that she could play at home. In my zeal to get the best instrument, I bought a keyboard that was technologically intimidating for her. When she was later in the nursing home, I bought a much simpler version of the instrument which is where I should have started.

The therapist, Helene, was almost infinitely patient in trying to get her to perform some simple exercises. I used to sit watching for the hour and I learned lessons about teaching. Maria struggled with any kind of sequence or simple pattern. On the other hand, she could run through a tune from *Oklahoma* or a Latin hymn from her childhood. Helene was startled by Maria's ability to play a whole song from memory. One of the marvelous things about this teacher was that she would simply take her lead from the student, a trait especially important when dealing with dementia. Maria's ability to play from memory as she had all her life did not surprise me much. As with other things but especially with music, the loss of short-term memory can leave parts of long term-memory intact.

We have been learning from research that the plaque in the brain destroys specific functions and activities. People who have no short-term memory may appear stupid but they are not. They can still have a deep appreciation of the arts. The *New York Times* recently had a story in the Sunday Arts section on Alzheimer's patients. It referred to a program at a local museum for these patients. The writer sounded completely mystified by the obvious capacity for art appreciation shown by the patients. It is not such a surprising phenomenon; another part of the brain continues to work well despite the loss of some functions.

During 2003, Kathy got me in touch with an adult day-care center in the West Village. She did some work there and assured me that it was a good place for Maria to go. Maria and I went together the first time and she agreed to go back each Wednesday. A car would pick her up at the door in the morning and return her in the afternoon; they would call ahead to check that I was at home. A varied program of music, art and physical therapy was provided by a staff that could not have been more cordial and hard working. They loved having Maria because, despite her illness, she was bright and relatively active. For example, she made friends immediately with a young man who had suffered a severe stroke and could not speak. I felt awkward in his presence and did not know how to communicate with him. I don't think Maria found it to be a problem; she was her usual self and brought him out of himself.

I was hoping that she would like going to the Center. I thought it was good for her to get out of the apartment and engage in activities that I could not provide. And, frankly, it was a relief for me each Wednesday. She soon became resistant to going; she continued to attend but with reluctance. It had nothing to do with the treatment by the staff; to a person, each of them was wonderful with her. I guessed that the reluctance stemmed from the vision that she was getting of what lay ahead for her. Many of the people who came to the center were at an advanced stage of dementia. Maria was not there yet. But I think that toward the end of 2003 she had begun to sense that the future was closing in on her.

## The Year of Living Inside (Jan., 2004 to Dec., 2004)

Although the drugs had seemed to work fairly well for almost two years, they suddenly seemed to be ineffective toward the end of 2003. I realize there may have been other factors at work that brought about the change. In any case, even I noticed a sharp change for the worse in Maria's behavior. Both on the physical and the mental sides there were serious changes that made living in the apartment dangerous. I had assumed that my next step was going to be home nursing help around the clock. But I started to wonder if even that would be adequate for the developing situation.

I arranged for a visit during the first week in January to the nursing home in Brentwood which is called Maria Regina Residence. We went out on the train and were given a tour of the place. Maria had lived on the property for two years when she was a novice; she had also taught there and visited many times. Her mother had even gone to school there almost a century earlier. It was a place Maria was very comfortable with, and many people in the facility, both staff and residents, knew Maria. We were therefore received with warm friendliness. Eating dinner from a good buffet in a pleasant dining room was an attractive feature of what we saw. I was aware that there were sections in the building which we did not see where the residents were at a more advanced stage of disease. But the attitude in the place was openness, efficiency, and compassion. The best thing was that we both had the same impression.

At breakfast the next morning, Maria's first statement was: "It is not a question of if but when." I was surprised at her succinct statement of where we were. Nothing she could have said would have provided greater relief for me. She was taking away the burden I would have felt if I had to try persuading her that going there was in her best interest. We discussed our feeling about the place which was very different from our reaction to the other nursing homes we had visited. We did not decide about time; I hoped to maintain my promise to do whatever was necessary when the time arose.

The director of the nursing home called me the next day. I think she had seen something that I could not see at that time. She asked if Maria was planning to come at the beginning of the next month. I said, "Oh, no. I was thinking about the future, maybe six months or a year from now." In the course of that month, however, I came to grasp that the situation was fast becoming intolerable. I don't know if the change for the worse was precipitated by the prospect of going to the nursing home. Maria did tell my sister – but not me – that she knew she should be in a nursing home because the burden was too great on me.

An incident at the end of the month sealed my decision to move more quickly than I had thought just weeks previously. We went out for a walk in the neighborhood and everything seemed peaceful and normal. But on the way back she suddenly darted into the building next door. When I tried to get her out she started screaming that I was attacking her. Fortunately, the super and the janitor arrived; and they immediately recognized the situation. Maria trusted the janitor who offered to take her home. She kept screaming to keep me away from her.

When she had been taken back to the apartment, I sat outside on the steps waiting for her to cool down. But she came out and walked up the stairs without saying anything to me. I figured she was safe up there and would eventually have to come down. But she knocked on a door and the woman took her in. Not knowing what to do, the woman called the police. The ID that Maria was carrying gave Montauk as her home address.

When I saw two New York City cops go by me, I suspected what they were there for. When one of them came out of the woman's apartment on the third floor, I told him that Maria lived on the next floor down. The policemen could not have been kinder both to her and to me. They spent about twenty minutes coaxing her back to the apartment, getting her a glass of water, and making sure she was safe and calm.

After I sat outside for an hour or more, I went into the apartment and she did not give the impression that anything unusual had happened. The incident is the kind of thing which care givers regularly confront. Looking back on the experience, I cannot find anything I should have done differently. I was just lucky that it did not turn out worse. I could have been taken in by the police for questioning; that would not have been unreasonable. She could have suffered serious injury. I concluded that the "when" had now arrived.

I arranged for an entry date at the nursing home. Michael O'Brien and his brother Kevin insisted on driving us out and they stayed until we were settled. On that day and in the year that followed she was given the best care possible. I cannot express how grateful I am for how she was treated. The staff listened to my suggestions, such as giving her the pills with yogurt rather than apple sauce, or giving her regular massages of her neck and back. I was allowed to brighten her room with some of her favorite art pieces, to bring a CD player, and to hook up a telephone recording device. Many people phoned her (Dulcie almost every day). Surprisingly, she was able to function on the phone even when she was barely able to communicate in person. On the last day of her life, as her consciousness ebbed, I was convinced she recognized Rosemary's voice when she called from Melbourne.

For a good while Maria managed to remember most of the faces and names of people who visited. She had a steady stream of visitors; Michael O'Brien came faithfully every week. Good friends such as Kathy Sperduto and Joan Grace, neither of whom was in the best of health, came when they could. Her dear cousin, Jim Tunny and his wife Betty Ann, were especially solicitous. Friends of mine, including Kieran Scott, Anthony Fasano and John Grieco, were supportive and on the scene. But on October 1, 2004, John Grieco, a friend of forty years dropped dead. He had been a constant support for me and a great friend of Maria's. I was devastated by the loss.

The one drawback with the nursing home was that Brentwood is about in the middle of the traveling distance between Montauk and New York. I had to allow about four hours round trip either driving from Montauk or taking the train from New York. However, in some ways I now had more time even if I spent eight or ten hours in visiting her. I considered getting an apartment in Brentwood but I decided that the train from New York would be less disruptive of the job I was trying to keep.

I had some regrets later that I did not move to Brentwood. When she could not feed herself, I would have liked to have been there every day instead of the every other day I tried to maintain. Helping a person to eat takes time and attentiveness. When she was in the hospital, one of the staff asked me how I got her to eat whereas they could not. I said: "Well, the first thing is it takes half an hour." Hospitals, rehab centers and nursing homes do not have the personnel to spend that much time with individual patients.

Until July, Maria could manage her own eating and had a healthy appetite. I had looked forward to the Spring and Summer when she could get out on the extensive grounds, even though by the late Spring she was confined to a wheel chair. One pleasant aspect of each day was going down to the chapel at 11:20 AM for the Eucharist and then going to the dining room for a leisurely dinner. I went more often to church than I had in years. It was a restful and comforting experience. With many people in wheel chairs or struggling with various ailments, the liturgical ritual of the Catholic Mass provided a community bond.

Most of the residents were nuns; the place had been built by the Sisters of Saint Joseph for their own use in the 1960s. With only a few modifications, they were able to open it to the general public. I could understand if some people would find the atmosphere of Catholic piety too confining But Maria adjusted easily to it. There was no pressure on anyone to conform to a religious code or a set of practices. I felt that as Maria withdrew from this world, she was often praying and in touch with another dimension of reality.

The physical therapists were wonderful with her, as were the woman who did her hair and the woman who did her nails. Such small touches brightened the environment. The woman who directed the second floor's operation was a model of efficiency and kindness. I got to know the place pretty well from sitting for many hours watching the nurses, the aides and the people who cleaned. Most of us most of the time can shut out of awareness the inner workings of nursing homes but the work there requires patience, skill and dedication. The pay will never be consonant with the importance of the work for an increasing part of the population.

When I had previously been in nursing homes I was ready to climb the walls after thirty minutes. Here I was surprised that I did not find the hours to be a drag. I found I could sit in silence for long periods. Of course, I was always aware of my situation in relation to hers. I could not imagine how she passed the time. She could not read or did not wish to read (she who used to grab the crossword in the *Times* every morning). Even television – the pacifier of babies and the aged – did not interest her. I tried various things but a set of video tapes of her favorite program, "As Time Goes Bye," was one of my few successes.

Throughout her illness and during the time in the nursing home, Maria showed little anger. I sometimes thought that she (and I) might feel better if she screamed and threw things. She remained remarkably calm under almost all circumstances. When she went to a hospital or clinic for a treatment, it involved being lifted up, pushed around, strapped down, and bumpily transported. She remained serene. I, not she, would get furious when she was left on a stretcher for an hour or more in a waiting room.

Her unlined face retained a strange beauty despite all she suffered. Some friends who dropped in told another friend that what struck them when they walked into the room was how beautiful she looked. It was therefore not mere blindness or bias on my part that she looked as beautiful at the end as she did the day we first met.

In October I received a call from a surgeon asking for my agreement that she have surgery for a "pressure sore." The sore which was there from before she had entered Maria Regina had not responded to treatment. The surgeon said it was necessary to operate; otherwise, "it could mean her demise." I obviously had to agree to the surgery. Until that time, I still did not understand the seriousness of a pressure sore; I thought it was just a bother and an irritation. When Christopher Reeve died that month, the press carried stories that most people with dementia die from pressure sores that become infected.

I was told that she would be in the hospital for seven days and in rehab for fourteen days. What happened was that she was in each place for about seven weeks. Neither place was bad but they were not as comfortable as the nursing home. I used to say that one's expectations have been shortened when all one hopes for is to get well enough to go to the nursing home. After she had been in the hospital for many weeks a surgeon said to me: "We want to get her out of here because the longer you stay in a hospital the more problems you develop." I thought that was surprising if somewhat depressing candor about hospitals.

When it came time to move from the hospital, I had a choice among a few rehab centers that had the proper machine to help her healing. My best choice was a place in East Patchogue, Long Island, which added a few more hours to my travel but which seemed a decent place. But after almost two months of treatment with machines and drugs, she showed little progress. I did not think it was anyone's fault; they did what they could. I was asked to agree to insertion of a feeding tube – a temporary tube – to improve nutrition. I would not have agreed to a permanent tube but after a while temporary tends toward permanent. At one point, I looked at her with five different lines running into her body. I had approved each thing separately but I began to wonder if the total result was just a form of torture.

The house physician was a nice enough man but not much involved with her case. When I asked him in early December when she might be able to leave, he replied quite casually: "Oh, I don't think she will ever leave." His candor shook me up. Until then I was concentrating on each day while I waited for the rehab to be over. His remark forced me to start considering that if the wound from the surgery had not healed then the end might be near. My sisters had seen this in October when they visited Maria in the hospital but for me it was a sudden awakening in December.

The Final Goodbye (Dec., 2004 to Feb., 2005)

On Christmas day, 2004, I knew that Maria was dying. I had gone out to the rehab center with Dulcie and with Elaine Roulet, another close friend of Maria's. This pair with their outgoing friendliness brought cheer to any room they entered. I knew that if they could not get a rise out of her, then she had passed a point of no return. When we entered the room, Maria closed her eyes.

Whether the movement was voluntary or not, it was shockingly different from the past, even a few weeks earlier, when the three of us visited her in the hospital. We shared Christmas day with her but with little response on her side.

I talked to the house physician again. He knew a little bit more about her case now. His prognosis was more guarded but no more optimistic. I asked him if had communicated information to her primary care physician but I found that he did not know who that was. I offered him the phone number so he could call. I must admit I was still naive about the communication of information among health care providers. It finally came home to me two weeks later when I asked one of the surgeons about the antibiotics Maria had been taking. The surgeon had no knowledge of that. When I gave the name of the person who prescribed the drugs to the rehab center they did not recognize the name. The light finally dawned: I was the only person who actually was aware of all the parties involved. Unless I functioned as the link, these people did not talk to each other.

At 10 PM on December 31, I got a call from a nurse in the rehab center. The nurse said Maria was not responsive. Did I want them to send her to the hospital? My question was how was I supposed to judge that? I asked: "Can't you call the attending physician to decide that?" He finally got back to me and we talked it out. We agreed that she was not likely to get much attention in a hospital emergency room on New Year's Eve. She was probably better off where she was.

The next week her primary care physician called. Dr. Ryan Cahill was a fine, caring physician serving the nursing home. He had always been straightforward with me, doing what he could for her but honest about the limitations of any treatment. I asked what he thought and he replied: "Tell me what you want and then I will tell you what I think." Not many physicians are that willing to listen. I said that the wound had not healed. One choice was to go back into the hospital for more surgery but that was unlikely to succeed. More surgery and antibiotics would probably just add to her discomfort. However, without further surgery she was likely to develop an infection. He agreed.

Then I asked him to describe to me what it is like to die of sepsis or septic shock. He provided a description for me. He assured me that pain could be completely controlled. We agreed that she should return to the nursing home and be given palliative care. Good Shepherd hospice was contacted to give us additional help in keeping the patient comfortable. When she was returned to the hospital she was given a quiet room on the first floor with ready access to any service she might need. Staff from the second floor where she had previously been came down to see her.

She stopped receiving nutrition because her body could no longer tolerate it. There are acrimonious debates in this country that surround "the removal of the feeding tube." The tube is not actually removed; nutrition is simply halted. Some people scream murder when there is such a move; they claim the patient has been starved to death. There are some debatable cases but most of the time the inability to take food is a sign that the body is preparing for death. In any case, the cause of death is not "starvation," an inappropriate name for allowing the person to die. In Maria's case continuing the feeding would have worsened her condition because the body could not absorb the nutrition.

When I arrived on Saturday, January 29, the nurse told me that Maria probably had only a few days to live. Obviously, I should have known the end was coming soon but it still caught me by surprise that it would be so quick. I moved into the nursing home, staying in a guest room that they had provided whenever I wished to stay overnight. My sister and brother-in-law came down from New Hampshire and the three of us went to the funeral home to make arrangements. Afterwards, I would be relieved that all of that preparation was in place.

I did make one quick trip to Montauk to pick up a few things that would be needed. On the trip out, there was an incident that touched me deeply. There is a friendly conductor on the Long Island Railroad whom I often meet. We exchange pleasantries; he often checks what I am reading or what movies I have seen. On this day, I blurted out "my wife is dying"; he was the first person I had said that to. He finished collecting the tickets and came back to sit and talk with me for an hour. One does not expect such compassion from a railroad conductor. It was one of numerous gestures of kindness I experienced from friend and stranger alike.

On the morning of February 1, I was waiting for Dr. Cahill. When he arrived and I asked him what he thought, he replied: "You have been here more than anyone else; you tell me." I was again surprised by his willingness to listen, rather than play the expert. After he heard what I had seen in the past few days, he checked her chart. When he saw that her kidneys were essentially closed down, he said she could not last long.

I stayed with her throughout the day trying to aid her breathing. Her lungs were filling with fluid. Listening to a person dying of pneumonia is disconcerting. There is obvious discomfort for the patient that cannot be removed but there is no apparent pain. I went out briefly for dinner and when I came back the breathing was more labored. I did not recognize the gurgling of a dying person. A nun who had great affection for Maria was with us. She recognized better than I did how close death was. She had seen it dozens of times; I had little experience.

I held Maria and tried to keep her mouth clear but, of course, my efforts were futile. When the staff tried to suction the lungs, I thought for a moment that her breathing had suddenly improved and then I realized that she had stopped breathing. The time was 9:50 PM; the last moments had been relatively peaceful. Two other nuns came in to pray and to provide immediate assistance. I called my sister and her husband who had gone over to their motel a few hours previous. They immediately returned and stayed with me until the funeral home came for the body.

Immediate Aftermath (Feb., 2005)

The next day I was mostly in a daze. Most of the funeral arrangements had been made and I had plenty of help in attending to whatever had to be done immediately. By the middle of the day, there was nothing more for me to do in the nursing home so I went into New York. I was waiting for a call from the funeral home which was trying to arrange an autopsy. Michael O'Brien had asked me if I would have an autopsy; he was concerned about the presence of Lewy Bodies in the family gene pool.

The funeral home had difficulty finding an available pathologist. Rather than sit alone in my apartment, I went over to school and met my graduate course. I could have canceled the class; the students were probably surprised that I came. I did not think of it as heroism. I simply found that teaching that day and throughout the semester was therapeutic for me. The students were wonderfully supportive and it gave me a chance to talk out my feelings. At about 10 P.M. that evening I got a call from a pathologist. She said she was willing to perform the autopsy the next morning. However, she needed a check for $4000 dollars before she would begin. Early next morning I was on the Long Island Railroad check in hand.

The delay for the autopsy pushed back the wake until the weekend and the burial until Monday. That schedule was probably a fortunate one because it gave time for people to read the notice in the newspapers and to travel from great distances. The day before her death I had written three separate obituaries. The first obituary was for the *New York Times*. I knew that it was a long shot getting a story into the *Times*. Our wedding had gotten a write up but that was when Tom Harris was with the paper. As it turned out, I gladly paid for the death notice in the *Times* that would be read by many people in New York and beyond. In the second case, *Newsday* did not use the obituary that I had written for them but they assigned a staff person to write the story. They had a fine picture taken on our deck in Montauk when they had done a feature on Maria. I was delighted with the picture and story that they ran.

The one newspaper I was sure would run a story and let people around the country know of her death was the *National Catholic Reporter*. I called the paper immediately but it took two days before I got through to the editor. He seemed interested and I immediately e-mailed the obituary that was tailored for that paper. They did not even run one sentence acknowledging her death. I repeatedly tried to get an explanation why, but with no results. I am still angry at that newspaper. Six months after Maria's death I was still getting letters from people who were just finding it out. The organizations we belonged to tried to spread the word but it did not circulate to everyone who would have been interested.

I knew that most people coming to the wake would be expecting the standard Irish Catholic format. If the choice were just for me, I would not have gone along with an open casket and many other features. I allowed the body to be embalmed though I consider the practice to be weird. A steady stream of people came for the two days. I met some people that I had not seen in twenty, thirty or forty years.

I had chosen a church for the funeral based on a helpful suggestion by Padraic O'Hare. The pastor in this church not only knew Maria but would be amenable to having what we wished for the burial service. I went over to the church with Dulcie and my sister Mary to talk with the liturgist about music, prayers, and the rest of the ceremony. Elaine, the liturgist of the church, had a more coherent picture of how to handle things than any of the three of us. Thus, the funeral was done with a beautiful simplicity in elegant surroundings. It included music Maria would have loved. John Rowan, the pastor, spoke with warmth about Maria. I provided the eulogy toward the end of the service.

Maria had given me instructions about burial in a plot next to her father and mother. That required a long funeral procession from Sayville, Long Island to Middle Village, Queens. At the grave site, Padraic delivered the final poetic testimony. Then fifty of us went for a meal at a nearby restaurant. That part of the day had been efficiently arranged by Michael O'Brien. The food, drink, laughter, and tears flowed in abundance. Maria would have loved it; her kind of gathering.

Joan Didion points out in her book that people are always concerned about getting through the funeral. They worry about falling to pieces. But people usually do manage to hold themselves together through the funeral. The ritual is designed to support the mourners, and a tight knit community provides an emotional balance. What may catch some people by surprise is the sudden hole in the world immediately after the funeral. For the next year and more, the rest of the world goes back to its ordinary business while the mourner may still be trying to find a firm footing on the earth.

Maria's story comes to its essential close with the funeral; this memoir is her story, not mine. I will add only some details about public forums of mourning by her friends immediately afterward. I estimate that I received about four hundred letters of condolence. Some of them were brief e-mails that could be answered briefly. But most were lengthy handwritten letters. If anyone had told me a year ago that I would be faced with answering four hundred letters, I would have said I could not do it. Strangely, I did not find writing replies to be burdensome. Writing a brief note of thanks to people who expressed their deep felt sorrow was therapeutic.

The range of letters was remarkable from people who knew her since childhood to a priest who visited her classroom for an hour in 1962 and never forgot her. I was particularly struck by a number of gay/lesbian former students for whom Maria was their chief support when homosexuality was not an open issue. I am sure she never thought of gay rights as a cause. It simply wasn't in her nature to discriminate against "outsiders." She often described herself as an outsider in institutions where she worked. That seemed odd, given that she seemed so easily accepted wherever she went. But I think she never forgot the feeling she had as an eight-year-old who was hustled off to the playground and not told that her father had just dropped dead. She seemed to have an instant rapport with people who are considered by society to be of low status. I used to sit back and marvel at this talent for talking to anybody.

Through the effort of Professor John Hull in England, ISREV established a web site. Members were invited to submit testimonies about Maria. Many of the group had already written to me. John Hull collected about two dozen of these remembrances and posted them along with a small selection of photos. Unfortunately, the digital camera had not come into general use before Maria's sickness so photos are not as easily and clearly transferred to the Internet. I used to kid her that the best picture she ever took was one taken while she was on a whitewater raft on the Colorado River. Since she was holding on for her life, she was not posing for the camera. The result is a picture with all the wonderful emotions of her inner life evident on her face.

Two gatherings shortly after her death stand out in my mind. Fordham University's religious education department organized a memorial on March 22 (The date sticks with me because we always celebrated that date as the first time we met). Professor Gloria Durka, the most steadfast friend one can imagine, organized the program along with her colleague, Kieran Scott. Kieran delivered a beautiful tribute to Maria, based on thirty-five years of friendship with Maria and myself.

I left for the memorial in plenty of time; the train ride from Grand Central is about half an hour. It is probably a reflection of my mental state at the time that I – who spends much of his life on trains – got off at the wrong stop. I showed up an hour and a half late after walking through much of the South Bronx. I felt just awful, having delayed the service and then missing most of it. Few of the current students had known Maria except through her writing. Nonetheless, her spirit was somehow present through the faculty that did know her. I should add that Fordham had not waited to pay tribute to her only after her death. They had honored her in December, 2002, when she could still appreciate the praise lavished on her by faculty and students.

A few days after Fordham's tribute I went down to Hollywood, Florida, at the invitation of Joseph and Mercedes Iannone. The Iannones have for decades done superb work in education first with families and parishes, then at St. Thomas University in Miami. I knew that being with them would be a comfortable and comforting situation. Since Maria and I had taught at St. Thomas, many people there knew and admired her.

On Sunday evening (the eve of our wedding anniversary), the Iannones got together an intimate gathering of friends who offered remembrances of Maria.

What was unusual, I recognized part way into the evening, was that everyone in the gathering had recently suffered their own loss or death. They understood the feeling of grief. Anyone in mourning can become too self-absorbed, forgetting that the world is filled with fellow mourners. This simple, poignant moment in South Florida was a fitting tribute to Maria's simple joy in the small things of life. She was a dynamo of energy for good even in her sickness and I like to believe that her presence did not end with her death.

# APPENDIX

Eulogy for Maria Harris by Gabriel Moran.

(Delivered at Lawrence Church, Sayville, Long Island, on Feb.7, 2005)

If it were solely up to me I would prefer silence at this point, which is mostly what I shared with Maria during the last months of her life. However, for such an articulate woman some few words should be said on her behalf to her friends who are gathered here today.

I know I am biased but I think that anyone who knew Maria would agree that she was an extraordinary person. So often I heard someone say: "Well, of course, everyone loves Maria." Each time I heard that I would think: What an amazing thing to be said of anyone. People seemed to mean it. She evoked a reaction of joy, admiration and love from so many people – whether women or men, young or old, gay or straight, people in high office or people consigned to menial work.

The reaction of women was especially noteworthy. They seemed to take pride in her accomplishments. I did not sense envy or jealousy. I think it was because Maria saw herself as surrounded by a sea of sisterhood within which and for which she spoke. Women sensed that and delighted in her talents. She treated everyone with respect, as if you were the most important person in the world. And it wasn't superficial. If you were a friend of Maria's, you were a friend for life.

She could cry up a storm on sad occasions. But she had a sunny personality. Her mother called her Mary Sunshine which was very fitting. She brought a brightness and enthusiasm to every group she worked with. We often team taught. I could not duplicate her talent for bringing out the best in every group. But I did learn from her and I became a better teacher.

Maria was a Sister of St. Joseph for 23 years. In the deepest sense, however, she never left the community of women; nor did the religious congregation ever exclude her. I was happy to share her with all the friends she had made, especially her dearest friend of fifty years, Joanmarie Smith. I only knew Maria for thirty-nine years. The day she walked into my office I think both of us knew within five minutes that our lives would forever be entwined. How that would happen was not clear. She figured it out pretty quickly; it took me a lot longer.

Her name in the religious order was Maria Crucis. She loved the name Maria and it seemed to fit her perfectly. I always thought that the name Crucis was ironic. She did not give the impression of carrying a cross through life. But in the last four years she earned that name. From the first moment when she was diagnosed, I never heard a word of self-pity or complaint. There was no "why me?" or "this is unfair." I think it was because she viewed all she had as gifts. When she had to relinquish each of life's powers, she could do so gracefully.

In bearing with the disease, she had a strength that I had not known she possessed. And perhaps she herself did not know she had such strength. She had never had a serious illness in her life. When she would get an annual cold and be miserable for a day or two, she would warn me that she would make a terrible patient. As it turned out, she was completely wrong about how she would handle a terrible disease.

In the late 1960s a group of seven older churchwomen gathered in Philadelphia. They decided that the image of the old in this country needed changing. The news media condescendingly called them the Gray Panthers, a name that they ran with. They succeeded admirably in what they set out to do. Maggie Kuhn, the leader of the group, said in an interview that she intended to continue the work as long as she lived. The interviewer said: "How can you say that with such certainty? Suppose you get sick and are lying flat on your back in a hospital?" Maggie Kuhn replied: "Then I will make that my work."

I believe Maria did just that. While she was in the nursing home and the hospital she was still a dynamo of energy for many people in this country and beyond. And for those of us who believe in the Communion of Saints the work continues.

In teaching about teaching, I have often cited a passage from a talk that Elizabeth Glaser gave at the 1992 Democratic convention. Glaser had become infected with the AIDS virus through blood transfusion and she had passed it on to her daughter who died. Glaser said: "My daughter lived 7 years and in the last year of her life she could neither talk nor walk, but her wisdom shone through. She taught me to love when all I felt was hate. She taught me to think of others when all I wanted to do was think of myself. She taught me to be brave when all I felt was fear." When I had used that passage in the past, I never dreamed that it could apply to a 70 year- old woman as well as to a 7 year-old child.

When we came to Maria Regina residence a year ago, I told friends that we were received like royalty. It was an unusual experience for anyone entering a nursing home to be surrounded by such warmth and love. She could not have received better care than she did here. When she returned from the hospital two and a half weeks ago, we received a second warm homecoming. She had come to die but it was the right place for her.

Both times we were greeted with a large sign that said: Welcome to Maria Regina. I read that sign in two ways: It could mean: Welcome into the residence whose name is Maria Regina. It can also read: Welcome to the one who is named Maria; she will be treated royally. The disease that Maria had was a trial of both body and soul. It was truly a cross to bear. But purified by suffering she has finally transcended the Crucis in her name. No longer Maria Crucis, she is now Maria Gloria, Maria Regina.

I conclude with an Irish prayer. I know she would love me to read this because she chose to read it at two funerals: that of her mother, Mary Tunny Harris, and that of her dear cousin, Brian O'Brien. The prayer expresses the sacramental principle that was the central theme of her writing, her speaking, and her life, the belief that God is revealed in all the elements of ordinary life. I cannot read it as well as she could but I don't think she would mind:

"May the blessing of the light be on you, light within and light without.

May the blessed sunlight shine on you and warm your heart till it glows like a great peat fire, so that strangers may come and warm themselves at it, and friends.

And may the light shine out of the two eyes of you like a candle set in two windows of a house, bidding the wanderer to come in out of the storm.

And may the blessing of the Rain be on you - the soft, sweet rain.

May it fall upon your spirit so that all the little flowers may spring up, and shed their sweetness on the air.

And may the blessing of the Great Rains be on you, may they beat upon your spirit and wash it fair and clean,

And leave there many a shining pool where the blue of heaven shines and sometimes a star.

And may the blessing of the Earth be on you – the great round earth.

May you ever have a kindly greeting for them you pass as you're going along the roads.

May the earth be soft under you when you rest upon it, tired at the end of the day.

And may it rest over you when, at the last, you lay out under it.

May it rest so lightly over you, that your soul may be out from under it quickly, and up, and off, and on its way to God."

# CHAPTER TWO: REFLECTIONS ON AGE AND SICKNESS: A MEMOIR

This chapter is an extension of the previous chapter, "In Praise of Maria." That essay was in part my reflection on mortality and my experience of Maria's gentle and courageous approach to dying during four years of a terrible disease. This current essay, as an extension of the previous one, does not have the finality of its predecessor. It does touch on some of the same themes, particularly the kindness of friends and the dedication of professionals.

The title of this chapter indicates that it is some thoughts on the experience of serious illness. It is not mainly concerned with medical details, though some of them are unavoidable, but instead on the thoughts a person has during a potentially fatal illness. Thus the reflections now are about the reflections then. The dead cannot do that so it is left to those of us who are still walking about. There is nothing very profound here but perhaps the ordinariness of the thoughts is in some ways comforting. When one is ultimately confronted with one's mortality, the reaction is not necessarily denial or desperate protests about the injustice of it all. When the great sports writer, Red Smith, was told at age 76 that he was dying, he calmly said: "If this is the end, it was a good run."

I usually shy away from memoirs of someone's sickness. The underlying assumption seems to be, "woe is me, no one knows the suffering I have been through," while in fact everyone knows or will know comparable problems. This essay is primarily therapeutic, to get it out of my system. It is also a thank you note to many people even if all their names are not here. Should anyone else find this interesting, that would be a bonus.

I wrote the memoir about Maria in part because a few similar memoirs by people caring for dementia patients had been helpful to me. Mainly I wrote it for the few hundred readers of the newsletter who knew her. The details of her illness were nobody's business except the people who really cared about her. I was surprised then to find that the essay was used in a course at a New York medical school. The professor, whom I don't know, said to the students concerning the contents of the essay: "We have to do better." I presume he was referring to the systematic problems of communication which I tell of encountering. Certainly I had only praise for the nurses, physicians, technicians and therapists that Maria and I dealt with.

In 2010 I was reinforced in those sentiments by the hundreds of people whose hands – quite literally – I passed through. One can perhaps best appreciate the skills and care of medical people in an emergency room. I was checked into an ER five times during the year. There is not much else to do in an emergency room for 6 or 8 hours except to watch the staff cope with unpredictable problems in a very confined space and with limited help. I do not understand how they sustain it day after day. On one occasion I was in NYU Medical Center for a blood transfusion that lasted for 4 hours and then I waited 8 hours for a bed to become available in the hospital. One nurse – I would guess from the Caribbean – while overburdened with duties, stayed with me for the entire 12 hours. I don't know what she is paid for her skill and care but I am sure it is not enough.

## Before

For a reason that I could not identify then and still cannot, I started reviewing my whole life in January, 2010. I had not been given to such searching in the past. My attitude has always been that whatever happened in the past I did what I could in the circumstances that were present. Disappointment, regret, or guilt about the past seems to me to serve no purpose. So it was a surprise to find myself totaling up the score for my life as a whole. For better and for worse it was now a life. I was approaching the seventy-five year marker; if I had not made a life out of it by now it was not likely to happen with a few years more.

Throughout the years I seldom thought of age. When I was asked how old I was I usually had to go back and calculate from the year of my birth. I barely noticed the often dreaded milestones, such as the fortieth or sixty-fifth birthdays. Then suddenly I realized I was an old man, the previous decade having disappeared in a flash. I started noticing the obituaries in the *Times*. I regularly am taken aback at the death of famous people; it is not a surprise that they died but that they had been still alive. When I check the age of these newly dead I usually find they are only a little older than I am; occasionally they are even younger. I figure when my obituary appears, someone who remembers me from a brief notoriety in the sixties will say: I can't believe he was still alive. The experience of our own age does not correlate with a simple objective number. For nearly everyone, "old age" is your age plus twenty. Cicero said that no one is so old that he does not plant crops in the Spring.

About a year before the onset of Maria's sickness she started putting together albums of photos. The half dozen albums provided a sequence of her life story. I have seen a few other people engage in the same kind of project, aware or not of their coming death. All my photos were inside my head but there seemed to be a similar impulse. I do not put stock in premonitions but perhaps there are sometimes warnings in one's body or the environment.

Possibly what inspired thoughts of mortality was my first trip to the ER two weeks into the year. I took a bad fall in Trader Joe's and quickly found myself in an ambulance to Beth Israel Hospital. I could have sued Trader Joe's; in fact they expected that I would and supplied the name of the person to contact in their legal department. However, it was my fault as well as theirs and I was just glad that I suffered no serious and permanent damage from hitting the floor and the edge of a delivery case about as hard as one can. The young people at Trader Joe's could not have been more solicitous. The manager who said it was his first day on the job could not have been happy when confronted with this old guy bleeding from the ear.

When I was wheeled into the ER I thought it was total chaos with bodies everywhere and with manned computers that looked like the deck of a spaceship. However, I got great care, far better than I would have expected in an ER. It did take time as they brought in at least three kinds of specialists before a surgeon did a little stitching in my ear and I walked home before midnight.

In April I went to see my primary care physician, something I had not regularly done. I had what turned out to be a minor problem. In a routine blood test, however, the physician found I was anemic, a problem I had never had before. He did not raise any great concern but said that the most likely cause of such anemia is internal bleeding. I had no pain and never saw blood; I had, however, lost a few pounds which was unusual. I saw a gastroenterologist who scheduled a colonoscopy for June but before I could get to that procedure the anemia brought me down – hard.

On June 5, I passed through the thin membrane that separates the Kingdom of the Well from the Kingdom of the Sick. Ordinary life in the Kingdom of the Sick contains practices that in the Kingdom of the Well would be embarrassing or frightening. The living environment in the Kingdom of the Sick involves screams of unbearable pain alternated with endless waiting in which nothing seems to happen. The one thing sure to the people in the Kingdom of the Well is that the Kingdom of the Sick is in a universe far, far away. In fact, of course, it is never more distant than a few moments journey. A sharp pain in the chest, a moment of distraction at the wheel, a patch of ice underfoot and – surprise – one has switched citizenships.

My instantaneous journey happened at 7:30 AM on a Saturday morning in Penn Station. I was on my way to Montauk where I was to host our annual family reunion; I had the shortest distance to travel of any of the family members. A few minutes before I would have been walking down the steps to the train platform, I went completely unconscious from a standing position. I must have hit the floor hard, landing on my lower spine first and then the back of my head. Bad luck for the back but lucky for the head.

If one is going to faint in Penn Station, I had the right day, the right time and the right place. If it had been 4 PM on Friday I might not have been found for hours. But given my spot between the police desk and the railroad office, within ten seconds I had two policemen and a woman from the Long Island Railroad taking care of me. They contacted the Fire Department and within ten minutes there were three EMS workers on the scene. In another ten minutes I was in the ER of Beth Israel Hospital. The only words I remember spoken to me were by the woman medic who said as we entered the hospital: "Thank you for flying today with the NYFD."

I had suggested Beth Israel to them because I had so recently spent time in their ER. I thought it might speed up things. It was two blocks from my apartment and I was just intent on getting home. I should have gone to NYU Medical where my physician is and the circle of specialists to whom he has access. At Beth Israel I met at least a dozen physicians (every one of them a woman), each of whom were very nice and no doubt skilled in her specialty. However, no one was in charge of me and there did not seem much communication among them. After numerous tests, especially for blood clots, I was released after three days.

What they did not treat was the excruciating pain in my back; I could not seem to get anyone's attention for that. The night physician scheduled an MRI which was rescinded by the morning physician. I later learned from an MRI and a bone scan that I had fractured the twelfth thoracic vertebra which the rheumatologist explained can radiate pain up to 12 inches. For the next month the pain in my back was perhaps a helpful distraction from the cancer but that was not the way it felt. Painkillers had little effect.

I did eventually get to Montauk for the last part of the family reunion. I do not remember navigating the railroad journey. I must have looked awful which

I was not aware of but there is a group photo in a restaurant that supplies the proof. My sister Dotty volunteered to come back to New York with me and stay for an unspecified length of time. Thus began a tag team of my sisters, Dotty and Mary, to take care of me for the next two months. They were my indispensable help, each of them coming down from New Hampshire with unconditional generosity of their time. I guess if it were not for them I would have been sent for rehab to a nursing home.

The colonoscopy revealed what I was expecting though the phrase "large tumor" was not encouraging. I got a quick appointment with the surgeon. After waiting 3 hours beyond my appointment time, I spoke with him for about 15 minutes. Like many (most?) surgeons he brimmed with self-confidence that he could fix me. He seemed blasé about the details, not putting much trust in the colonoscopy picture or the CT scan.

My surgeon's confidence perhaps rubbed off on me. I did not doubt that he could get the cancer. I trusted in his skill despite his offhand attitude. It is not always easy to distinguish between confidence based on talent and arrogance based on an inflated ego. An advantage to having access to one of the nation's great medical centers is that the surgeon's skills are constantly tested.

Some years ago when I had a torn rotator cuff I could not get a clear diagnosis for months until I met the right person, an orthopedist specializing in shoulders. His office was in the World Financial Center, part of the World Trade Center complex. The size of the crowd in the waiting room looked to me like Port Authority Bus Terminal except nearly everybody was a guy my age. After hours of waiting I was tempted to quit but I finally got to see him. I walked in and raised my arm and he said: "I know what's wrong with you; I can fix it; your shoulder will be better than it ever was."

His confidence would have seemed misplaced except that he did this surgery several times a day. True to his word, I had a completely healthy shoulder several months before the typical recovery time for rotator cuff surgery. When I saw him several months after the surgery he took a quick look at my rapid recovery and then asked me to talk to a man in the next cubicle who was fearful of having the surgery. The only time after that I saw him was on television on Sept. 11, 2001. He was one of the few physicians immediately on the scene tending to the wounded where he stayed throughout the day and night.

My cancer surgeon does this procedure several times a week. This was all new to me but I knew that he knew what he was doing. The technology has improved considerably over the last few decades so that what was once a death warrant can now be treated. I was astounded to learn that the surgery could be done laproscopically; I cannot begin to imagine how that is possible. The surgeon admitted that they do not really know what they will find until they open you up. I asked if the laprosy is as good in showing whether the cancer is confined. He said it provided a better picture than they could get before.

I went that day to the NYU Cancer Institute accompanied by a professor from NYU. When I had first realized that I would need someone to accompany me for some medical visits, I was at a loss. The close friends I have do not live in Manhattan. I did not want to ask someone to take a half day off from work to be my companion for a medical appointment. It happened, however, that because I had to cancel two speaking engagements at NYU word of my illness got back to the chair of my former department. He immediately contacted me and said he or someone else in the department was ready to help in any way they could, including accompanying me to appointments.

I was relieved to have a solution to that problem. Even more so, I was surprised and touched by the outpouring of support that was backed by action. I had been retired for two years from full-time work. University departments are not known for being well- springs of human kindness, and certainly not for retired members. Even before retirement I was not a prominent member of the department. During Maria's illness I thought that perhaps I should retire because I was not pulling my weight. The professor who was then chairman very kindly said: "Don't worry about it; teach your classes and we'll take care of the rest."

The department is now filled with bright young people who have recently graduated from top universities. I had come to NYU for the religious education program that died at the time this department was formed. At seminars when we identify ourselves to an outside speaker, my self-description is utility infielder in the department. I taught courses in three or four programs without being located in any one of them. The current department chair, besides being the top person in his field nationally, is one of the kindest and most caring people I have ever met. The department response to my sickness was no doubt rallied by him but many people, including the department secretary, surprised me with their generosity and genuine concern.

My NYU colleagues were one surprise but not the biggest. I was constantly taken aback by the letters and calls that I received. A dear friend,

Anthony Fasano, asked me if it would be okay to inform the organization of former Christian Brothers. I said I was neither trying to hide my illness nor publicize it. I was aware that this network was efficiently run but I was unaware of its extent. I heard from people I had not had contact with in thirty, forty or fifty years. Some sent cards; more used email which is an easier and quicker way to express sympathy. Most of the letters were thoughtful and generous in feeling. I found it nice to have people say the things that are usually reserved for funerals when it is a little late. I suppose many people thought my funeral was imminent.

The genuine concern that so many people showed was the central element in my experience of serious illness. I am still somewhat bewildered by it, in part because it made me wonder about my own concern for sick people whom I know. If only just a handful of people had shown concern for me I would have readily understood. Especially since Maria's death and my retirement, I have not been an integral part of anyone's life. Why should anyone be concerned, then, whether I live or die when they have much more pressing concerns?

The question is not asked in self-pity; my aloneness is just a fact of life, in large part my own choosing. I live what for many people would be a lonely life although I can never remember feeling lonely (perhaps that is itself pathological). My chief interlocutor these days is probably the building super, a friendly and hard working Puerto Rican, José, who is known to all as Daniel. He keeps the building spotless and as far as I can tell is friendly with everyone in all ninety-three apartments. He was very helpful and concerned during my illness. When each of my sisters stayed in the apartment, he said to me: "If they need anything at all, tell them to just ask me for help." Not the stereotype of a super in a Manhattan apartment building.

I knew that my four siblings would be concerned about my health. We have been together a long time and keep in touch. I certainly would be missed at our family gatherings, just as Maria still is. But that nieces and nephews were concerned surprised me. I tried to remember when I was young having any interest in the health of some old uncle. Perhaps to the extent my mother was concerned with the sickness or death of a sibling, I took some notice but not much. Weren't people in their 70's supposed to die?

The simplest description of love that I know of is St. Augustine's words: *Volo ut sis*. That translates as "I want you to be." It is a simple but profound feeling that gives ultimate affirmation to another being. Nothing is sought; no possession is claimed; no particular actions are demanded. One human being simply says to another: I want you to be. The other person is not necessarily a close friend or even a regular acquaintance. I have often quoted a line of Gorky's referring to Tolstoy: "So long as this man is alive I am not alone in the world." I have wondered, however, about the twenty years Gorky lived after Tolstoy died. At my mother's funeral, I quoted a line of Gabriel Marcel's: "To say I love you is to say you will never die." The promise of love is thus rudely contradicted by death; I want you to be but death says that will not be. Yet at some level human beings in the face of all evidence to the contrary affirm that love is everlasting.

## During

The surgery ("re-section") was scheduled for July 7. The surgeon said I should expect to stay in the hospital for about 5 days or as long as it took for my digestive system to be functioning. After that, he said, I would need a month to recover my energy. I thought a month seemed more than enough time. In fact, however, he was exaggerating in the other direction. Whether or not his prediction was part of his conveying confidence, a more realistic guess for recovery would have been three or four months. Certainly the thirty pounds I had lost to the anemia and cancer could not be gained back in a month.

The surgery was scheduled for 3 PM which had its drawbacks. We were in the middle of an extreme heat wave. I was very weak and with my system cleaned out and no food or liquid that day my body reacted. While being prepared for the surgery my heartbeat suddenly doubled. I had had no anxieties up to that point and my only fear then was that the surgery would be postponed. Quick action brought the heart back to normal. Everything went smoothly after that.

I admit to a bias about anesthesiologists based on a small sample. They struck me as grumpy old guys who had no desire to be part of the medical team. They know their specialty and no one should interfere. One would like to think that the person holding you in suspended animation is concerned with more than his fee. The anesthesiologist at NYU shattered my stereotype. He was very friendly, careful to explain every step, and precise in everything he did. He seemed laid back but when action was needed with my heart beat he did not waste a second. When he found I was a professor emeritus at NYU, while he is an assistant professor, he kidded about that all the way into the operating theatre. Wheeling me down the corridor he shouted for everyone to get out of the way because a professor emeritus was coming through. His voice calmly guided me to sleep.

The next thing I knew I was waking up and speaking with both the surgeon and my sister. I don't remember anything said; he apparently assured me that everything went as planned. The whole first day and night was a haze although there was surprisingly little pain. In fact, the severe pain in the back that I had had for the previous month finally got some relief from the morphine after the surgery. The morphine was set for 1mg an hour but I had a button that enabled me to get another 1mg up to every 20 minutes. After I had pushed the button numerous times I figured it must be morning but I found that the clock said 1AM.

The days after surgery were not very pleasant but it was all part of the game. I appreciated the many visitors who came to cheer me up. A Buddhist minister, who is a former student, regularly visited. She was insistent on my learning Buddhist techniques of healing. It took me all of the five days to get my digestive system stable. I also learned to walk in the corridor with the help of a cane. When it came time to leave the hospital, the crowds of people in the elevator and on First Avenue were intimidating. Tony Fasano provided invaluable help to getting a cab and getting us into the apartment. From then on it was a question of getting solid food into the system and through the system.

The big day was a week later when I went to see the surgeon and the oncologist for the pathology report. The lymph nodes would show if the cancer had spread. I understood that there were three possibilities: no cancer remaining, chemotherapy, or the cancer had spread beyond the colon.

I don't think I was naïve but I approached the moment without anxiety. I was prepared for whatever was coming. If he had said, "sorry, it has spread to the liver or pancreas," I would not have been surprised and not terribly dismayed. If I had six months or a year, I would not change my life much. It is true I had been thinking throughout the whole experience that maybe I would be a better person, more generous with my time and money. I did not imagine having a new personality but a slightly better version of the person I am. Perhaps if the news had been that I had only a few months remaining I might have changed for the better – or maybe for the worse.

The news turned out to be the best I could have expected. The tumor was large but it had not broken through the wall of the colon. The surgeon had examined fifty lymph nodes before declaring me cancer free (the oncologist told me they typically do a dozen). I did not need chemotherapy or radiation. Cancer free means that current machines cannot detect the cancer cells. I was told my chances were about three to one of a non-recurrence of the cancer. Those are pretty good odds although when betting on one's life one would like a little better ratio. The surgeon, true to his style, quickly exited and left me to talk to the oncologist.

I was told that my chances might increase another four or five percentage points if I took part in a major research study of stage-two colon cancer patients. The key word was "might"; there was no guarantee of any personal benefit. In the study, a patient is randomly assigned to one of three groups: the first gets no chemo, the second gets six months of it, the third group a year of chemo.

I talked at length with the oncologist about the study. She assured me that the effects of chemo are not as bad as they used to be. I could do the 36 hours on Monday and Tuesday, while being ready to teach on Thursday. I don't doubt her honesty but I have never met anyone for whom chemotherapy was anything but a horrible and debilitating experience. If the choice had been chemo or die, I would have taken the chemo (I think). Otherwise, I could not agree to the 67 percent chance of taking it with no promise that it would improve my chances of survival. I really would have liked to contribute to the important research. But if I have only a short time to live I don't wish to spend six months or a year of it drugged.

After

The letters and calls resumed when I was at home. I cannot believe the number of people who offered me a place where I could rehab. Some of them I barely know or can't quite remember from the past. The generosity of people just amazed me. While thankful to all of them, I had no inclination to go anywhere beyond my apartment which I had come to like very much after a year's residence there. Each morning during the recovery I would try to add a block to my early morning walk (Manhattan is especially lovely before 7 AM), sometimes picking up a bagel and a good cup of coffee for my sister.

The night before I had had surgery I received back from the publisher a manuscript of mine with a request for major revisions. I told the editor I would get back to her in a week or ten days. Working on the revision during July and August provided something useful to do when I could not travel very far from home. That proved to be good therapy although I did not do a good job of revising. My mind was not as clear as I thought it was. I had to do another major revision two months later. I did manage to keep moving on it and the book, *Living Nonviolently*, is due to be published next March.

After being home from the hospital about a week I said to my sister that I suddenly had the feeling that I was now inhabiting my body. I realized that for the previous six weeks I had been a sort of spectator to what was done to me. I later was struck by a passage in Simone De Beauvoir's *Coming of Age*. She says that when she had her first serious illness in old age, she suddenly realized that the woman being carried on a stretcher was herself. I know exactly what she describes. It is perhaps a reduced version of the near death experience in which people say they looked down from the ceiling at those who were trying to revive them. One clearly is alive, not dead, but there is perhaps a defensive move by one's body to tamp down emotions of fear, flight, and pain.

I felt bad about canceling a number of obligations which I had for the summer. Some of them I did not feel terribly bad about, such as being a reader of a dissertation for the University of Queensland. I have regularly quoted Woody Allen that 85% of life consists in showing up. Whatever else I did I in my career I was there and on time. I had never had to cancel an agreement to produce an article or to show up as a speaker. People were very understanding of my problem even if it caused them the inconvenience of finding a last minute replacement.

I unrealistically had hoped to attend the International Seminar on Religious Education that was meeting in late July in Ottawa. I had to send my regrets at the last moment. I received many expressions of sympathy from colleagues in that organization; some of those friendships go back thirty years. One commitment I was determined to meet was my Fall graduate course in international education. It was a little presumptuous to assume that in the first week of September I would be ready for the bell but I was.

Throughout the Fall I had a number of medical problems that required attention. I was often not clear whether they were related to the cancer. Several of my physicians used the same metaphor, that my body had experienced an insult. Every cell of the body has to be informed and heard from before good government can be restored. I could not complain.

I referred earlier to a colleague whose full-time work was with children who are dying and children whose parents have died. Not much bothered her; the rest of life looks pretty good when you work constantly with the tragic. I think perhaps my experience of the past year has increased my equanimity during life's minor crises. I noticed that in October when I was mugged on the subway. When the same MO had been used on me in London some years back I was discombobulated. This time I was surprised at my own reaction which was mainly one of disappointment. The subway is one of my favorite places where I have peacefully traveled for forty-five years. I was disappointed at someone abusing the subway.

As a good citizen I thought I should report the crime to the police. I have always felt intimidated by the police although my encounters with New York City cops have always been cordial. This time was no different. A detective carefully gathered all my information although I was not a very observant witness. He followed up and tried to track the perps through their use of my bank card. The robbers used my card to get food at what is probably the worst fast food chain in the country. The woman at Chase Bank agreed with me that they should have found themselves a better restaurant. I have to admit that the experience was mostly entertaining; the police squad room was more Barney Miller than CSI.

In the memoir I wrote about Maria I described a conductor on the Long Island Railroad who sat with me for an hour the weekend she was dying. Artie and I have remained friendly though I see him less frequently. In the summer, he was concerned about my health when I traveled on the train with my sister. On a subsequent trip when I was alone, he insisted on taking my phone number so that he could check that evening that I was okay. He did in fact call that evening, and when he did not see me over the holidays, he called again to check on my health. That is service one does not expect from railroad conductors but it does confirm for me that despite all the terrible things that happen there is much kindness in the world.

As I did when Maria was in the nursing home I continue to marvel at the work that people do with the sick, the aged and the dying. I know they are doing it to "make a living" but so many of them obviously have more invested in their work than the need for a paycheck. The nurses are the most extraordinary as well as the physical therapists. Success is measured in such tiny steps or in resisting something that would be worse. I do not know how anyone works a twelve-hour shift with people who are not in a condition to be friendly and appreciative of what is done for them.

Life is now rather simple. I have started on a new writing project. The topic will not get many readers but these days I write what is of interest to me regardless of the number of potential readers. I am fond of a statement by Arthur Koestler that any serious writer would trade a hundred readers today for ten readers ten years from now, and one reader a hundred years from now. My neighborhood provides me with a surplus of both life's necessities and entertainments, especially theatres and restaurants. A recent *Times* article on our most high class restaurant said that within a two block radius of it there are sixty-five food establishments. No need to go hungry.

However, my chief entertainment in life is walking the streets of Manhattan. Even after forty-five years of such walking there is always something surprising to see; the diversity of life is never boring. But mostly I am just happy to be walking at all. Every day is a bonus.

April, 2012

## OLDER THAN DAD: AN INTERIM REPORT ON LIVING AND DYING

I am now at the exact age at which my father died. I would guess that for a man it is often a significant milestone when he becomes older than his father ever was. That may also be true for women and their mothers but I am not inclined to speculate on that. For most boys dad is the one who represents the world of grown ups and the one who sets a standard. Nearly all boys have to struggle to get out from the shadow of their fathers whether the father is loved, admired, feared, hated, or even absent.

Even when the boy is grown up and has established himself far from his father's direct control, the father's image is still out there ahead of him. The father's death does not entirely remove the sense of an overarching figure. But it is a sobering moment to enter a time zone where the father never was. Finally, the man is truly orphaned; the moment can be confusing, liberating or frightening.

I remember being surprised at the preliminary findings of a longitudinal study of men that was published when the men were in their late forties. As longitudinal studies begun in the 1920s would tend to be, the subjects were upper middle class white men who were successful at business, politics or the arts. What struck me was that nearly all of them were still very concerned about their fathers' opinions of their success in life. In some cases, the son was still trying very hard to prove himself superior to his father. Sometimes the young man had followed the same path as his father had; sometimes he had tried to find a completely different path. In neither case did he avoid having to carve out a position different from his father's.

At present, Mitt Romney is the latest politician who is trying to outperform his father, George Romney. Mitt has protested, a little too strongly, that he has had to work for everything in life that he has; he is not the beneficiary of his father's wealth. Everyone, of course, can see that there are benefits that a boy has from a father who has been a governor of a large state and a rich car manufacturer. George Romney for a short time was also the favorite to become president of the United States. One understandable but clumsy metaphor did him in when he said he had been brainwashed about the war in Vietnam. Mitt is determined not to follow in his father's footsteps even though he has a strange tendency to make embarrassing off-the-cuff remarks and to use clumsy metaphors.

What may turn out to be the worst case of a boy's attachment to and at the same time rebellion against his father is George W. Bush who by some bizarre path became the president of the United States just like his father. The younger Bush professed affection for his father and there is no reason to doubt him. But from numerous comments that are well documented, the younger Bush was out to better his father's one-term presidency. The tragedy of the United States war in Iraq lies in how much of its origin revolved around Saddam Hussein's relation to the older Bush. One reason that W. gave for going to war with Hussein was that "he tried to kill my daddy."

More important, however, was that the younger Bush wished to complete the job at which in his view his father had failed. Concerning his father's decision not to march troops into Baghdad, W. told his biographer: "My father had all this political capital built up when he drove the Iraqis out of Kuwait and he wasted it....If I have a chance to invade...if I had that much capital, I'm not going to waste it." He did in fact have the opportunity and he did what he said he would do. The result showed that the older Bush had been wiser than the younger.

When W. was getting ready for war he was asked whether he consulted with his father; his answer was that he consulted a greater father in heaven. Actually, in his memoir, *Decision Points,* W. does recount a conversation with his father about going to war. The father says: "You know how tough war is, son, and you've got to try everything you can to avoid war....But if the man won't comply, you don't have any other choice." I cannot imagine worse advice from father to son. Everyone else in the world knew there were other choices. If only it were true that the son knew "how tough war is" he would not have recklessly started a war; infrequent participation in the Texas Air National Guard did not convey the horrors of war. As for the line "if the man won't comply," it sounds like a cliché from a B-list movie.

Fortunately, most of the rebellions of sons against fathers are played out in harmless ways; the whole world is not dragged into their petty conflicts. I am not aware that I rebelled against my father although I realize that it is difficult for any man to recognize that fact in his own life. My father was a quiet man whose outward demeanor must have hid emotions that I seldom saw. As a child I admired him and I still do for his care of my mother and his hard work to support the five of us children. I was the fourth child born in the middle of the depression. It must have been an economic struggle but I never heard my father voice concerns about money. I seem to have imitated my father in trying to be in control of every situation and not letting any emotion be evident.

I do know that I tried very hard to imitate my brother who seemed to be able to do all kinds of things, especially build things and fix things. I was utterly inept at all things mechanical. In this respect I was like my father who could not fix anything. I would sympathize with my father when my mother, who in all other respects was a loving mate, would berate him for his lack of skill at doing home repairs. Eventually, I stopped trying to imitate my brother and decided I could make it through life without any of the skills that men are supposed to have.

I joined a religious order of brothers not really knowing what I was doing. Perhaps I was just running away from home and from having to compete with my father and my brother. It was a means to a good education and to the only kind of work I thought I would be good at, that of school teaching. I concentrated in school on receiving good grades which were easy to get even though I did not learn much. As a high school teacher I was not very effective at controlling a room full of forty or fifty teenage boys. Skill at teaching was mostly beside the point. The system was repressive but I was not good as an enforcer. I would not have survived at all without help from my confreres. Luckily for me I was lifted out of the high school and had the opportunity to get a PhD so as to teach in college.

Once I got some space to operate on my own I published some books and essays which got me notoriety in my small world. There followed my rebellion against church authorities. I think I went through my teenage adolescence about fifteen years late. I imagine that could be interpreted as rebelling against my father although I was far removed from the family setting. There was some strain in the relation with my parents to the extent that they became aware that I was considered a radical in my religious views; but any outward tension was with my mother rather than my father.

I lost an appointment to the job I wanted at Boston College because I ran off at the mouth and convinced the college's president that I was reckless and irresponsible. He was not far wrong. He did me a favor because I was forced to start rebuilding my life. It took me five years to get a job but New York University was a far better fit for me.

Having returned to New York after a few years in Boston, I never again considered leaving. The one woman I ever loved somehow put up with me for twenty years before we finally married and were quite happy until her sickness and death. Some people at the time thought I had waited until my parents had died before marrying; that might have been a subconscious factor although that was not what I was thinking about.

My father worked very hard until his late 60s. He worked his way up to ownership of the local bus company. But private bus companies were a dying business. When he had the chance to sell what was left he took the opportunity and retired. I thought he would find the change very difficult. Men who have been devoted to work all their lives often find retirement bewildering and tend to die quickly. It was a pleasant surprise for me to find that he seemed to adjust very well to retirement. He and my mother seemed to enjoy each other's company and be content with their lives. They regularly traveled to visit the children and the grandchildren. Since I and my four siblings lived all over the country my parents were often on the road. My father liked to drive, a characteristic I certainly did not inherit.

Although I was glad that my father seemed content in retirement he was also a puzzle to me. When I would visit the family home, I would look at my father as he was reading the newspaper or watching a baseball game. I would think to myself: How can he be so content when all he has to look forward to is dying? Shouldn't there be some anxiety that his life is running out? Doesn't he give any thought to the future and to the fact that it does not include him?

Now that I am at the age that my father reached I have a better understanding of his attitude. Old age, if you have fairly good health and adequate financial resources, can be liberating. One doesn't have to worry about the future; one can let go of a lot of what bothers younger people. Each day is here to accept and live. The experience is heightened if one has had a close brush with death, a quite common experience in old age. When I wake up in the morning, my first thought is surprise that I have one more day to live. I have no pressure to get results at a job. I can concentrate on enjoying the day and trying to be kind to the people I meet. I walk the streets and ride the subways and meet with friends; I love to study the thousands of faces I see each day in Manhattan. I continue to write every day even if publishers know that what I write does not sell.

Since I had cancer surgery two years ago there has not been an hour of any day that I have not been aware of the cancer. That may sound gruesome but I am not anxious or fearful. Cancer is simply a lifelong companion. At any moment one of the cells can go rogue and the game is over. Of course, at any age death is a possibility. Old age is different in that death is now conceivable and imaginable in a way that is almost impossible earlier in life. In old age, one either tries desperately to flee from the shadow of death or else one relaxes and accepts each day as a gift while also accepting the fact that this day realistically could be the last.

I periodically visit the NYU Cancer Center to see the oncologist. My first two trips to that building were scary: the first to arrange for the surgery, the second to receive the pathology report after the surgery. Since then I have come to almost enjoy the experience. The waiting room always has a lot of people; each one of them is either dealing with cancer or is a care giver to a cancer sufferer. I sense in the room a gentleness, peace and calmness that I do not find elsewhere. People don't shout or complain or bicker. The smaller irritations in life seem to be placed in their proper context. The oncologist and her assistant are careful and kind. Whenever I look at the oncologist, I think: You must regularly have to deliver very bad news to people. I would not know how to do that or perhaps I just don't have the courage.

After the surgery I had several small afflictions that hung on. A bad leg brought me to the emergency room three months afterward. I then went to a rheumatologist who did a set of tests that found nothing. After that I went to a physical therapist for a number of sessions. She was helpful in giving me exercises for all my aging joints but I did not get relief from the numbness in my leg. Since the discomfort did not seem to be symptomatic of something worse, I decided I could put up with it even though it restricted my daily walks.

Recently, however, the leg gave out from under me and I hit the pavement hard at Fourth Avenue and Eighth Street. My first thought after landing was surprise that nothing seemed broken. I felt a twinge on my left side that a few hours later I recognized as a broken rib. That was not worrisome because I knew the routine with broken ribs from three previous experiences ("take an aspirin and wait two weeks"). I considered myself lucky to have only a bruised knee and a broken rib; my previous two falls had sent me by ambulance to Beth Israel's emergency room.

One rather nice thing about this fall on the street was that at least ten people rushed to my aid. That was contrary to the stereotype of the Manhattan resident who would step over his or her grandmother lying in the street. From more than forty years of walking these streets I know that is not true. Undeniably these streets can be mean and there are a scandalous number of people who are forced to beg for help. Like most people I don't give money on the subway and I am selective as to which beggars on the street I give help to. The individual develops a hard shell in the face of overwhelming problems. However, I have found that many people in this city have a store of compassion just under the shell. If they are sure of what is going on they are anxious to help and they will lend a hand. A Japanese woman spoke reassuringly to me while I lay on the ground; a white man helped me to my feet.

A fall to the pavement did get my attention. I had been thinking of seeing my primary care physician whom I have not seen for a long time. I once went seven years between visits to him which was not a wise policy. But during the recent past I figured the oncologist would discover if there were any grave problems. I saw the primary care physician who referred to me to the neurologist who will send me to the physical therapist.

In a lifelong struggle with skin cancer I go to a dermatologist at least every six months. Laser surgery is a lot better than the old time scalpel. However, when the problem is on the face as it often is, fixing the problem still requires the skill of someone wielding needle and thread. I admire my skin cancer surgeon's skill at sewing. My dermatologist fancies himself a therapist to his patients. I am considering giving him up after all these years. I don't know how to get him to stop prying into my life below the skin. On my last visit he asked me if I was depressed. I was surprised at the question. I did ask myself why anyone would ask me that. Did I come across as depressed? I did not think so.

I was reminded of a scene in the fine movie of last year, *Fifty-Fifty*. The main character is told he has cancer and has a fifty-fifty chance of survival. The physician sends his patient to a psychotherapist to deal with the psychological repercussions of that diagnosis. It turns out that he is her first client. She tells him he is depressed; she knows that to be so from her studies. He insists he feels fine. She says that his feeling fine is a false feeling to cover up the depression. He wonders whether she could be right but nonetheless he still feels fine.

Forty years ago I did have bouts of depression so I think I know how depression feels and how I feel. After long reflection on the dermatologist's question I concluded, perhaps paradoxically, that at present I am less inclined to be depressed than at any previous time in my life.

My dermatologist wants me to get out more, travel, meet women, fall in love. Wouldn't it be great to have a woman as an intimate companion? Actually living alone is a more attractive arrangement. Fifty percent of households in Manhattan are of single occupancy. Nationally, one third of households are, and sixty-two percent of the elderly widowed live alone. Some people view these statistics as sad and tragic. A recent book, *Going Solo,* finds the situation mixed. Many people living alone are lonely and would prefer another arrangement. But there are also many people who prefer the advantages of living alone. This is a different world from the seventeenth-century colony that fined people for "the selfish pleasure of solitary living." The *Times* report on apartment occupancy found that people living alone had more friends and were more socially active than the rest of the population.

I realize that living alone can become impossible as one becomes very old. That does not seem like a good enough reason to seek a living companion. I did not say it to my dermatologist but if I were unsatisfied living alone I would be more inclined to seek a community of men rather than a woman. Some people might immediately deduce homosexual leanings. I have never been inclined that way. (I doubt that gay men today would be attracted to a communal arrangement). I did live for several decades in communities of men and I think I could do it again. I would want more privacy than in the past but I have maintained and cherished many male friendships over the years. I could be comfortable living in either an all male community or a community of men and women.

I was scheduled to teach a course this semester in International Education. I was not surprised but I was disappointed that the course did not have a sufficient number of students enrolled. I offered to teach those students who were interested in an arrangement off the books. They would get credit; the one drawback was that I would not get paid. I assured the department head that I did not care whether or not I was paid. He agonized over finding some arrangement in which I would receive payment for teaching. I finally told him that I would have been willing to pay him to let me teach the course. I have more money than I will ever spend; I need work not money. He relented and reluctantly allowed me to proceed.

It took me forty years to learn how to teach but I think I finally got the hang of it. Unless I am completely deluded I do a better job now than at any time in the past. I retired from full-time teaching when I was most enjoying it but I felt obliged to step aside and let a younger person have a chance. I hoped that I would be able to get part time work on a steady basis but that has proved difficult. Erik Erikson wrote that the old person needs to be needed. Teaching is one of the few things in life I can do well. But one cannot be a teacher unless there are students.

Fortunately, a teacher does not need thousands of people who chant his name. In *A Man for all Seasons,* Thomas More says to Richard Rich: "Why not be a teacher? You'd be a fine teacher, perhaps a great one." Rich responds: "If I was, who would know it?" Thomas More answers: "You, your pupils, your friends, God. Not a bad public, that." I know there will come a time when I am incapable of doing the job. If I do not recognize that condition, I hope a friend will tell me. For now I am content with sharing what I know with any number of students so long as they wish to learn. I have never had a moment of regret for running away from home to become a teacher.

## A WINDOW ON EMERGENCY ROOMS

NOTE: The following reflections were written in August, 1989. The account of a stay in an emergency room is included here because – sad to say – things have not changed much, except possibly for the worse. I reflect toward the end of the essay that emergency rooms are being swamped and cannot handle the problems which they daily face. It happens that the hospital I describe here has recently gone bankrupt and closed its doors. The resulting situation is a gaping hole in health care for this part of the city.

I recently spent eight hours in the emergency room of St. Vincent's Hospital in Manhattan. The interval was from 4 PM on a Tuesday afternoon until I got a hospital bed at one minute past midnight. Although eight hours is a very small slice of one's life, that length of time can feel like a lifetime under some circumstances. Like most people I have had occasional experiences of emergency rooms; in my case several times previously in Manhattan. But I had never been in a position to experience the total pattern of the operation. Despite being half delirious with pain, I was acutely aware of everything around me. In fact, I think it was because of the delirium that I was forced into being a curious observer of my surroundings.

I will focus on the time in the emergency room although the hospital room was largely a continuation of the experience. When I got a hospital bed, it was the third bed in a room for two beds. I never really saw the other two people during my stay. I picked up that one had AIDS and was always desperate for methadone. The other person had been shot in the stomach. A team of physicians had been working for two weeks to save him, apparently with success but without any seeming gratitude on his part.

The description that follows is not a story about how insane our health care system is. Rather, it is a tale of the extraordinary dedication and care that takes place in an overburdened system. The people working in the system every day are no doubt keenly aware of the limits of what they are doing. I must have passed through the hands of fifty people, some of them several times. Unfailingly, the people were kind, friendly, caring, and as efficient as the system allowed.

In some ways this is a terrible story, a nightmare come true. However, it is the kind of interesting experience that teaches you things you would not otherwise have chosen to learn. There is no sarcasm in what follows nor an implication that I know the right way to do things. I am just interested in being a reporter of events that are reported here from a particular angle.

I started my day, accompanied by my wife Maria, with an 8 AM treatment called lithotripsy. The word means stone smashing. In the past five years it has become the most common way to remove kidney stones. It involved 1200 precisely aimed sound blasts. The cost, like so many other medical treatments today, is staggering. When one is sick – and also rich – there is no better place to be than Manhattan. I wasn't rich but I had an insurance company backing me. You can fill in the blank for what is also one of the worst places to be sick if you are poor and lack insurance.

The medical resources on Manhattan Island are beyond imagination. In my case, there is a whole institution on the East Side devoted to nothing but lithotripsy. Eighty physicians perform this one procedure. Every person in the place is dedicated to lithotripsy. That fact generates confidence that you are in the hands of people who know what they are doing.

On the whole, I have no complaint about what was done. But through miscalculation that was in part my fault, the shock in my internal system was not clear to me when I left the recovery room at noon. By 2 PM I was at home in severe pain. Not being able to keep water down, I could not get relief from the prescribed pain killer. Maria reached my physician by 3 PM and told him of my problem: excruciating pain and a fast rising temperature. He told me that I had to keep trying to get water into my system. If I could not succeed at that, I should go to the emergency room at 4 PM where he would meet me.

By 3:45 it was obvious to me that I had to get to the hospital. The problem then was how to get there. I doubted a cabbie would take me. But the first cab that Maria stopped was a very solicitous Korean driver. He was so anxious to get me there quickly that I was relieved to get to the hospital in one piece.

At the hospital, the waiting room for the emergency room is only a half dozen steps from the street. The first person one encounters about half way into the room is a compassionate but unyielding guard. No matter what tale is recounted, the guard's message is to see the triage nurse. Triage? I thought my mind was playing tricks and that I had misunderstood the word. But that is indeed what she is called. She takes a first look and listens. You say: "Unbearable pain in the kidney." She replies: "Have a seat and I will get you for registration as soon as possible."

Triage is a nineteenth-century military word for treating casualties on the battlefield. When the medical supplies are inadequate, one has to decide who can be treated. The metaphor of war is overused in our society but it perhaps did apply here. At least, the wounded kept coming through the door. They arrived in cabs, from buses, on foot, or by stretcher. A few steps from a busy corner on Seventh Avenue, the drama gets played out twenty-four hours a day.

At about 5 PM the triage nurse indicated that Maria and I could go to the registration desk, receive an identification bracelet and produce an insurance card. After that, we were allowed into the emergency room proper. I finally found someone to take the papers and she said to have a seat. There were a couple of empty chairs at the back of the room where it connected to the waiting area.

During the next hour I kept waiting for my physician to appear and to snatch me from this whole scene. I never got a sense of how big the room was, but every bit of space was in use. Only the staff moved on foot and they seemed in perpetual motion. It was not frenzied rushing about; in fact, the atmosphere was eerily calm. One almost had the sense of a slow motion film. The patience of everyone in the room was unbelievable; that included the patients. There were screams of pain, of course, but one's own pain existed in this sea of calm. The patience of the staff was the most remarkable thing to me. Unlike the rest of us, they could presumably have been somewhere else, perhaps in a different line of work.

I was reminded of a movie, *Dog Day Afternoon*, which is about a hostage taking in Brooklyn. It was an exciting movie except that its portrayal of the police negotiator was totally false. In the movie, the negotiator ran about wild, furiously screaming at everyone. In actual fact, however, the negotiator's method is to keep talking in the calmest possible tone. The police officer who had the job for over a decade was involved in over three hundred negotiations and he never lost a hostage. His actual pattern of hostage negotiation would not make a very exciting movie. Neither would the emergency room I was in.

At about 6 PM, I was called and given a cot. The woman who led me there began asking me questions about where I hurt. I said: "First, you have to know that I had lithotripsy this morning. I am suffering from complications that are the result of it." She said: What is lithotripsy?" That response was not encouraging. I heard her asking outside the curtain how to spell lithotripsy. Actually, it was not so surprising that she was unfamiliar with the term. She was on the lower end of the hierarchy, a fact that I did not know when I assumed that the first person to tend to me was to be my major medical assistance.

As it turned out, they came by the dozens, most of them with a particular test to perform. There was a vast and apparently precise hierarchy operating in the room. Some people were easy to spot: heavily armed police or weighted down paramedics. Others looked like college-age or even high school students. Most of the room was decidedly youthful. After a while one could guess at hierarchical places according to such signs as gender, race, nationality and age. But the rules were not universal. Most black men were near the bottom but occasionally one would be near the top. White women were above the black and Hispanic women, but an Indian or Filipino woman was hard to locate.

After I had been asked the same questions repeatedly, I finally said to an authoritative looking black man: "Look I am only here to meet my physician. He was supposed to meet me at here at 4 PM." The technician answered kindly but firmly: "No, everyone is cared for and evaluated by the staff in this room. Then your physician is informed and he will intervene. I have been in this room for twenty years. Believe me, I know how the system works." In some respects this information was disappointing. But it was the first confident assurance I had received. There was a logic at work and I was not caught up in some hopeless comedy of errors.

My physician was not on the scene but he did send precise instructions through another physician. Within the hour I got the shots I needed to relieve the pain. I also got hooked up to the IV that would sustain me and become my inseparable companion in subsequent days.

People kept testing my vital signs. After a while I realized that they were not really interested in the particular numbers, but only in making sure that the numbers were not off the chart. All the tests and questions had to do with what I would call the routinization of pain. The patient has a sense that there is a world still under control and that help is arriving. Perhaps more important, the young staff are learning how to provide calm and steady treatment within an environment that could overwhelm them.

At about 7 PM I was rolled out of the room for an x-ray upstairs. At this point I was conscious but a bit hazy. I do remember being in a sea of stretchers parked in a corridor. Eventually, I got through the x-ray room and seemed to be alone in a corridor. At that point, a friendly man appeared and said: "I am the admitting physician. I just have to ask you a few more questions." At the end of a friendly chat, he offered to take me back to the emergency room. That was not his job but he thought it might speed up things. When I asked how long it would take before I could get into the hospital, he smiled and said he did not know. I believed him. One thing for sure was that no one lied to me and made promises on which they could not deliver.

When I got back to the emergency room I had lost my place. Visiting hours in the emergency room are the first ten minutes of each hour, twenty-four hours a day. Maria had lost me on the 8 PM turn because I had gone upstairs. When she came back at 9 PM, someone knew exactly where I was in the room. I was impressed. They did have a tracking system in all that movement.

The next few hours were a waiting game for admission to the hospital. As noted above, even the head of admissions would not speculate when that might be. Everyone we asked was hesitant to guess. I had, however, passed some line so that now the questions and tests were stages of the admission process. As night wore on, the room became quiet. One could hear conversations more clearly. On one side a voice was saying she could not go home because there was no one in the apartment and she did not have money for a cab. On the other side, a woman was pleading to go home to the two children and a cat that were waiting for her. Some people actually did stand up and walk out, a feat that seemed miraculous in the setting.

At midnight I finally got the call to roll. Two very pleasant black men turned me over to the nurses on the fourth floor. During my stay in the emergency room I had witnessed only one shift. Actually for some of the staff, eight hours is only part of a shift. I was impressed by their concern and compassion. What truly amazed me was the thought that they do this every day, 365 days a year. They deserve a better system: more space, bigger budget, better equipment. But the machines will always need the dedicated people.

Emergency rooms throughout the United States, especially in the cities, are bearing the burden of a health care system that is priced out of sight for many people. Millions of people have no access to health care. The one place you can go with some hope is the emergency room, a place never constructed for the purpose it is now serving. As I watched this scene in a relatively affluent part of Manhattan, I kept wondering what it looks like in parts of Brooklyn and the Bronx.

One of the few good features, as I have indicated, is a certain egalitarianism under which the proceedings take place. When you go to the triage nurse, the only discrimination is how sick you are. Overwhelming pain is a quick leveler, even for those people who are rich and – up to that point – powerful.

I suspect it is a tendency of human beings to think: no one knows the suffering I have; surely it is greater than anyone else's. If we have enough sense to look around the world, the city, or sometimes the room, one is humbled by the view and saved from self pity. Usually, we just have to penetrate a veil that separates us from those who are suffering far beyond what pains we have. On the good days, however, it is easy not to see that veil at all. Dostoevsky wrote that we ought to treat everyone we meet as we would a sick child in a hospital. That approach might make some of our institutions come to a quick stop and reconsider what they are doing, but that might not be such a bad thing

# CHAPTER THREE: DEATH EDUCATION: DOES ANYONE NEED IT?

Since the 1960s in the United States there has been a death and dying movement. Central to this movement has been the claim that everyone needs "death education." Many universities began offering courses on death. The movement has tried, with limited success, to have courses offered in secondary and elementary schools.

The reflections in this book have emerged out of the struggle to teach the young. For twenty-five years I taught a course called "The Meaning of Death" to undergraduate students in a large urban university. The course was limited to fifty students who signed up in the first few days of registration. At the beginning I feared that the course might attract the suicidal, the morbid. or students looking for an easy course. Almost never was that the case. The students were among the best and the brightest, and as psychologically balanced as any group of college students can be these days.

The young think of death as far away and, for the most part, they are right. I was always surprised, therefore, that at least some young people do wish to reflect on dying and the meaning of death. I was always uneasy about the academic integrity of the course, starting with the presumptuous title that was not of my choosing: "The Meaning of Death." I had to admit in the first class of the course that I don't know the meaning. Perhaps *meanings* would have been a better word in the title but the problem goes deeper, namely, whether death is the proper subject matter for a college course. It was cross listed in two schools and had four departmental listings, which is indicative of its maverick nature. Because it was listed as a religion course, some students were religious studies majors who might have come expecting the study of ancient sacred texts on death. Many other students who signed up for the course were indifferent or hostile to religion.

In the first years of the course I realized that the most common reason for a student choosing the course was that someone close to the student had recently died or was dying. The student might have been looking for therapy more than for an academic course. A classroom is not a place designed for therapy but people take comfort wherever they can find it. I explained in the first class meeting that the course was not aimed at therapy. If a student wished to speak about a personal experience of death – as many did – that was their choice, but I would not play at being a therapist.

The course delved into any place and any medium that might help in the understanding of death. The casual transgression of academic disciplines did not seem to bother students but it did concern me. I do not think this approach is a good model for other courses. I used this grab bag approach because I did not know how else to get hold of death.

From this experience I can see the value of a college course on death offered as an elective. As for requiring high school and elementary school students to study death and dying, I am skeptical. Advocates of death education say that the traditional college age is too late for beginning one's education in this area. That is true and I return below to the need to begin "death education" in early childhood. Before describing how to answer the need, however, are we certain about the need itself?

## A New Need?

Is there a need for death education and, if so, is that something new? Has the world always needed it but failed to recognize the need until recently? I noted above that the movement seems to have emerged in the late 1960s. Is there any special significance to that date? Was this movement part of a package deal that saw all aspects of the culture and its education shaken up? Like other fads of that time it may have peaked long ago and now is the preserve of a few faithful followers. Or like other aspects of the 1960s, it might be a movement that is still gathering momentum. As it was in 1968 (or 1468) the fundamental issue of death is not going away. The death rate on earth is one hundred percent; one out of one dies.

The question is whether this time and this place are in need of a particular change in education. Are there factors that have reshaped the fundamental idea of mortality, forcing us to face new questions about the universal experience of dying? Anyone can list both positive and horrific factors of the past century that have affected the human experience of dying. Whether or not that list essentially changes the experience of dying cannot be confidently asserted by anyone.

A common claim is that we need death education because the issue of death is hidden in contemporary culture. Is it true that individually and collectively people avoid the subject of death? At first glance, the claim seems wildly off the mark. Popular culture seems saturated with violence and killing, war and terrorism. Whether one watches the news or a drama on television, death is usually the lead story. The blockbuster movies that Hollywood sends around the world are most often technically brilliant but powerfully violent exercises concerned with death.

The person who claims that death is a taboo topic must either be oblivious of the surrounding cacophony or else is speaking paradoxically. I think that someone who says that the culture is silent on death is referring to the absence of reflection on one's personal mortality. That is, the reality of one's own death is seldom engaged or discussed. The culture does its best to hide from general view the sick and the dying. The constant portrayal of death on the movie or television screen could be part of the evasion of real dying. Watching characters on a screen be blown away can lead to a belief that one is facing death while in fact the experience is a distancing of oneself from one's own mortality. The idea conveyed is that death is what happens to other people.

The claim is also made that the absence of reflection on dying is a recent development. Any clear comparison with the past on this point is hampered by the limitation of material from previous eras and our inability to know the experience of ordinary people from 5000 or even 500 years ago. We can try to construct a picture from materials such as funeral markings, religious rituals, popular poetry, and diaries. We have the pronouncements of a few philosophers and religious leaders but the relation between their words and society at large is not clear.

Plato, as the first great philosopher in the West, is often cited as expressing the attitude of ancient thought concerning death. Plato put the case simply and starkly that philosophy is a "meditation upon death." He argues that "those who philosophize aright study nothing but dying and being dead."[1] The trial and death of Socrates comes to us from Plato's writings. The attitude of Socrates to his own dying undoubtedly shaped the outlook of his young disciple, Plato. The death of Socrates, along with the death of Jesus of Nazareth, became in the West the preeminent examples of how one's dying should be approached, namely, with clarity, courage and hope in a better life. Dying was what human life moved toward and therefore dying was what a human being constantly prepared for.

The philosophical marker that is often cited as a radical altering of this pattern is a seventeenth-century statement of Baruch Spinoza. Directly contradicting Plato, Spinoza wrote that "the free man thinks of nothing less than of death; his wisdom is a meditation not upon death but upon life."[2] This statement in 1677, the year of Spinoza's own death, may be emblematic of a change that was in the air in seventeenth-century Europe and whose effects continued into the twentieth century. The focus of the new sciences shifted concern from death to life, a change that might be seen as healthy and hopeful. Some commentators, however, have seen the move as a flight from death, a living in pretense. The modern affirmation of life is seen to be a denial of death.

If modernity is deeply committed to a denial of death, then the belief that the modern era has reached a crisis point could be tested by the resurfacing of death in dramatic ways. The argument can be made that that is just what occurred throughout the twentieth century. Of course, what has been the modern attitude continued to be celebrated in many quarters. For example, Harvey Cox's world-wide best seller in 1965, *The Secular City*, acclaimed the arrival of the modern in religion and, predictably, had almost nothing to say about death. The twentieth-century questioning of the modern attitude to death arrived in the United States later than it did in Europe. Many of the most prominent philosophers and theologians of the twentieth century had direct experience of the disillusioning war between 1914 and 1918. The devastating experience of that "great war" shows up in the work of many writers in the first half of the twentieth century.

The philosophical work that is often cited as signaling a turn from the theme of modern progress to one of acknowledging the stark reality of death is Martin Heidegger's *Being and Time*, published in 1927. Not only does death return, it becomes the defining element of human life (or what Heidegger calls *Dasein*). "As soon as a human being is born, he is old enough to die right away."[3] Although Heidegger posits that "man is a being toward death," this characteristic is not evident, Heidegger contends, because human beings do everything possible to avoid thinking about death.[4]

A similar theme emerged in the writing of Sigmund Freud, who like Heidegger, cast a shadow across the twentieth century. Freud, almost in spite of himself, eventually came to posit a "death drive" which struggles with the force of life and finally wins out. "The aim of all life is death," Freud wrote, "all living creatures strive to die; indeed death appears to be an object of desire."[5] Thus for Heidegger, Freud, and their descendants death returned with a vengeance, not as a gentle reminder or a fact of life but as an overwhelming power and an obsessive concern.

The writings of Heidegger or Freud may have brought into the open the modern flight from death. It would be too much to claim that their work was the cause of the shift away from contentment with modern progress. A new prominence of death was no doubt the result of a confluence of scientific, political, aesthetic and cultural causes. I will comment on two of the most obvious and powerful causes of the emergence of death: war in an era of world-wide communication and medical technology in its fight against death.

Warfare has presumably always been a reminder of human mortality. It brings early death to masses of healthy young people. However, the scale of war has changed dramatically, beginning with the United States' Civil War in which over 600,000 young men were killed. Weapons of offense had outstripped tactics of defense. That war was a prelude both to World War I and to civil wars at the end of the twentieth century. Sandwiched between these later and earlier wars was the horror of World War II, including the Holocaust, and a half century of cold war in which the annihilation of hundreds of millions of people was coolly contemplated.

Large numbers of deaths can obscure rather than heighten awareness of an individual's dying. In the second half of the twentieth century, however, war came into the living room. Television became increasingly capable of instantaneous transmission of deadly combat. The rise of the death and dying movement coincided with the war in Vietnam, the first televised war. Television was sometimes accused of deadening people's sensitivity to war and killing. It probably did have that effect but it also had a cumulative effect: disgust and despair at the killing of over two million people in a war whose purpose was never clear. Since that war, the United States has often sent its military when the television cameras have shown great suffering. The United States has also tended to pull out its military when television pictures of dead U.S. soldiers bring pressure on the government.

World-wide communication is a force for spreading the ideals of justice, rights and democracy. The same media can be exploited in the service of killing for what is believed to be a noble cause. Dramatic killings can achieve disproportionate effect through television and the Internet. The bombing of the World Trade Center in 2001 killed fewer than three thousand people. That number would not rank it among the top calamities of the twentieth century, let alone all human history. But people from around the world could view the dramatic unfolding of the event; several million people watched the incineration as it happened. A documentary film, that included footage from 118 amateur photographers, claimed that the bombing was the most documented event in history.[6] Did this event change the perception of life and death in New York, the United States or the rest of the world? Some permanent effect is likely in the lives of those who were close to the event. What it has done on any large scale to people's attitude to death will take decades to become clear.

The second major influence in the contemporary perception of death is modern medicine and its attendant technology. The change here would seem to be for the good; human beings are able to live longer and to live more healthily. Until 1900, fewer than half of the people who entered hospitals returned alive. The physician's little black bag contained very little help in staving off death. Most deaths occurred in the home so that family members, including children, gained familiarity with death.

In the United States the funeral industry had been founded in the mid-nineteenth century. Death became more isolated from ordinary life even as the claim was made that dying was natural. Together with the rural cemetery, the new funeral profession tried to prettify death. But starting about 1880 new medicines and machines made dying a more complicated process watched over by the expert called "doctor."

The big leap in medical technology did not occur until the second half of the twentieth century. Fantastic feats of surgery and the use of "wonder drugs" transformed the care of the sick. New problems appeared in deciding when and how death happens. The fact that more than eighty percent of deaths in the United States occur in hospitals has the effect of removing death from the general public's awareness. Death is kept out of sight, if not out of mind. Today's diseases and the research information about those diseases can provide a person with knowledge that he or she has a month, six months, or a year to live. If as Dr. Johnson said, "getting hanged in a fortnight wonderfully concentrates the mind," then being told that one has liver cancer is likely to encourage a person to reflect upon his or her own dying.

Not surprisingly, Elisabeth Kübler-Ross' *On Death and Dying* was published just as the revolution in health care had begun.[7] Technology was extending people's lives and also the process of dying. There was now a population who were simply waiting to die. Kübler-Ross' study would have been inconceivable fifty years earlier. Published quietly by a small press, the book found a ready audience. It was on the best seller list for years and continues to be read today.

If death had been in the closet until the late 1960s, Kübler-Ross' book seemed to signal that death was now an in-topic. Philippe Aries, a maverick historian who had changed the perception of childhood, turned his attention to dying.[8] Aries gave a series of lectures in 1973 on the theme that death is a taboo topic that no one writes about. When the published lectures appeared in 1974, the book was reviewed in the *New York Times* with a series of other books just published on death.[9] That fact might indicate that the book's thesis was incorrect and that death was out in the open. Aries was not convinced. A sudden explosion of writing is not conclusive evidence that a topic is being thoughtfully examined in its proper context. In the decades that have followed there has been an increase in the number of books, especially textbooks, on death.

## Dying in Education

The ABC television program *20/20* once did a segment on "Death Education."[10] The treatment of the topic revolved around a high school course that included a visit to the morgue, and an elementary school class on its visit to a funeral home. Like many stories on television news magazines, this one had a shock appeal and was directed especially at parents. The commentator advised parents to find out if death education was being taught in their local school and, if so, whether the course was optional. All but one of the teachers interviewed on the program seemed unprepared to be teaching a course on death. A teacher shown to be using an unorthodox form of therapy said she had one day's training. A student who tried to commit suicide said that the course had made death seem desirable. Fourth graders required to touch a dead body showed fear and revulsion on their faces.

The television producers could have found more positive examples to give the program balance. Even with its bias, however, the program raised a serious question concerning what schools should do about the reality of death. What is appropriate for death education, where and when should it occur?

The people on the program repeatedly referred to "teaching death education." They were using a standard phrase but one that obscures understanding. We cannot begin to explore how death belongs in education so long as "death education" is the name given to a course in school. That use of language prevents any discussion of how the question of dying should be included in education from infancy to old age, and within the family, school and other institutions.

Logically, the only people who teach death education are those who teach the teachers of dying and death.

Education in regard to death has two kinds of teaching: 1) teaching someone how to die 2) teaching someone how to understand death. At the beginning of a course on death, I would acknowledge that the first of these two kinds of teaching is the more important, but I could not do that in a classroom. Someone else had to teach them how to die. The small but important job that the classroom can do is to provide a language for people to understand and discuss death.

## Teaching People How To Die

Teaching is showing someone how to do something. Most teaching in the world is nonverbal and communal. Starting in childhood and continuing throughout our lives, the examples of fellow human beings shape our own attitudes and lay out a path for us. The teaching might begin with the death of a parent or a grandparent or the death of a public figure. By middle age, everyone has been taught how to die by a parent, a relative, or a friend. Quiet influence is especially the case when it comes to the dying as teachers. Often unwittingly, the dying person becomes a powerful teacher. In the play, *Wit*, the professor who is dying of cancer discovers that she has become a different and perhaps more effective teacher than she was in the classroom.

Not surprisingly, two of the best known contemporary works on death begin with their respective authors acknowledging the dying patients as the teachers. Elisabeth Kübler-Ross writes in the Preface of *On Death and Dying*: "We have asked him [the patient] to be our teacher so that we may learn more about the final stages of life."[11] Similarly, Sherwin Nuland, at the beginning of *How We Die*, writes: "Even when I had no idea I was learning from one or another of the vast number of men and women whose lives have entered mine, they were nevertheless teaching me, usually with equal unawareness of the gift they were bestowing."[12]

We learn how to die because we are taught how to die. Not everyone is a ready learner and many people disregard the lessons that are all about them and within their own bodies. When one is young it is easy to dismiss much of the teaching; other people die but surely one's own death is not imminent. Some children, teenagers and young adults do have to be fast learners because of their surroundings or their own ill health. In middle age and old age, suffering is a powerful teacher. The infirmities of age as a premonition of death stimulate reflection on one's own mortality. Erasmus said that his kidney stone was his great teacher: "That is our philosophy, that is the true meditation on death."[13]

Practically every religious tradition has recognized that to teach someone how to live includes teaching him or her how to die. And since dying is such a difficult part of life, a part we might deny or hide, dying is one of the first things taught, usually in the form of ritual.[14] Birth is a form of death to a previous intra-uterine life so that the infant already has some experience of dying on which to build an education. Infancy for a human being is a dependent and fragile existence. A concept of death is not present but an infant survives with a sense of the precariousness of life.

Young children cannot and should not be shielded from all encounters with death. Philippe Aries, in his study of deathbed scenes, found that until two and a half centuries ago the pictures always included children.[15] Then adults began to shield children from all direct knowledge of death. The intention was to preserve the child's innocence, and so was born a separate part of life called childhood. Some of the protections of childhood were good. Children should not have to be overwhelmed by life's complexities and horrors. But dying is an unavoidable aspect of life. Trying to cut off the child from encountering death requires a truncated sense of life and the effort is bound to fail. The task for adults, especially parents, is to allow death its place in ways that do not terrify or overwhelm.

Many small children experience the death of a pet animal. The occasion is a teachable moment in the child's short life. The child should be allowed to recognize and accept what has happened. Adults need do little explaining, although a funeral ritual is often helpful. What parents should not do is rush in a replacement cat, dog, or goldfish in the attempt to deny that any serious change has occurred. A child's grieving for a time over a departed animal is not unhealthy.[16]

A more serious experience that is common for children is the death of a grandparent or another relative. Most likely the death occurs in a hospital or nursing home where children are unlikely to be found. Among religious and ethnic groups for whom viewing the body is standard practice, the question of the child's presence is always raised. If children are brought to a funeral home, they should be carefully prepared beforehand as to exactly what they will see, hear and touch. When possible, a child should be brought to view the body before other people arrive. When children ask challenging questions, as they do, the answers should be as simple and truthful as possible. If the child wants to know where grandma has gone, the adult should formulate an answer in terms that make sense within the family's tradition.[17]

Less directly but surely, every child meets death in stories, movies, television programs, and in local events or the world news. Children do not shy away from stories about death. Fairy tales, the secret literature of childhood, are filled with stories of violence and death. Not every story is appropriate for every child. Exposure to too much mayhem, whether fictional or real, is not good for children. The issue is always restraint and guidance on the part of adults so that death is kept in perspective and one's emotional response is proportionate to the occasion. A child absorbs the adult's attitude to death, the effect of which is greater than any explanations by the adult.

## Teaching People To Understand Death

The reason why courses in school are called "death education" is the assumption that unless something is taught in school it is not part of one's education. If confronted with that proposition, most professional educators will say that they recognize teaching and learning beyond the schoolroom. However, that is not the way they ordinarily speak. Teaching is assumed to be telling things to children; and teachers are assumed to be people who work in classrooms. Any other use of language is considered an extension of the primary meanings of teaching and teacher.

Death is one of several important issues that do not fit easily into school curricula. Its most obvious relative is sex which for more than a century has been a contentious issue in schools.[18] Advocates of death education sound similar to enthusiasts of sex education: the ignorance of students and the negative attitudes in the culture require schools at every level to offer courses that will shape positive student attitudes. The urgency of the situation is thought to demand aggressive techniques to reverse prior beliefs and attitudes. It is said that the earlier that students are exposed to sex education and death education the more likely they are to develop positive attitudes to sex and death.

When schools talk about "teaching sex education" and "teaching death education," why is "education" part of the course name? Subjects that are secure in school curricula have recognizable names such as physics, mathematics or history. Often the curriculum name includes the idea of study or discussion: biology, psychology, sociology; the course teaches a language to study life, soul, society or dozens of other subject areas. When something does not fit into the curriculum, the term "education" is often attached (driver education, physical education, sex education, drug education, moral education, religious education). It is a kind of overstatement to shore up support but actually stirs up doubts about the academic integrity of the topic. The peculiar language subverts the classroom's genuine contribution to education in an area that the school does not and cannot control.

In many countries religious education and moral education are curricular subjects. Parents may be hoping that the students are learning morality and (the parents' own) religion, but the schools shy away from claiming to teach religion or morality. In such curriculum areas, schools worry about remaining "objective" so they introduce a second layer of abstraction: they teach "moral (or religious) education." But "morality" and "religion" are already abstract and objective terms; teaching religion is not the same as teaching Christianity, teaching the New Testament or teaching baptism. Nonetheless, for many people "religion" still suggests a subjective attitude.

In contrast, teaching religious education, moral education or sex education allows for the denial that a teacher is imposing any actual view of religion, morality or sex. The parent may know what morality is but the school knows what moral education is and, therefore, parents are in no position to criticize a moral education or sex education course. The risk in this second level of abstraction is that the subject matter becomes abstruse technicalities that hide but do not replace whatever biases inevitably operate in the lives of curriculum makers and classroom instructors.

Dying, as the most extreme subject matter, might throw light on this important educational issue. If one can deal with death in education, other things might fall into place. Conversely, the controversies surrounding sex education or moral education might suggest which paths to follow and which mistakes to avoid in trying to include death in education. There is a need for a term to specify the limited but helpful role of the school in sexual education. Professional educators have tried to replace the term sex education (for example, with sexuality education) but "sex education" has retained a popular hold. The term "sexology" might be appropriate as a curriculum name but it has not had much success.

Death, in contrast to sex, does have an academic name, thanatology, meaning the study of death. Many people might assume that the term thanatology is an invention of the 1960s, but it was coined in the mid-nineteenth century (before, for example, the term sociology). Any aspect of existence can be a legitimate classroom topic if there has developed a language for discussion and methods of research in that area. When a sufficiently large body of literature exists, the subject can be taught and learned in a classroom setting. Despite the fuzziness of its method, thanatology is something that is taught in the university and something in which one can get an academic degree.

Just as psychology or anthropology are not courses taught in elementary school, so also thanatology is not a fit candidate. There is need for elementary school teachers to know psychology and there are psychological questions raised by young children. Those psychological questions are best addressed in the particular contexts in which they arise. Similarly, one can hope that any teacher of the young would have engaged the reality of death and reflected upon various aspects of human mortality. Questions about death can arise in just about every school course imaginable. The questions ought to be answered as candidly and as truthfully as possible. On matters of sex, death, or religion, children often simply wish to hear an adult speak without embarrassment, evasion, or smugness.

The classroom is a place for a peculiar kind of conversation about things that one already knows. While the library and the Internet are chief sources of information, the classroom is a place to question the information, to challenge biases, and to sharpen needed distinctions. By crossing the threshold of a classroom the student agrees to nothing less and nothing more than to put his or her words on the table for examination. The student should already know how to read, speak and write; the classroom is for learning how to read better, speak better, and write better. In the classroom one person may do most of the talking but the form of speech should always be dialogical: posing questions, provoking thought, inviting replies. The restrictions of a school course should generally exclude requiring students to do such things as to visit a morgue or a funeral home.

While it is the case that *the* truth about death will not be achieved, the same can be said about much else in life. If things continue to be said about one of life's important aspects, classrooms should provide that the speech does not sink into banal clichés and that the conversationalists are not oblivious of helpful resources. Anyone who speaks on death has to know when to be reticent; at all times he or she has to exercise humility. The person with strong religious convictions needs to show some restraint in claiming to know exactly what happens at death. The same principle applies to people who are absolutely certain that nothing follows death. A dose of agnosticism ("not know") would be helpful for all parties. The fact that no scientific proof is available does not make continuing inquiry useless. Rather, it raises interesting questions about the nature of evidence, belief, and choice as applied to death and to much else.

The result of taking a course on thanatology is not that one solves the mystery or riddle of death. By confronting the worst that life offers one is relieved of the burden of always hiding the truth and avoiding reality. Strangely enough, a course on death is less likely to bring on morbidity than joy. It is a chastised joy, to be sure, when one opens her or his eyes to suffering and death but the joy is genuinely concerned with life.

Colleagues would jokingly ask me why I did not teach a course called The Meaning of Life rather than one with the title The Meaning of Death. My response was that a course on the meaning of death is a focused way to ask the meaning of life. These days we are offered psychological gimmicks and endless new products as the way to a happy and successful life. A course on death should be a reminder that life has other things in store for us. As William James warned, "the skull will grin at the banquet table" unless human beings admit the unwanted guest and provide it with its proper place.[19]

# CHAPTER FOUR: IS DEATH A GROWTH EXPERIENCE?

*On Death and* Dying by Elisabeth Kübler-Ross was one of the top selling books of the twentieth century. It was on the best seller list for ten years and continued to be widely read after that. The book affected attitudes to the dying in ways that are not always obvious. Scholars tended to dismiss the book as unscientific; it was certainly vulnerable to criticism. But the book made an imprint on the culture and provided a new language about dying. It has been said at times that the field of thanatology consists of footnotes to *On Death and* Dying. That statement was an exaggeration and was unfair to hundreds of authors who have studied issues of dying and have written books that have their own distinctive approaches. Nonetheless, the statement is an extraordinary tribute to an unlikely icon.

As often happens with books that achieve such popular success, the acclaim of disciples is countered by critics who are intent on showing the book's weaknesses. What I think may be worth doing with *On Death and Dying*, now that sufficient time has passed, is something that was seldom done, namely, to give an appreciative but critical reading of the book. At the least, it should be acknowledged that she opened a conversation about death and grief that others have continued. It might be helpful to examine how her assumptions and findings have given direction to the work of others who care for the dying and who present their own conclusions about the processes of dying and grieving.

Elisabeth Kübler-Ross grew up in Switzerland, where despite paternal opposition, she trained as a physician. She did volunteer work that included a visit to the death camp at Maidanek, which she says helped to shape her attitude in later life. She accompanied her husband, Emmanuel Ross, to New York and then to Chicago. Having also received psychiatric training, she began work in a Chicago hospital where she discovered her vocation.

Kübler-Ross acknowledges that it was in part because she felt lonely and miserable that she was open to working with dying patients.[20] A project brought to her by four seminarians gave concrete expression to her interest in the dying.

Her small team of investigators proposed to the hospital administration that they be allowed to interview dying patients.

The hospital staff were initially resistant to the idea but eventually Kübler-Ross received a go ahead. She then found that the patients were also skeptical of the project. It took some time and some mistakes about where, when and how to interview the dying, before she could break through the assumption that the dying just wish to be left alone. She eventually got an interview room in which to work and became sensitive to whatever were the physical and temporal constraints of the patients. She began attracting many people to her seminars, although not the medical school students.

As the work progressed, Kübler-Ross found that the dying were anxious to talk. They were tired of silence, evasion, or outright lies about their condition. The dying often felt that they were being treated as inanimate objects by physicians who seemed incapable of discussing death.

There is always a danger in such situations that people try to make a simple reversal. If you ask people whether the dying should be told that they are dying, a large majority will say: "Of course they should; they have a right to know." Kübler-Ross took a somewhat different approach in saying: "No patient should be told that he is dying."[21] Instead, one should listen and respond to the patients' questions until they are ready to discuss the fact that they are dying.

A colleague of mine, who worked for more than two decades with the dying, said she had been asked hundreds of times: "Am I dying?" She claimed that she had never said yes, and that she had never lied. Her usual response to the question was: "Why do you ask?" With just that opening, dying patients would begin a conversation about the fact that they knew they were dying and that they felt frustrated by people pretending it was otherwise.

After two and a half years, Kübler-Ross wrote up her experiences that she had had with about two hundred patients. The book consists of transcripts of conversations and her interpretations. She warned that the book was "not meant to be a textbook on how to manage dying patients, nor is it intended as a complete study of the psychology of the dying."[22] However, with the book's success, nurses, counselors, chaplains, family members and others who were confronted with the process of dying, could hardly resist using *On Death and Dying* as their textbook. The book was translated into twenty languages.

Kübler-Ross used as an organizing tool the idea of "five stages of dying," a phrase that has become a standard piece of popular culture. Novelists, comedians and movie directors, as well as practitioners of popular psychology, invoke the five stages of dying, sometimes as if proven science, sometimes as a rigid orthodoxy, sometimes in playful variations.[23]

Like many such books that are written quickly about a promising new idea, *On Death and Dying* was vulnerable to some obvious criticism. Two hundreds cases in one urban hospital did not impress people who were looking for scientific rigor. If one is going to claim that every dying person progresses through stages, the obvious failure of the book is that it does not follow any individual through all five stages. Many cases are cited for illustrating each stage, but, even there, the interpretation of what each case illustrates is often very ambiguous. Despite these drawbacks, or possibly because the book does not follow scientific procedures, *On Death and Dying* had amazing appeal. The raw nature of the data and the naive approach to method made the book almost impenetrable to criticism.

Kübler-Ross never followed up *On Death and Dying* with the proper scientific controls. That probably would not have worked anyway. The book has inspired dozens of doctoral dissertations but none that has served as a comprehensive support for her book or a serious alternative. Like many authors whose first book is a sensational success, Kübler-Ross in her subsequent career made occasional references to *the* book but mostly she became involved in other projects that could not match the popular and commercial success of the initial work.

Outsiders often express regret at an author's failure to live up to expectations but the author may feel that he or she has gone on to more important things. In Kübler-Ross' case, she used her talent and fame to spark interest in the hospice movement, with its palliative care for the dying, and to raise awareness of the care of AIDS babies. History may show that her greatest work has been in helping to found hospice in the United States.

When Kübler-Ross became interested in the spiritual side of dying, many people were disappointed and some people ridiculed her. Her reputation suffered when she became involved with a charlatan named Jay Barnham who claimed to channel spirits. Her writing suffered in quality. The speeches she gave after 1980 and her autobiographical memoir are filled with dogmatic pronouncements and carelessly formulated generalizations.[24]

Much of what she later wrote seems to undermine the early book. Although she would blithely dismiss this criticism, many of her supporters, as well as opponents, see this later development as unfortunate.[25] My interest in this chapter is not to join with Kübler-Ross' severest critics or to bemoan her failure to continue in the direction that *On Death and Dying* suggested. Instead, I will attempt a close critical reading of *On Death and Dying*, with references to her later writing when helpful for interpretation.

Stages of Development

Did Kübler-Ross write a theory of development? I doubt that was her intention but such a theory is what most readers took from her book. She may not have given much thought to her choice of the word "stage." That term, and the naming of five stages, inevitably fixed *On Death and Dying* into the history of developmental theories. Such theories exercise fascination for people who are trying to figure out where the world is going (a population that might include just about anyone). Despite the disclaimers of their authors, "stage theories" become employed for their supposed predictive power.

Kübler-Ross' original intention, stated at the beginning of *On Death and Dying*, was admirably modest. She writes: "I am telling the stories of my patients who shared their agonies, their expectations, and their frustrations with us."[26] But once the book was published and became famous, she was subjected to questions about her method, theory, and sequence of stages. She never attempted an overall restatement or a theoretical defense. Very often, she simply concedes the point of a specific criticism: "Yes, a patient can skip a stage....Yes, a patient can regress to an earlier stage....Yes, a patient might be in two stages at the same time."[27] The trouble with conceding one small point after another is that eventually no pattern remains. Unlimited variations in a sequence undermine the idea of a sequence. Perhaps she would not be perturbed by that conclusion; however, she certainly insisted that the stages should lead to "acceptance" and that once arrived there the patient should not regress.

I think it is worth offering an interpretation of the "five stages of dying" that would retain for it some theoretical validity and some practical significance. I suggest that Kübler-Ross did make an important discovery about dying but that the famous five names can be misleading. What can be defended is an understanding of the process of dying that is simpler and at the same time open to more variation. It is worthwhile to try to find a pattern for the experience of the dying.

In one of her ill-advised comments on the five stages, Kübler-Ross said: "This is not just typical of dying, and really has nothing to do with dying. We only call it the "stages of dying" for lack of a better phrase."[28] Taken seriously, that comment would completely undermine her book. What I think she was trying to say is that the stages of dying are so important because they reveal the structure of life itself. Precisely because the focus is on dying, the stages are about living which inevitably includes dying.

Kübler-Ross' five stages give the obvious impression of being one more theory of development. As such, this theory of dying would take its place next to economic, psychological, social, moral, religious and other theories of development. However, the fact that this theory ends in death makes it unusual, to say the least. Theories of development, whatever the field, are about improvement, progress and success.

I wish to argue that Kübler-Ross' "stage theory," instead of being one more developmental theory, is a challenge to the very idea of development itself. If dying is at the end, what sense can be made of theories that promise improvement and success? One would then have to ask of any theory of development: Does it stand up to the particular progression that Kübler-Ross claimed to document?

## The Development of Development

A brief history of the idea of development is needed to situate the stages of dying. Development is not just a modern idea; one could say that it helps to define what modernity is. It has emerged as a more comprehensive term than either evolution or progress, each of which has some notes in common with development. The two greatest users of the term development in the present are economists and psychologists. Each group tends to assume that they own the idea and they tend to be oblivious of its use outside their respective fields. Of these two groups, the economists clearly have the longer hold on the term. The language of developing and developed nations is firmly set in popular language.

The psychologists were relatively late on the scene, but if one finds a course named "human development" in a university catalogue, it is most likely in the psychology department. A question that does not seem to have a place in the university is whether theories of psychological development are biased in the direction of the economically developed world, and conversely, whether the idea of economic development reflects one psychological mind set. The world could use a study of the development of development that might better situate particular theories of development and initiate dialogue between them.

The idea of development seems to have arisen from a protest against, but also an assimilation of, ancient and medieval systems of thought. (The division of ancient, medieval, and modern is itself a product of the idea of development). The early moderns liked the idea of history having meaning and direction, an idea that had roots in Greek, Jewish and Christian histories.

Christianity had begun by proclaiming an end to history, an ambiguous phrase that can embrace nearly opposite attitudes toward history. Much of early Christianity took the "end" literally. History would give way to a meaning at its end or conclusion. That did not happen. Gradually there was a shift to the belief that the end was not imminent but immanent, that is, the meaning of end was absorbed into history. The meaning of history was to be found in history itself which was thought to move toward a third age or third stage. This vision of a third age, beyond the conflicts of the previous two, has haunted Western history since the twelfth century. A movement upward and forward toward a better state is the background for modern development.

While the idea of progress had arisen many centuries earlier, theories of progress or development awaited the late renaissance and early modern era. Even with the belief in history's meaning, Christianity had retained the idea of a final judgment beyond history. For the individual, heaven and hell still fixed the limits of possibility. The choice was between taking the path that God had laid out or else rebelling against the road to heaven. At the collective level, the choice was between a fair and an unfair distribution of the goods that had been provided by a benevolent creator. Modern developmental theory is the attempt to retain the direction toward a better life while eliminating the end point toward which history moves. Not only the Christian heaven but Aristotle's teleology had to be dismantled.

Can we get rid of an end point but retain a clear direction of progress? Is it possible for us to be moving clearly in one direction if we are not moving toward anything? There are two ways to imagine a positive answer to that question. The first image is "growth," a movement forward and upward. The second image is movement around and within a sphere to achieve a harmony.

*Growth.* The image of growth has dominated most theories of development. In fact, "growth and development" is often taken to be a single phrase. Economic development occurs if humans put together their ingenuity and the organization of resources with the result that the goods of the world can grow indefinitely. At the level of individual psychology, when humans use their own creativity, new paths can be constantly opened for human exploration. The image or metaphor of grow seems endlessly applicable with a sense of infinite possibility.

Economics, which set the standard for development, has found the metaphor of growth more than congenial. No one argues about the value of higher gross domestic product, quarterly rates of expansion, or a rising stock market. Development means upward and forward. Politicians in the 1990s adopted the phrase "growing the economy" to indicate betterment of life. Some psychologists might question the metaphor of growth, but this particular metaphor enveloped modern psychology from the beginning and it has retained its dominance.

One factor that explains psychology's attachment to growth is that "developmental psychology" was at first about children. Human development as growth – the metaphor coming most directly from biology – seemed to be appropriate for children. Jean Piaget's classic studies of cognitive power go up to age twelve; Piaget said he had no interest in studying "growth and development" beyond that age.[29] Piaget, as biologist and logician, was focused on how the body and the mind's judgments grow together. But if one extends "human development" to include adults, the metaphor of growth runs into trouble. Should adults be growing when they are no longer growing up? Do people actually grow old?

What may be seen as a small problem of logic in psychology became a major issue in ecology. Since the 1960s, the ideal of growth has been subjected to severe criticism. The assumption that bigger is better, it turns out, can have disastrous consequences when applied throughout the environment. The United States, with its gargantuan appetite for the world's resources, has often been compared to a cancer in the world's body politic. And, indeed, cancer is thought by some people to be the disease that appropriately symbolizes our world-wide environmental problems, that is, a disease in which some cells grow wildly at the expense of others, oblivious of the problems caused by their unrestrained growth.

Despite the now obvious problems with growth as a metaphor for human development, it retains its rhetorical place as a cultural cliché. James Hillman, the maverick psychologist, suggested that human development might better be described as shrinkage, but not many are ready to follow that lead.[30] Gail Sheehy, at the beginning of a book on development, describes a woman who, after countless travails of life, declares: "I will never adjust downward."[31] One can sympathize with the woman but still wonder whether she could use a different metaphor for her life's journey. Similarly, I think Elisabeth Kübler-Ross picks up an inadequate metaphor from today's psychology when she writes in the next to last sentence of her memoir: "Our only purpose in life is growth."[32] It is not obvious how death fits in with growth.

*Integration.* There is a second metaphor for development, one that is more compatible with Kübler-Ross' findings about the dying. The movement in this development is not toward an object that can be pictured nor is it an expansion that is measurable quantitatively. The closest one can come to illustrating this movement is to describe it as a series of cycles moving toward a harmony around the center of a sphere. Movement forward can also be downward; movement upward may be a going backward. Only after a pattern of many cycles can one judge whether there is progress toward integration of the whole.

In this form of development, a movement to the future is at the same time a recovery of the past. Quite often as people age, the memory of what happened decades ago sharpens, even as their short term memory falters. In this development, the journey of life would not be conceived as moving toward an end point but toward a unity of conflicting forces in one's life. Progress is not just forward and upward but in and out, around and back, aesthetic and playful. In this image, death is not the end point of life but is the center around which all human activity dances.

Modern sciences, including psychology, have not been very successful at incorporating death into theories of development. Most developmental theories could be compared to describing the progress a man makes as he takes an elevator to the top of a high-rise building. What is left out in these theories is the fact that when he reaches the top the man is then pushed off the roof. Freud was led to theorize about a death drive that struggles with a pleasure principle. Freud had few takers for his death drive, which seemed to be a counsel of despair.[33]

Erik Erikson proposed a series of tensions in life, the last being the struggle between integrity and despair.[34] Dying might be situated better here than in most theories of development, but Erikson did not address death in any detail. Robert Jay Lifton proposed a corrective to previous developmental theories by making the experience of death central. Lifton's writing career included a constant awareness of death and its presence throughout life, but his theory of development was left fragmentary.[35]

I would argue that Kübler-Ross' *On Death and Dying* could contribute to our understanding of development by providing a better understanding of dying and how living moves toward dying. Incorporating stages of dying into developmental theories would make all of them more realistic. The pattern of dying could mean progress toward a unity, a progress that neither smuggles in an end point nor relies on an image of growth.

I think that Kübler-Ross did discover a pattern in the lives of patients who had time to prepare for death. The pattern may more resemble medieval writing on mysticism than modern theories of development. In the mystic's journey there is movement between the positive and the negative, light and darkness. The pattern can be repeated many times. The culmination of the mystic's journey is a "unitive" state in which the separation of subject and object is overcome.

Kübler-Ross is thought to have discovered a pattern with five stages. Her five stages were actually four stages and a conclusion. Furthermore, the even number of stages is more significant than the number four. There might be two stages or there might be six, eight or ten stages. The stages could be given various names; the four that she happened to choose are appropriate. So also would be terms such as resistance, evasion, deliberation or protest.

I suggest that the movement toward dying is characterized by a dialectic of "yes and no." In the next section I will document from her book that this pattern is what Kübler-Ross found. At its simplest, the pattern has two stages. A yes to life, throughout our lifespan, is a no to death. We avoid, deny, and resist dying every day. When people are informed that they have a fatal disease, their first reaction is to say no to death, yes to life. That is what they were already doing but they now do it more emphatically. Eventually, a second stage is entered where the no to death is overtaken and a despairing yes to death is a no to life. This two step process can be repeated many times. As dying approaches, the yes to death keeps deepening.

The resolution in the life of the dying person comes about when the yes and the no are not seen as excluding each other. Having circled back to encompass all of one's life, the dying person accepts that life includes dying and that one's life is now complete. Thus, the stages of dying culminate in a yes to life which now includes death. Dying is now understood not as an unintelligible catastrophe at the end point but as a force that has been present since birth. The wise among us possess this knowledge long before the x-ray results show terminal cancer. They know that to live fully one must risk dangers, that every day has small dyings that prepare the way for the final dying, and that one must find a meaning in dying in order to find a meaning in living.[36]

Stages of Dying

A contentious issue that surrounds theories of development is whether an author is describing what exists or what should exist. The question arises about all ethical statements, but it becomes especially acute when applied to developmental theories that eschew moral judgments but seem to smuggle in notions of the good, the better and the best. The question can be and has been raised about Kübler-Ross' stages of dying; and it would also apply to my interpretation of her stages as a dialectic of yes and no.

Authors very often try to defend their theories by claiming that they are just describing the world. For example, a book on adult development that rivaled Kübler-Ross' book in popularity was Gail Sheehy's *Passages: Predictable Crises of Adult Life*. Sheehy insisted that she developed her catchy names for stages of adult development after she read 115 biographies. "Therefore, those patterns are descriptive not prescriptive."[37] This defense seldom works. Readers embrace the theory because it offers direction out of the unpredictability of life, an idea encouraged by the subtitle of Sheehy's book.

Kübler-Ross regularly struggled with this question when she was asked whether "acceptance" should be the goal for every patient. She clearly implies that acceptance is the ideal toward which patients should move but she nonetheless said acceptance was not the goal. She acknowledged that this "may sound as if it were a contradiction and I think it's a matter of semantics."[38]

She is right that the question is "semantics" but that is the crucial point here. How does one state these theories and how is one to understand the words? One can sympathize with Sheehy and others who wrestle with the choice between description and prescription. It is the wrong "semantics." The first term, description, is excluded as soon as the author chooses, organizes, and interprets data. But the second term, prescription (to write beforehand), is a grandiose and indefensible claim, no matter what data have been collected. When applied, for example, to language itself, the result has been a fruitless argument between people called descriptivists and prescriptivists.[39]

The metaphor of prescription is taken from the medical profession. On the basis of symptoms, the physician describes a problem and the lab tests confirm the description. The physician then writes out the prescription for the pharmacist. If the prescription is correct, the problem is solved. Even in the medical profession, the language of description and prescription is of limited value.

Consider an alternative metaphor drawn from the legal profession. If accused of a crime, I hire a lawyer to be my advocate in court. From conversations between lawyer and client, a strategy is devised to argue before the judge or jury. If one approach to my defense is not working, another might be tried. It is a fallible process of persuasion to get to the underlying truth that I am innocent. The task is not to prescribe but to advocate. Success is found in being judged not guilty. In trying to chart a developmental theory of any kind, the truth is what is sought but it is too complicated for our language to encompass. The best that one can do is advocate a way of speaking that is better than any available alternative.

Advocacy should be based on language that is persuasive because it is historically well-grounded and because the writer or speaker is aware of contemporary connotations. The names that Kübler-Ross chose for her advocacy of four stages (denial, anger, bargaining, depression) are appropriately ambiguous. They can signify something good or bad, depending on the context. At the right moment each of them is good; when the circumstances change, each of them can be bad. Only "acceptance" which she chose for the culmination of the stages is good by definition.

In Kübler-Ross' advocacy of a language to describe the process of dying, her best choices are "denial" and "acceptance." In fact, she could have worked through the whole process with only those two terms. That surmise is suggested by her statement that "denial is usually a temporary defense and will soon be replaced by partial acceptance."[40] What can she mean by "partial acceptance" and what about the in-between stages? She must be implying that acceptance is not a last stage in a sequence of five, but a theme that runs throughout the four stages and is gradually being filled out.

Corresponding to partial acceptance, she could have referred to "partial denial." She does not in fact use that phrase. She uses denial as the initial reaction that almost everyone experiences in receiving a death sentence. "There must be some mistake....I'm too young and healthy to be dying....I need a second opinion." In popular speech, a person being "in denial" is thought to be in the worst way possible. And, indeed, if a person were in complete denial about everything, he or she would be cut off from reality.

Perhaps surprisingly, Kübler-Ross has a good word to say about denial. "Denial functions as a buffer after unexpected shocking news, allows the patient to collect himself and, with time, mobilize other, less radical defenses."[41] The person is not denying his or her mortality, just denying that this disease is the end. The response of a friend of mine to being diagnosed with prostate cancer was "I am going to die with this disease but not from this disease." The determination to deny this disease's finality at this time is a healthy basis on which to affirm one's life. It is a no to death, a yes to life.

Denial can thus be a good attitude at the beginning of the process. Persisted in completely to the end, denial is not a good. Kübler-Ross is somewhat ambivalent on this point. She describes one case in which the woman seemed to be in denial until the end. Kübler-Ross later wonders "if I was not a bit too ready to support her denial."[42] But elsewhere she thinks that the proper approach to a particular patient is "to allow him to stay in the stage of denial."[43]

If she believes that acceptance is ultimately better than denial, I think she must also argue that a counselor should try to help the person beyond denial. The caveat is that denial and acceptance become ambiguous when interpreting another person's life. Denial can have many forms and degrees. Frontal attacks on denial almost always fail. Therefore, a counselor should be trying to help a person beyond denial while being aware that the counselor's perception of what constitutes denial may be skewed.

Kübler-Ross named the second stage of dying anger. It is an appropriate name for the moment when the dying person cannot sustain complete denial. "Yes, I am dying and I'm mad as hell about it." Anger is generally thought to be a vice or a failure of temperament, especially in Eastern spirituality. Christianity, while listing anger among the capital sins, also recognized "holy anger," a proper response to some evil. East and West may have a profound difference here or perhaps the difference is more at the level of applications and connotations.[44] Anger seems to be an understandable reaction when it becomes clear that one is fatally sick.

Some of Kübler-Ross' most helpful comments in *On Death and Dying* are in the chapter on anger. For the dying patient, it is important to know that feeling anger and letting the anger out in nonviolent ways is a healthy reaction.[45] Just as important, it is indispensable for the care giver to be prepared for anger and to know that the anger is not personally directed. The dying patient is not angry with the nurse, counselor, family member, friend, or whoever is in the general vicinity. The patient is angry at the disease, at the situation, at God. When asked what to do about a patient angry at God, Kübler-Ross replied: "I would help him to express his anger toward God because God is certainly great enough to be able to accept it."[46]

Although the care giver has to be understanding about anger, that stance is not equivalent to being passive in the face of anger. One can tell the patient that some behavior is unacceptable. There may be a need to talk out the anger; some of the anger may have a reasonable basis and the cause of the anger can be corrected. In any case, a vigorous human response is called for. In the play, *Whose Life Is It Anyway,* the patient is angry that the social worker does not criticize him for his outbursts. Treating a dying patient as a human being includes conversation, criticism of bad behavior, and even sharing a joke.

The third and fourth of Kübler-Ross' stages repeat the pattern of no to death, yes to life, followed by yes to death, no to life. She calls these two stages bargaining and depression. The pattern of no/yes to death is repeated but now at a deeper level. The chapter on bargaining is the shortest in the book, the one chapter on the stages of dying without a transcript of a conversation. That is unfortunate because there would be no shortage of data. Bargaining might start in the first stage and continue in the third, fifth, and seventh stages. The dying person will try to bargain with everyone and everything.

The religious person has God to bargain with. Logically, God would be the only one who could commute the death sentence. But even people who say they do not believe in God try to strike a deal with the forces of the universe. Anyone in the immediate environment, anyone imagined to have power, becomes a fit candidate for negotiating a deal to put off death. So long as one bargains, one can keep denying that death is approaching.

When the fourth stage reverses the third, the no to life now takes the form of depression. This stage parallels anger but now the emotions are more deeply set and are indicative of the person being further along on the journey. The term depression is almost totally negative in its connotations. But as is the case with each stage, Kübler-Ross finds a positive aspect along with the negative. For this stage, she distinguishes the good and bad into two kinds of depression; reactive and preparatory.[47] The bad depression is directed to the past, the good form of depression is concerned with the future.

Reactive depression is a guilty feeling about what the person has or has not done during his or her lifetime. Unresolved personal problems weigh heavily upon the person, something that the dying should not have to carry. Being depressed about the past is no help to anyone. Kübler-Ross recommends vigorous counseling to help the person get beyond this reactive depression.

As for preparatory depression, she recommends a nearly opposite strategy. This depression results from a realistic assessment of what lies in the near future. The patient's whole system is beginning to shut down. Trying to cheer up the patient will not work and may be burdensome. That fact does not mean the person should be abandoned to his or her depression. The best that one can do is to be physically present and provide whatever verbal and physical contact that the dying patient wants.

Finally, there is "acceptance" which is not a stage but a resolution of the two, four, six or more stages that have preceded it. Do most people reach this state? Kübler-Ross begins the chapter on acceptance by asserting that "if a patient has enough time (that is, does not suffer a sudden unexpected death) and has been given some help in working through the previously described stages, he will reach a stage during which he is neither depressed nor angry about his fate."[48] Since her patients in the study had both of these conditions fulfilled, she found that "the majority of our patients die in the stage of acceptance."[49] That conclusion is the most that she can claim about the universality of acceptance. Clearly she thinks acceptance is the way to go but neither she nor anyone else can know in what state most people die.

Kübler-Ross insists on a distinction between acceptance and resignation. The latter term she describes as simply giving up. In contrast, acceptance, while not connoting an embrace of death or a pleasant experience, does suggest that one is actively open to receive death when the time has come. Unlike the four stages that preceded acceptance, here the positive and negative aspects have been separated into two different terms: acceptance and resignation. Only the positive one, acceptance, is deemed acceptable.

Acceptance is characterized as peaceful and calm. Kübler-Ross sometimes speaks of acceptance as directed toward one's mortality, at other times toward the fact of one's imminent death. This double meaning might seem equivocal unless one grasps how the two are related. Acceptance is not primarily about the fact of dying. It is about accepting one's life that is soon to include dying. The person has concluded, "This is who I am, this is a whole life, this is the meaning of my life." If it were a question of the fact of death, one would simply recognize or acknowledge that fact.

Persons, situations and the universe have to be "accepted" rather than just acknowledged. William James defended Margaret Fuller against the ridicule of Thomas Carlyle for her saying, "I accept the universe." James commented that "at bottom the whole concern of both morality and religion is with the manner of our acceptance of the universe. Do we accept it only in part and grudgingly, or heartily and altogether? Shall our protests against certain things in it be radical and unforgiving, or shall we think that, even with evil, there are ways of living that must lead to good?"[50]

Kübler-Ross chose the right term, acceptance, with its profound philosophical and religious significance. She did not do such a good job in describing acceptance. At least, she did not leave enough room for interpreting what acceptance might mean in particular cases. Part of the problem, I suspect, is that she assumed a context which is not fully described in the chapter on acceptance. What she describes there is the dying person withdrawing into a state of solitude, detached from outside concerns.

While she is right that the living have to "let go" so that the dying person can accept death, that does not mean the absence of a community. There are many documented cases in which the patient waits until family members leave before dying. In such cases, a caring community is not the problem; it is the possessive attitude of some people who are attending the dying. The dying person wishes to finish life surrounded by those who love and care, but the circle of community can vary greatly in its shape; the community should not be too narrowly confining. The dying person needs solitude not loneliness, a solitude that includes not feeling abandoned.

Kübler-Ross' opening statement on acceptance is: "He wishes to be left alone..." She goes on to say "or at least not stirred by news and problems of the outside world." This second comment is more to the point. She describes someone sitting with the dying, holding their hand, listening to the song of a bird, simply being present in silence. The whole point of stages of dying is the realization that the dying person needs the help, understanding, and presence of a community. Final acceptance should be a confirmation not a rejection of that attitude. Kübler-Ross seems here to be concentrating on death as a biological event, whereas human death is a personal and communal event.[51]

A second way that Kübler-Ross may too narrowly circumscribe the meaning of acceptance is by describing it as "almost void of feelings." That may be accurate but if acceptance is the culmination of stages of emotions, it might also be called the integration of all those emotions. The fullness of feeling could appear to be the same as the absence of feeling. If final acceptance can be said to include all the emotions, it would not be surprising that at times elements of anger or resistance are still evident. Admittedly, it is difficult to reconcile acceptance with "rage, rage against the dying of the light." But someone who is a fighter to the last might still have reached acceptance.[52]

The claim that the dying person is void of feelings is tied to Kübler-Ross' description of the dying person as going back to early infancy, "to the stage that we started out with and the circle of life is closed."[53] That image, the one which she used in entitling her autobiography "The Wheel of Life," seems to me unfortunate and misleading. It is related to the dangerous tendency to confuse child-like attitudes in the old with childishness. Eighty-year-olds are not children and should not be treated like children. Death experienced as the completion to life should not be interpreted as a denial that a life has occurred.

The image of a closed circle or wheel is to be distinguished from the cyclical movement that I described earlier. One should not declare the circle closed even in death. A cyclical movement always leaves open possibilities that we may not be aware of. I think that Kübler-Ross' description of acceptance as a closed circle is part of the reason for her turn in the road after *On Death and Dying*. She not only turned to the spiritual but to a spirituality opposed to the body. She then repeatedly made such statements as: "Death, as we understand it in scientific language, does not really exist....My real job...is to tell people that death does not exist....One way to not be so afraid is to know that death does not exist."[54]

These statements would be puzzling from anyone; but from someone famous for investigating the dying process, the statements seem bizarre. Kübler-Ross, like everyone else, has a right to her beliefs and a right to change them. But what she repeatedly said in speeches and essays does not seem to make sense.

In her memoir, she says on page one that "death is one of our greatest experiences," while later in the book she says that "death does not exist." She also says that death is "a transition to a higher state of consciousness where you continue to perceive, to understand, to laugh and to be able to grow."[55] The metaphor of growth survived in her speculation, even apart from bodiliness. If one views death as a "transition" it seems unintelligible to say "death does not exist." Many religions see death as a transition but they do not deny that dying is real, that it is often painful, and that it is the dissolution of the life we have known.

In *On Death and Dying*, the chapter that immediately follows the chapters on stages is entitled "hope." Perhaps there is a neglected theme there that Kübler-Ross might have pursued further. She begins the chapter by saying "the one thing that usually persists through all these stages is hope."[56] That suggests an attitude of crucial importance, one which comprehends stages of dying and goes beyond acceptance.

Unfortunately, her description of hope is unclear. She says "it gives the terminally ill a sense of special mission in life" but then adds "in a sense it is a rationalization for their suffering at times; for others it remains a form of temporary but needed denial."[57] That description of hope is reductive. She goes on to equate hope by the dying to counting on a cure or to being able to talk about their dying.

Christian theology developed hope as a "theological virtue," the one that links faith and love. Although somewhat neglected in Christian writing, hope could turn out be a virtue that is especially appropriate for today's skeptical world. Hope does not claim to know the future nor does it promise a reward. Thomas Aquinas notes simply that "the difference between hope and despair is the difference between possibility and impossibility."[58]

The individual today wants to be in control of his or her life. Death is a shocking reminder of the power and forces which are far beyond the individual. The only choice left is hope or despair, and as Gabriel Marcel writes, "hope is the will when it is made to bear on what does not depend on itself."[59] It is difficult to see how acceptance of one's own dying is possible without the accompanying feeling of hope – that, "at the bottom of the heart of every human being, from earliest infancy to the tomb, there is something that goes on indomitably expecting, in the teeth of all experience of crimes committed, suffered and witnessed, that good and not evil will be done to him."[60]

# CHAPTER FIVE: THE NEW EUTHANASIA

This chapter is about the changing meaning of "euthanasia," how and why the word has been changing, and whether that change is helpful. The cases that are discussed in this chapter include people who end their own lives with the aid of someone else, people who are put to death without their consent, and cases where people are allowed to die either because a treatment was originally withheld or because it is subsequently terminated. The term euthanasia has spread out so as to cover all of these disparate situations but unfortunately that can produce inconsistency and confusion in the term's usage.

The movement to a positive meaning for "euthanasia" has been a somewhat surprising development in recent decades. The term's etymology is positive, that is, it means a happy or good death. But the word was coined as a euphemism for a practice that was widely and severely condemned. As happens with many social movements, a small group of believers doggedly insisted in the face of widespread disapproval that euthanasia – mercy killing – should not only be allowed but should be seen as an important good. In recent years, the movement seems to have achieved considerable success.

One extension of the term euthanasia has been to include physician-assisted suicide. The logic here is understandable; a happy or good death might include the patient asking for an end to life. Thus, it is said that euthanasia can be voluntary as well as involuntary. Voluntary euthanasia certainly draws more support and approval than does involuntary euthanasia. Euthanasia as a term has managed to gain a more positive meaning by the introduction of this distinction. Voluntary euthanasia is intended to be less harsh in meaning than the connotations usually associated with the term suicide.

A more questionable change in the movement to make euthanasia a positive term has been its extension to cases of allowing a person to die. The practice of allowing death to occur has a long history of being morally acceptable. Euthanasia automatically acquired a more positive meaning by this wider inclusion. One can argue that there is nothing illogical in this extension of the meaning of a "good death." Nevertheless, one can be suspicious of this move which has more to do with political acceptance than logical consistency. Discussion henceforth was not to be about the contrast between allowing someone to die and killing someone; it was about two kinds of euthanasia.

Whether or not the intention was to mislead, these two kinds were inaccurately named "active" and "passive," terms that obscure the heart of the issue. Once the language of two kinds of euthanasia was in place, there was a claim that no significant difference exists between killing and letting die. The latter, "passive euthanasia," it was said, actually involves activity. The result is that "euthanasia" and "active euthanasia" can then be used interchangeably. The implication is that "passive euthanasia" should disappear. "Euthanasia" was rehabilitated by the creation of "passive euthanasia," which began disappearing immediately after its birth.[61]

I do not think that this change of language was the result of a plot or a conspiracy. Language is not so easily controllable and probably no one had charted the course of this change. The shift in "euthanasia" happened among a public that may have been open to persuasion. But a change of language can either help to clarify points of debate or it can cloud an issue that is in need of further inquiry. How we use the term euthanasia is in some ways a minor question but it is tied up with important changes that need debate.

Until recent decades, the meaning of "euthanasia" was clear. The *Oxford English Dictionary* gives a summary of its meaning as "the action of inducing a gentle and easy death. Used especially with reference to a proposal that the law should sanction the putting painlessly to death of those suffering from incurable and extremely painful diseases."[62] Up to the middle of the twentieth century, both friend and foe would have concurred on that meaning of euthanasia. The attitude of the medical profession was succinctly stated in 1973 by the American Medical Association: "The intentional termination of the life of one human being by another – mercy killing – is contrary to that for which the medical profession stands and is contrary to the policy of the American Medical Association."[63] This brief document then allows that there can be a cessation of "extraordinary means" to keep a patient alive.

One of the first and most famous mercy-killing trials was held in Manchester, New Hampshire in 1950. The entire city had been shocked at the announcement that Dr. Herman Sanders, a highly respected physician, had been indicted on a charge of first degree murder. He had four times injected 10 cc.

of air into the vein of a dying patient. According to Sanders, the patient had asked him to do so. He duly noted on the patient's chart what he had done. The trial attracted national and international attention. The jury acquitted Sanders, apparently on the basis that there was no proof that his actions were the cause of death. Juries in subsequent mercy-killing cases also refused to convict any physician of murder.

## Physician-Assisted Suicide

The phrase "physician-assisted suicide" brings up issues of the law and ethics. There is a question about the right to be assisted in the committing of suicide, a right that implies a duty for someone else. There are also questions about whether a physician is the person who should assist, whether all physicians should be required to assist, and in what ways a physician should assist.

By referring to "physician-assisted suicide," one avoids the simple, blunt question: Is it all right to kill oneself? By bringing in the physician, a kind of approval is given or implied. "The current assumption about physicians' role in assisted suicide demonstrates that we remain in the grip of the norm that first took hold in the mid-nineteenth century, when physicians displaced clergy as the principal and even exclusive custodian of death and dying."[64]

By including the physician, we seem merely to be discussing various medical treatments. But the question of suicide raises the issue of the physician's proper professional role. There are some cases where people are physically incapable of ending their own lives, but there are many others in which a person is fully capable of the act. If the principle on which suicide is judged to be acceptable is the patient's "autonomy," then always referring to the physician's assistance fails to be forthright about what is being discussed.

Many physicians would object to being required to help kill the patient. The two roles of healer and killer are not easily combined. If not the physician, then who would do the assisting? It is difficult to imagine a new professional specialty of suicide assistant. In some cases, a close friend might be able to assist. One famous case involved the television reporter, Betty Rollin, who recounted in detail how she helped her mother to die.[65] Rollin prepared the lethal dose of the drug and then left before her mother took it. Although there were legal grounds for Rollin's arrest, the state's attorney general refused to indict her.

Rollin had made a distinction between helping her mother to secure the means of death and actually administering the drug. Some people might find the distinction trivial but, especially for physicians, it might be important. If a friend or a physician administers the lethal drug there might well be a question about the patient's consent. Even people who thought that Dr. Jack Kevorkian was raising the right issue disagreed with his "suicide machine." He claimed that he was only helping to die those who had asked for his help. But most of his clients were aged; many of them were depressed.

There are degrees of coercion by powerful people, even when they do not intend to coerce. The physician – part father, part guru, part scientist – always has to be careful about dominating the patient who is frightened, in pain, and feeling helpless. The person's mood may change from day to day, hour to hour. When a person says "I just want to die," he or she may really mean it or the person may be going through a bad patch. People can change their minds about most things and they can act differently in the future. The obvious exception is if they ask someone to end their life and the decision is carried through.

There is a need for strict safeguards that protect the patient's consent if physician-assisted suicide is widely accepted. The assistance that the physician provides should probably be limited to information, which might include a prescription, but not include that the physician administer the means of death.

The extremes in carrying out physician-assisted suicide are illustrated in two cases, one reported in the *Journal of the American Medical Association*, the other in *The New England Journal of Medicine.* The first article was a mere seven paragraphs long but it caused a firestorm of criticism directed at the journal's editor and became the subject of dispute with prosecutors in Chicago. The essay entitled "It's Over Debbie," was published anonymously. It is so extreme that one might suspect it is fiction done for the express purpose of stirring up controversy.[66]

The article's brevity is inherent to its intended point. A gynecology resident is awakened in the middle of the night and directed to a unit unfamiliar to him. "Bumping sleepily against walls and corners...I grabbed the chart from the nurse's station on my way to the patient's room, and the nurse gave me some hurried details." What he found was a twenty-year old girl, Debbie, who was dying with ovarian cancer. "The room seemed filled with the patient's desperate effort to survive....It was a gallows scene, a cruel mockery of her youth and unfulfilled potential. Her only words to me were, 'Let's get this over with.'" The resident concluded that "the patient was tired and needed rest...I could give her rest." He does so by injecting her with 20 cc. of morphine sulphate. Within four minutes her breathing stopped.

In this description, one detail after another violates the standards that most advocates of physician-assisted suicide would maintain. The description seemed designed to mock any standards. A half-awake resident in unfamiliar surroundings hears a young woman speak five ambiguous words. He tells a nurse to prepare a lethal injection and immediately kills the patient. It is difficult to believe that a resident would so cavalierly risk his career, not to mention arrest, even if he was totally convinced of the value of physician-assisted suicide.

The contrasting case of a patient named Diane was recounted by Dr. Timothy Quill.[67] He had worked with the patient for three and a half years when she was diagnosed with leukemia. Although intervention with this disease had a twenty-five percent success rate, the patient had no desire to undergo chemotherapy and bone marrow transplant. "All she wanted to do was go home and be with her family. She had no further questions about treatment and in fact had decided that she wanted none." Quill talked to her several times and at length to be certain that she understood what she was doing. "We arranged for home hospice care....left the door open for her to change her mind, and tried to anticipate how to keep her comfortable in the time she had left."

The patient, Diane, went a step further. "When the time came, she wanted to take her life in the least painful way possible." The physician told her where to get information and he prescribed the barbiturates in the amount necessary for suicide. Several months later she said her final goodbyes to her husband and son and asked to be left alone. After an hour they found her dead. Quill told the medical examiner she had died of acute leukemia which, he later said, was the truth but not the whole story.

Timothy Quill clearly believed that Diane's suicide is a model case that would persuade almost anyone that a physician should sometimes offer careful and indirect help to the commission of suicide. His empathy, care and candor were widely admired as he continued to champion the cause of physician-assisted suicide. The patient, Diane, also exemplified carefulness and courage.

There are two sentences in the essay, however, that raise a concern. Quill writes that "It was extremely important to Diane to maintain control of herself and her own dignity during the time remaining to her." As the description of her indicates, "dignity" was equated with control. Quill assumes the same meaning in saying "I was setting her free to get the most out of the time she had left, and to maintain dignity and control on her own terms until her death." Although one should not belittle the value which is put on being in control, it is sad that "dignity" is thought to depend solely on retaining control. The vast majority of the world will never die with the rational control that is put forward in the article as the only way to die a dignified death. In many other cultures and in many homes, hospices, and communities of this culture, people are treated with dignity despite their lack of rational control.

This concern that suicide is seen as a necessary protection of "dignified dying" is at issue in the Dutch experiment. The Netherlands has been engaged for several decades in the world's most extensive experiment of assisted suicide. The guidelines, which were given final approval in 2002, stipulate that the patient must face a future of unbearable and interminable suffering, and he or she must make a voluntary, well-considered request to die. The physician, along with the patient, must be convinced that there is no other solution, and must consult with another physician. Finally, life must be ended in a medically appropriate way.

These regulations seem reasonable and well-designed to protect the patient's interests. However, the legalizing of suicide seems to create an atmosphere that is lax in the observance of the guidelines. For example, two government studies in 1990 and 1995 found that more than half of Dutch physicians felt that it was appropriate to suggest euthanasia to patients. Since "voluntary" may not be so clear-cut as it is often assumed to be, it is not surprising that the studies found many "non-voluntary" cases, or cases where there was no "explicit consent."[68] Consultation with another physician is often perfunctory. A report in 2000 found that seven percent of assisted suicide cases had complications associated with the methods used to achieve a speedy death.[69] In many of these cases, the physician administered the lethal medication after the patient's failed attempt at suicide.

Supporters of physician-assisted suicide say that these problems with the application of the law can and will be solved. The more important question, however, is whether Dutch (as well as U.S.) physicians are adequately trained for and properly sensitive to managing pain and relieving suffering. Suicide can become a routine way to deal with intense suffering. Some of the problems lie in the medical school's preparation of physicians to provide palliative care. Another aspect of the problem is an overly restrictive policy on narcotic drugs for the dying. A survey of 1400 physicians and nurses in five major U.S. hospitals found that eighty-one percent of respondents agreed that "the most common form of narcotic abuse in caring for dying patients is under treatment of pain."[70]

It is somewhat paradoxical that the demand for physician-assisted suicide has arisen just when great progress has been made in the control of pain. Although suicide is being urged in the name of patient "autonomy," the physician and the health care system still set the options within which choice is made. The only choice offered to many people may be between inadequate care and suicide. "One might ask," writes Carol Tauer, "whether a medical system that is the subject of so many complaints and so much wariness is a system that ought to be entrusted with additional power, the power to kill."[71]

Allowing to Die

What historically has been distinguished from killing – either by one's own hand or by another's – is a tradition of allowing death to occur. The argument now is that there is no "bright line" that separates killing and allowing to die. Before we overturn a long tradition here, the distinction deserves careful consideration. It is important to attend to the precise formulation of the distinction.

Before the advent of modern medicine the discussion of allowing to die used the language of ordinary and extraordinary means. A physician or a patient was required to use all ordinary means to sustain life. In recent times, this distinction has become unclear. The distinction implies that some things are simple and ordinary while other things are complex and extraordinary. Focusing on the things used in the treatment misses the point. The main issue is the kind of treatment that makes sense for the patient's overall situation.[72]

The Vatican Declaration on Euthanasia in 1980 proposed a distinction between proportionate and disproportionate means.[73] This recognition is significant because the Catholic Church had much to do with shaping the language of ordinary and extraordinary means. The test for treatment should be the burden laid upon the patient. If the treatment simply prolongs a person's dying of a painful disease, there is no proportional benefit for the dying patient. Thus, an IV line to provide nutrition and hydration cannot be called either an ordinary or an extraordinary means in today's medical practice. While a feeding tube makes eminent sense for someone recovering from surgery, the same instrument makes no sense for someone who has suffered irreversible damage to the neocortex and has no prospect for regaining consciousness.[74]

Pope Pius XII was prescient in addressing this question in 1958. Hardly a liberal reformer, Pius XII was simply applying a centuries-old tradition. He wrote that "it is unnatural to prevent death in instances where there is no hope of recovery. When nature is calling for death, there is no question that one can remove the life-support system."[75] The Pope did not merely say that disconnecting life support was allowed; he called the indefinite continuance of such instruments "unnatural." People often refer to not using "artificial means" for extending life. But most of medicine and much else in human life is "artifice" that protects and extends life. The artificiality of the means is not the problem; the "unnaturalness" is the problem, that is, the kind of artifice that goes directly counter to the organism preparing to die. Pius XII referred to extraordinary or heroic means but he pointed to the burden on the patient and the survivors. The whole situation, including economic concerns, has to be considered in judging whether the application of the means is proportionate.

In the United States the courts have been both the arbiters of the ethics and the judges of the law in the care of the dying. The first benchmark case for the removal of a respirator was that of Karen Ann Quinlan. On one side, Lawrence Casey, a Catholic bishop in New Jersey, testified that extraordinary means to keep her alive were unnecessary. But the court-appointed guardian argued that "one human being, by conduct or lack of conduct, is going to cause the death of another human being." And the lawyer for the physicians said it was "like turning on the gas chamber."[76]

After the court allowed the respirator to be removed from Karen Ann Quinlan, courts assumed that there is a sharp difference between a respirator and a feeding tube, although ethically there seems little difference. The operative principle in both situations is that removing the technology allows the patient to complete the process of dying. There may be a strong emotional difference if removal of a respirator leads to death in a few minutes, while death occurs after several days when a feeding tube is removed. There is also an emotional difference between not starting a life-support system and discontinuing it. But not to turn off a machine can be as much a decision as turning it on.[77]

People who oppose removing a feeding tube usually argue that such a procedure is starving the patient to death. That description is no more accurate than describing the removal of a respirator as smothering someone to death. One of the signs of impending death is an inability to eat; the organism is preparing to shut down. A feeding tube is not the same action as eating and the removal of a feeding tube when the patient is prepared for dying is not starvation.[78] Hospices generally recognize the difference and do not introduce the invasive technology of a feeding tube; that is, the patient is allowed to die. In hospitals, respirators and feeding tubes are routinely attached to the dying.

In the case of Nancy Cruzan, the parents asked for the removal of the feeding tube after she had been in a coma for three years. It took them four more years of court battles before the tube was removed; she expired twelve days later.[79] Her tombstone reads "departed: Jan. 11, 1983; at peace: Dec. 26, 1990."

Courts look for evidence of what the patient's own wishes would be. These days, some people have living wills which state a person's wishes if he or she is unable to make known those wishes. Despite all the talk about living wills, only a small minority of people actually have one. Even when people have living wills, hospitals and physicians often disregard them, sometimes because the living will is too vague.[80] A living will that simply says "I do not wish to be kept alive artificially" is not precise enough these day.

When the patient is a child or a young person, the parents are usually in the best position to decide but often they are forced into long legal battles with the hospital, the physician, and outside advocacy groups. When the parents of Jamie Butcher, who had been in a coma for seventeen years, tried to remove the feeding tube, they were opposed by an advocacy group for disabled people, Nursing Home Action.

Concern for protecting the rights of disabled people is certainly praiseworthy but the attempt to intervene in the Butcher case made no sense. The parents had done everything possible until they finally decided that Jamie should not be in a coma for a longer time than for the seventeen years he had lived before the accident. The court-appointed referee, James Finley, ruled that the advocacy group had no standing in the case: "We have caring parents who have taken care of their son his whole life. There wasn't any dispute that they are loving, caring, decision-makers."[81]

People do occasionally recover from long comas so that precipitous action here should be avoided. But today's technology does make it possible to determine if there is any glimmer of activity in the cerebral cortex. That determination shows whether the patient can ever regain consciousness and participate in a human community. How long one should wait before disconnecting life-support machinery cannot be made into a rule. But surely at some point – after eight years, seventeen years, x years – it makes no sense to continue keeping the body functioning.

In the case of Paul Brophy, his wife, mother, children and parish priest joined in appealing for the discontinuance of life support. "What we have here," said the Catholic priest, "is an intervention that is not working." Only the chief physician disagreed. His lawyer said that starving a person to death is not a death with dignity. The physician said that the patient was in good health except for being in a coma. "I am not in the business of killing people," the physician said. When asked how long he was prepared to keep the patient alive, he referred to a case that went on for more than twenty years.[82]

This physician and protesters in several of these famous cases presumably believe that they are defending the right of individuals not to be killed. Unfortunately, however, their actions have the opposite effect. By equating the removal of the machinery with the act of killing, they have joined the advocates of euthanasia in their claim that there is no ethical difference between killing and letting die. That judgment can be especially cruel on parents who have had to face this decision. Stephen Carter's opinion on the Cruzan case is both explicit and outrageous: "The thing that is precious in the human, the thing that makes life worth protecting, does not vanish because higher brain function is lost. Consequently, the starvation that occurs when feeding and hydration cease – not the underlying injury that caused the coma – is the cause of the end of that precious human substance. And it is the family, the unit to which the state has delegated the decision, that has made the choice to cease the feeding and, thus, to destroy that precious substance."[83]

In such statements, thousands of the parents of dying children, and thousands of the children of aged parents, are accused of being state-delegated executioners. In the Cruzan case and in thousands of similar cases, the family members neither wished to kill the patient nor were they the cause of death. They simply recognized that after years of their sorrow and care the disease or injury made recovery impossible. They removed the machinery that was delaying the completion of the dying process. Up to a few decades ago in the United States, the cause of death would be evident, as it still is in much of the world. The temporary intervention of machinery does not change the cause of death.

In these situations "acceptance," the term made famous by Kübler-Ross, is helpful to recall. Acceptance is an attitude that one comes to after a long struggle of denial and resistance. Human freedom exists on two levels: a fundamental attitude of yes or no, and a range of options to choose from. Even when the options have narrowed down to a single possibility, one still has the freedom to say yes or no. When dying is imminent, life that now includes one's death is all that is available for choice. Acceptance is a yes to dying, not the desire to kill or to end one's own or another's life; it is a recognition that a life has been completed.

Daniel Callahan uses the helpful analogy of a man shoveling snow from his driveway during a storm. If the snow is light, he might be able to keep up with it and keep the driveway clear. As the snow becomes heavier there will come a point when the shoveler recognizes that his efforts are futile and that the driveway will be clogged with snow no matter how hard he works. When he stops shoveling the snow it is not because he wants his driveway covered with snow but because he accepts the fact that the snow storm is in control. The cause of the driveway being covered with snow is the snow storm, not the cessation of shoveling. In this case, the storm eventually ceases and shoveling can begin again. With some diseases and injuries, the storm never ends; acceptance of death is final.

It is best when the dying patient is the one who can express this acceptance, if not verbally then by a prior written directive. The person who refuses a medical treatment does not desire to die but instead accepts the fact that resistance to dying no longer makes sense. The person's judgment may be distorted. Physician, counselor or family member might sometimes try persuading the patient that the treatment would be worthwhile in a particular situation. In Kübler-Ross' distinction, the patient may simply be giving up (resignation) rather than having reached acceptance.

Sometimes the decision has to be made by someone acting as a proxy for the dying patient. A family member or close friend will usually be the one who can decide what is best for the patient's interests. However, there can be conflict of interest when, for example, the heirs to a sizeable estate are involved. Many hospitals now have an ethics committee or a committee of the person to protect the rights of the patient. The courts or the hospital administration are not in the best position to decide when acceptance of death is appropriate. No one is an infallible judge. But if someone has to decide when death is to be accepted, one hopes for a loved one on the scene, who can decide to accept that death should be allowed to happen.

## Killing

In recent years it has been claimed that any line separating killing and letting die has been erased. The argument is that what had been called allowing to die amounts to the same thing as killing. The change in the meaning of "euthanasia" has facilitated the shift for advocates of assisted suicide who can now argue that the question is solely and simply about various means of achieving the same result, that is, a good death.

Central to such an argument has been the claim that "active" and "passive" are the two kinds of euthanasia so that the issue turns on whether a positive act is performed. Ronald Dworkin, commenting on a recent court decision, writes that "though the distinction between acts and omissions is often valid... that distinction does not seem important in this context." He then concludes that "removing life-support systems already in place, which the *Cruzan* case said states must allow, is as positive an act as is an injection."[84] He is correct that allowing a patient to die involves positive acts, but the kind of act performed, its meaning and intention, are crucial.

Intention is an important factor in human action but the intention is not always clear That is especially the case where large doses of potentially lethal drugs are given to a patient. Is the intention to relieve pain or is it to bring on death? Does it make any difference? Many people are inclined to say it does not matter. And yet both legal and moral traditions have always considered intention to be one of the major factors in determining the legality or morality of particular actions.

It must be admitted that there are times when it is unclear to an outsider and even to the actor what his or her intention is. A son removes the respirator from his father who is dying. If the intention is to allow his father to breathe his last and complete a peaceful death that is one kind of action. If the son's intention is to get hold of his inheritance, that is a different kind of action. The external behavior is the same, but the moral value differs. Is the son completely certain of his intention?

If one provides a pain killer that might hasten death by some days in the distant future, the intention to relieve pain seems obvious. If one administers the same drug and death follows in a few minutes (or hours? or days?), can one still claim that the intention is pain relief? The traditional language was "double effect," rules for intending a good effect while acknowledging an unintended bad effect. The new medical technology, especially pain-killing drugs, has complicated the issue. Nevertheless, one cannot abandon the principle of double effect; it applies to practically all human actions. We are seldom in control of all the effects of our actions.

In most circumstances, the difference between allowing death and killing is clear. The fact that there are cases where the difference blurs and genuine debate is possible does not eliminate the difference between an intention to kill and an intention that is not to kill. Night and day are different, although it may not be clear exactly when one passes into the other. Analogously, thirty miles per hour and seventy miles per hour on the road are different. The difference between twenty-nine and thirty-one miles per hour may be difficult to determine but it does not follow that there is no difference between speeding and not speeding.[85]

To those who say there is no clear line between letting die and killing, Robert Burt responds: "From my perspective, however, it is precisely the tenuousness of the logical distinction that recommends its preservation as a way of giving expression to the inherently limited force of rationality." He goes on to ask "how the format for decision-making can be structured so that this ambivalence, this tension, can be most effectively and visibly preserved. On this score, terminal sedation has clear advantages over physician-assisted suicide."[86]

The decisions in two United States Circuit Courts approving physician-assisted suicide opened a new level of discussion about euthanasia.[87] The U.S. Supreme Court overturned both decisions by a vote of nine to zero. The unanimity of the Supreme Court was somewhat misleading because several opinions indicated an openness to challenge the traditional distinction.[88]

The Ninth Circuit Court in the state of Washington ruled that a prohibition of suicide violated the fourteenth amendment's equal protection clause that requires all persons similarly situated...be treated alike." Judge Stephen Reinhardt said that the prohibition of suicide "places an undue burden on the exercise of that constitutionally protected liberty interest."

As to whether disadvantaged persons might be pressured into suicide, the court said that was "ludicrous on its face." This dismissal of a serious issue was shocking. "It did not occur to Reinhardt that helplessness might undermine voluntariness, that an individual's wish for continued life could be clouded by a disability that undermined accustomed self-confidence, even though the diagnostic label of 'mental incompetence' might not clearly apply."[89]

Judge Robert Beezer in his dissent took a more balanced view. He said that the change in health care "has forced us to step back and reexamine the historic assumption that all human lives are equally and intrinsically valuable. Viewed most charitably, this reexamination may be interpreted as our struggle with the question of whether we as a society are willing to excuse the terminally ill for deciding that their lives are no longer worth living. Viewed less charitably, the reexamination may be interpreted as a rationalization for housecleaning and burden-shifting – a way to get rid of those whose lives we deem worthless. Whether the charitable or uncharitable characterization ultimately prevails is a question that must be resolved by the people through deliberative decision making."

The Second Circuit Court of Appeals in New York State made a similar ruling shortly afterward. It said that those on life-support systems are being treated differently than those who are not, in that the former may "hasten death" but the latter may not hasten death through physician-assisted suicide. The premise here is that refusing life-saving treatment "is nothing more nor less than assisted suicide." Chief Justice William Rehnquist, in the Supreme Court's ruling, reaffirmed the difference between allowing to die and killing: "The distinction recognized and endorsed in the medical profession and in our legal traditions is both important and logical; it is certainly rational."[90] The Supreme Court saw no unfair discrimination. "*Everyone*, regardless of physical condition, is entitled, if competent, to refuse unwanted, life-saving medical treatment; *no one* is permitted to assist a suicide."

The Second Circuit Court used inflammatory language in describing the allowance of death. "The withdrawal of nutrition brings on death by starvation, the withdrawal of hydration brings on death by dehydration." The Court also used two spurious arguments in referring to "active/passive" and "natural." It claimed that "the writing of a prescription to hasten death...involves a far less active role for the physician in bringing about death than through asphyxiation, starvation and/or dehydration." I noted earlier that it may be desirable to restrict the physician's role but the issue is muddled by contrasting the act of writing a prescription and the act of disconnecting a respirator. Both are actions but they differ in meaning and intention. Removing a respirator is a condition for death to occur; writing a prescription for lethal drugs can be a contributing cause of suicide.

Even more muddled was the Court's contention that by the discontinuance of a life-support system "a patient hastens his death by means that are not natural in any sense. It certainly cannot be said that the death that immediately ensues is the natural result of the progression of the disease." As I commented previously, no human action is merely natural. The moral issue is whether the natural is being shaped for good and human purposes or whether the natural is being violated with a violent intrusion into the cycle of life and death. The introduction of life-support systems and their discontinuance are deeply personal acts that affect the rhythms of human nature. One might well make the case that some hastening of death is sometimes compatible with the natural process leading to a human death but only in cases where as the Court said "death is imminent and inevitable." When intervention stops and death immediately ensues, the death is indeed the result of the disease. The intervention has merely stopped a previous intervention.

In a 1999 case before the Supreme Court, Justice Anthony Kennedy contrasted "active intervention" and "nature taking its course." The phrasing could have been better. Lawrence Tribe rejected Kennedy's opinion; but Tribe's statement that "none of these patients is in a state of nature" introduces worse phrasing. Talking about a "state of nature" is a distraction from the important question about the limits of the control of natural processes in a human life.

The erasing of the line between allowing death to occur and killing someone can be looked at from opposite directions. Looked at from the side of allowing death, the act of letting die can be said to be not "essentially different" from killing. However, erasing the line can also be a move from the opposite direction so as to make killing seem a form of letting die.

What is natural and what is not natural remains an issue. If the result were the only thing important, without regard to what is natural, why would one merely hasten death instead of bringing it about immediately and certainly? Why would a quick acting bullet to the back of the head not be preferable to hastening death through drugs?[91]

The question is a serious one. When the state executes prisoners it looks for means that appear to be medical procedures. The guillotine or the firing squad are too revealing of what the state is doing, arrogating to itself the power to kill human beings. If the state is licensing physicians or other specialists to kill, the language for this permission ought to be clearer than "hastening death."

An American Hospital Association study found that seventy percent of deaths in the United States included "negotiated settlements regarding technology."[92] In the majority of cases there is a clear difference between killing and allowing death to occur. The joint effort should be directed at comforting the patient physically and spiritually. No doubt there are cases when the effort to reduce pain has an immediate connection to the ending of the life. Physicians should be given some leeway of interpretation lest they generally under-medicate those who are in pain. But extreme cases do not make good law.

A legal approval of physician-assisted suicide creates a new context of medical treatment. Then the unclear line shifts to voluntary and involuntary which many Dutch physicians seem to cross. The result is that euthanasia "solves the problem of a runaway technological medicine with a final resort to technique. It opposes the horror of a purely technical death by using techniques to eliminate the victim."[93] I would subscribe to the two guidelines that Robert Burt offers:

1. Intentional, unambiguous infliction of death in any context should be rigorously avoided and socially disapproved.

2. Where death cannot be avoided, ambivalence about its moral status is unavoidable and should be self-consciously honored through design of practical techniques for highlighting, even amplifying its presence.

In our attempt to master death through rational means we are in danger of creating new horrors. The attention of the country ought to be on improving health care rather than finding a quick and technically efficient solution. We now have medicines and technology that can do wonders in curing many diseases. But dying is part of what physicians, researchers, and the rest of us must still accept and we will always feel some ambiguity when our decisions concern our own or another person's dying.

# CHAPTER SIX: CONSIDERING AND RECONSIDERING SUICIDE

Talking about dying must include considering suicide. Albert Camus wrote that "there is but one truly serious philosophical problem and that is suicide."[94] How immediately and practically the considering of suicide for oneself is a theme that can be explored within a more general examination of suicide. The considering of suicide refers to a phenomenon that is presumably as old as the human race. Are there any perennial truths that the considering of suicide reveals?

*Reconsidering* suicide implies that one is open to new considerations and a different attitude to suicide. The premise of reconsideration is that suicide is so different in the present that a revision of past judgments is called for. Some of the changes concerning suicide are easily documented. For example, the number of teenagers and young adults committing suicide has taken a startling jump in recent decades. David Satcher, Surgeon General of the United States, felt compelled in 1999 to issue a Report on Suicide for the first time in the two-hundred year history of that office.[95] Whether greater numbers are symptomatic of a change in the nature of suicide is one question to be asked.

The biggest obvious change affecting suicide has been the difference in medical practice since the middle of the twentieth century. The effects of this new medicine have been complex. We now know more about medical conditions that contribute to suicide and about medicines that can be helpful in stabilizing potentially suicidal lives. That knowledge has led to a more compassionate, less harsh judgment in most cases of suicide.

The other side of medicine's reshaping the question of suicide is the possibility of prolonging the dying process almost indefinitely. Some people wish to end their lives because they have reached a point where nothing remains to their life but machinery keeping them alive. In such cases, dying seems to be more appropriate and more desirable. The situation of a ninety-year-old in an intensive care unit, who is being kept alive by a feeding tube, is genuinely new in human history. So also are questions about a person refusing to use such technology. A study in the 1980s found that nine percent of people who are on kidney dialysis came to a point where they simply decided to stop. The decision clearly means that their lives are ending. Is that suicide?

The answer to that question raises the issue of whether all forms of ending one's life should be covered by a single term. We may need a new term if the nature and forms of ending one's life have drastically changed. Attempts at neologisms usually do not work and I do not propose to offer one here. At present, descriptive phrases are sometimes used, such as "voluntary death." If there is essential change in reconsidering suicide, a new term is likely to emerge.

"Suicide" was itself invented in the seventeenth century as part of a shift of attitude, or at least as the signal of the beginning of a shift. Previous terms, such as self-murder or self-homicide, carried a strongly negative judgment. "Suicide," meaning to kill oneself, left open the possibility that the killing is neither a crime, nor a sin, nor a sickness. The first citation in the *Oxford English Dictionary* is from 1651: "To vindicate one's self from inevitable calamity by Sui-cide is not a crime."[96] John Donne had already broached that position in his 1644 essay *Biathanatos:* A Declaration of that Paradox or thesis, that selfe-homicide is not so Naturally Sinne, that it may never be otherwise."[97]

A survey of eighteenth- and nineteenth-century uses of suicide suggests that there was limited success in "suicide" becoming a neutral term. "Suicide" picked up most of the meaning of "self-murder" and to this day it remains overwhelmingly negative in its meaning. Advocates of legal, ethical, socially approved suicide will probably not succeed without the birth of a new term that is not burdened with the connotations of "suicide"[98]

For considering and reconsidering suicide an impressive body of literature has been built up in recent decades. These studies allow for some measured judgments about the past and some medical understanding of suicide's past and present.[99] One must nevertheless approach the subject with humility. Suicide remains one of the great mysteries of human life. The reflections in this chapter can only nibble at the edges of the mystery.

## Suicide in Education

I noted earlier the parallel between "sex education" and "death education" insofar as both of these names are used for courses taught to children in schools. That usage places an impossible burden on school teachers of the young because neither sex nor death fits comfortably into a classroom. Education in matters of both sex and death should begin in infancy and continue into old age.

Education belongs in the home, in the work setting, in leisure activities, and in all of school life, not just the classroom. When the classroom for children is given exclusive educational rights to delicate and controversial issues, there is pressure to preach against what is not socially accepted. Or else teachers wishing not to be accused of advocating the socially unacceptable may take the safer route of silence.

Jocelyn Elders lost her job as Surgeon General of the United States when she casually acknowledged, in response to a question, that masturbation should be part of sex education. She was stating an obvious truth, namely, that a sexual education cannot neglect discussing a nearly universal practice, such as masturbation. The classroom's part in education should not be to advocate or to condemn a practice but to understand it. If education were thought of as lifelong and life-wide, the teacher in a classroom of children could concentrate on the students learning how to ask the right questions and how to understand the history and meaning of each aspect of human experience.

If an official can lose her job for saying masturbation should be included in sex education, it would no doubt be dangerous to say that suicide should be part of everyone's death education. However, similar to sexual education, the main burden for education in matters of dying and death should not be placed upon classrooms for children. Unless suicide is acknowledged as a practice throughout history, it is likely to emerge from hiding as an emotionally charged subject for the classroom. The teacher in the sixth or ninth grade may prefer to avoid the subject, or if it is unavoidable, the schoolteacher may just condemn suicide as disgusting, sick, horrifying, immoral or criminal.

The trouble with telling young people that a practice is unspeakably bad is that, while a majority may consciously accept that judgment, the condemnation creates a fascination for some people. Even for those people who are rationally convinced that the practice is not to be entertained, an allure may remain. Talk about suicide can be a prelude to committing suicide; but everything depends on the *kind* of talk. Discussion of the history of suicide, its conditions, causes and prevention, is not a guarantee that suicide will not be attempted. But trying to suppress suicide through silence or unequivocal condemnation is even less of a guarantee that suicide will not happen.

The mechanism of psychological repression is better understood today than it generally was in the past. Although it may seem dangerous to acknowledge some practices concerned with sex or death, they can be more dangerous when hidden in the shadow of consciousness. On a scale of practices that are dangerous, suicide would seem to hold first place. Sexual experimentation can have unwanted or embarrassing effects, but there are usually remedies and corrections. Suicide does not have the same room for experimental error so a society's dire warnings are understandable but they are of doubtful effectiveness.

## Suicide in History

Western society after the fourth century C.E. offers a case study in the control of suicide. The early Christian movement, instead of clearly condemning all suicide, seemed to offer reasons for ending one's life. Jesus had said "I lay down my life....No one takes it from me."(John 10:17-18). Jesus' followers did not presume to have the same power over life and death but they did expect to share in the same joys of heaven. Jesus went willingly to his death in anticipation of being raised by his Father. So, too, Christians believed that death was entrance into eternal life and reunion with their loved ones.

Becoming a martyr was highly honored in the early church. However, the martyr was not someone wishing to die but a person willing to die rather than renounce the faith. As G.K. Chesterton formulated the difference, "A martyr is a man who cares so much for something outside him, that he forgets his own personal life. A suicide is a man who cares so little for anything outside him that he wants to see the last of everything."[100] In principle the line was clear but there were borderline cases. Apollonia, who died in 249 C.E., did not wait for her executioners to push her into the flames; she jumped. Was that martyrdom or suicide?

There were enough questionable cases in Augustine's time that he felt the need to condemn suicide as "detestable and damnable wickedness which is never justifiable."[101] Augustine thereby extended the commandment forbidding wrongful killing to include oneself. The Hebrew Bible has more than a dozen suicides, including Sampson and Saul, that do not receive divine censure. Jewish law allowed suicide if it was necessary to escape murder, incest or idolatry.

A turning point came in 73 C. E. after the suicide of 964 Jews at Masada to avoid Roman idolatry. Although Masada is to this day celebrated in Jewish memory, the Jewish attitude to suicide shifted toward a more universal condemnation of the practice. The social and religious acceptance of suicide could threaten the continued existence of the community.

Augustine, like the Jewish leaders, saw his own Christian community endangered by the prevalence of suicide. Augustine was very successful in setting the direction of Western church law and even secular law. Suicide became "the sin against the Holy Ghost," the one sin for which repentance was impossible. Thus, Judas Iscariot, the clear case of suicide in the New Testament, was consigned to hell. Anyone who attempted suicide was condemned as a sinner and a criminal. If the suicide was successful, punishment was directed to the corpse and to the possessions and the relatives of the dead person.

What happened in the centuries after Augustine could not have been foreseen by him. Alfred Alvarez, in his history of the Christian attitude to suicide, writes: "The Christian ban on suicide, like its ban on infanticide and abortion, was founded on a respect for life....Yet what began as moral tenderness and enlightenment finished as the legalized and sanctified atrocities by which the body of the suicide was degraded, his memory defamed, his family persecuted."[102]

The theology of the Middle Ages, including that of Thomas Aquinas' *Summa Theologia* and Dante's *Inferno*, was unambiguous in the condemnation of suicide. Church law could not have been more severe. Was this total condemnation effective in stopping suicide? We cannot be certain, given our sketchy knowledge of the lives of ordinary people in the distant past. However, the most extensive studies of medieval suicide paint a picture surprisingly similar to today's situation A commentator on Alexander Murray's *Suicide in the Middle Ages* observes: "The profile of medieval suicide does not seem to differ in essentials from modern suicide. Its causes were various and personal; mental illness and overwhelming stress were frequently acknowledged. So the Middle Ages were not peculiar; they were neither too primitive for suicide to exist; nor too religious to obviate individual desperation."[103] A similar conclusion is drawn by Georges Minois in surveying the Middle Ages. For reasons of poverty, sickness, jealousy, hopeless love and honor, suicides had their way despite peril to their souls, posthumous injury to their bodies, and the distress caused to their relatives.[104]

Although the invention of the term suicide in the seventeenth century signified a shift, which was already occurring and presaged further change in the centuries that followed, neither church law nor secular law changed quickly. Most European nations decriminalized suicide in the eighteenth and nineteenth centuries. English law still made it a felony until 1961; Ireland until 1993. The United States was always more lenient but some states still have a law against it.[105]

The larger change over the centuries was one of attitude, a tendency to find exculpatory factors for the individual while the act itself was still condemned. The most common factor was a judgment of *non compos mentis*, not guilty by reason of insanity. In seventeenth-century England, one out of ten suicides was so judged; by the nineteenth century nearly all cases of suicide were taken to be indications of mental sickness.[106] That judgment seems largely vindicated by twentieth-century scholarship. Studies in Europe, the United States, Australia, and Asia have shown the "unequivocal presence of severe psychopathology in those who die by their own hand; indeed, in all of the major investigations to date, ninety to ninety-five percent of people who committed suicide have a diagnosable psychiatric illness."[107]

The distinction between the action that is thought to be criminal or immoral and the actor, who may not be morally responsible, has allowed even the stiffest opponents of suicide to exercise compassion in actual cases of suicide. Thus, Jewish law continues to have a strong stricture against suicide but Jews refrain from judging the individual case of suicide.[108] The Roman Catholic Church, since the Second Vatican Council, has moved toward a similar position. Everything is done to comfort grieving relatives. No disrespect, such as exclusion from consecrated burial grounds, is shown to the deceased. The Catholic Church is here living up to one of its most basic principles: God alone is ultimate judge. No religious official can judge the mind and motives of the person who has committed suicide.

The recognition that mental illness affects most people who commit suicide has, on the whole, been a positive and helpful development. The only drawback is that the "presence of psychopathology" could be equated with a complete explanation of suicide. Differences among kinds of suicide could be obscured and different kinds and degrees of mental illness might also get downplayed. The presence of mental sickness answers some questions while raising others. Underneath the mental disturbance there are still questions about what suicide means both to the individual attempting it and to the community where it occurs. One can continue to ask these questions even while drugs are being prescribed or psychotherapy is tried.

The explanation of mental illness does not do full justice to the complexity of suicide. Concerning the label of insanity, James Hillman writes: "Justice is performed by defamation of character. To be saved from being found a murderer, one was defined a lunatic....The 'sane' suicide was consequently hushed up or disguised as an accident."[109] Despite greater openness today about suicide, there are still many disguised cases and a strong resistance to the idea that someone "rationally" decided to end his or her life.

Is Suicide Natural?

The question of whether some activity is "natural" is usually related to a concern with morality. In the first half of the twentieth century the main school of ethics denied that there is a connection between the natural and the moral. In the second half of the century, for a variety of reasons, such as war crimes, ecology, and feminism, the question returned. To say that the natural is moral (or the moral is natural) would be too simplistic. Nonetheless, the question of what is natural cannot be avoided nor can the question of some link between the natural and the moral.

One route that people take in assessing what is natural for humans is to look at the historical record. If something has always been present, as far as we can tell, that fact would seem to count for its being natural. For example, the Kinsey Reports and subsequent studies of homosexuality strongly suggest that homosexuality has always been present in the human population. In the past, one of the most frequent uses of the term "unnatural" has been in reference to homosexuality. Data that show the existence of homosexuality throughout the centuries shift the burden of proof to those who call it unnatural. The question becomes not how can homosexuality be natural but why should it be called unnatural.

If one approaches "natural" in this way, another ambiguous term that usually shows up is "normal." If something is always present, cannot it be called "normal"? The only unequivocal meaning of norm/normal is mathematical; the statistician decides what is the mean and median. To be normal is to fall within some expected range toward the middle of a group. Talking about what is normal can work against any minority of people in the population. In statistical terms, the left-handed or the homosexual person is not the norm. The danger comes when being different – outside the norm – slides into being thought sick, immoral or unnatural. The term "abnormal" certainly acquired these connotations so that it would be unfair to say that a left-handed person or a homosexual person is abnormal. Homosexuality is neither normal nor abnormal.

A consistent meaning of humanly natural refers to what we are born with, the powers of the unique person. Historical studies help to determine the range of those powers. The "natural" in this meaning is amoral, simply the given capacity from which human actions flow. The activities of a person are morally good if they are in accord with these powers, transforming possibility into actual practices. An action is immoral if it violently conflicts with the human organism and the capacity to partake in the human community. An immoral act is in this sense unnatural, a direct attack on what constitutes the naturally human.

A common way to dismiss all talk about what is natural and unnatural is to say that since murder or rape or stealing are present throughout history they cannot be called unnatural; that is, they are natural to human beings.[110] This objection misses the mark. Murder or rape is indeed the activation of natural powers but they are destructive uses of the natural and therefore deserve to be called unnatural. The capacity to murder is natural; the act of murder is unnatural. If anyone and everyone engaged in it there would eventually be no human nature and no human community.

This relation between the terms natural and unnatural is not so paradoxical as it may seem. A similar use of language is found elsewhere. For example, the capacity to act rationally is the precondition for acting irrationally; animals other than humans cannot act irrationally; they act non-rationally. There is a clear distinction between the irrational, as a destructive force, and the non-rational, as a different way of doing things. Similarly, only a professional can act unprofessionally; other people are simply non-professionals. Acting unprofessionally connotes moral failure. Thus, a humanly natural being is the only one that can act unnaturally. What is not natural may be a positive complement to the natural, but what is unnatural has almost always indicated a distortion or destruction of the natural.On the question of whether suicide is natural, it is helpful to acknowledge that the *capacity* for suicide is. James Hillman writes: "Without dread, without the prejudices of prepared positions, without a pathological bias, suicide becomes 'natural'. It is natural because it is a possibility of our nature, a choice open to each human psyche."[111] I agree with the second sentence that suicide is a possibility of our nature but the first sentence may imply too much. The actual performance of suicide is other than natural – either a personal act that is more than natural or else a supremely unnatural act. On the face of it, no human act is more unnatural – the destruction of the human person and its human nature.

The judgment in past centuries that suicide is an unnatural act remains generally convincing. But in addition to recognizing the exculpatory presence of mental illness, two other qualifications are needed. First, it seems possible that some individuals today are not violently opposing their natures so much as listening to their organism telling them: enough, it is time. Contemporary medicine has extended their life but a stop seems called for.

The other qualification of suicide as unnatural is the dimension that Hillman digs for. The person who chooses suicide is taking an option available for all of us, a power natural to the human. The suicidal person can be a threat to our complacency, forcing us to ask ourselves if we have chosen to live or merely not chosen to die. He or she forces us to ask what kind of life we are living and whether that is all there is. Hillman writes: "The impulse to death need not be conceived as an anti-life movement; it may be a demand for an encounter with absolute reality, a demand for a fuller life through the death experience."[112]

In summary, suicide is both natural and unnatural. It is natural insofar as the *capacity* for suicide is humanly natural. The act of suicide, however, is, with some possible exceptions, unnatural, a destruction of the nature in the person who commits the suicide. One can also say that suicide is a normal occurrence in the human race, that is, subject to statistical predictability. For the individual person, however, suicide is not normal. Alexander Murray concludes his survey of suicide in the Middle Ages with the observation "How normal the picture has been."[113] What that means is that in comparison to the Middle Ages the present era has similar patterns of suicide.

Although suicide may be normal for the human race, Emile Durkheim, in his classic work, *Suicide,* found great variations among ethnic, religious, educational, age and other groups.[114] What is normal among Swedish Lutherans is not normal among Jews; the Swedes have a high rate of suicide, the Jews have a low one. In educational terms, the normal rate of suicide goes up according to the educational level. In comparing war and peace, the normal rate of suicide goes down in wartime. Durkheim was looking for a sociological law that would encompass all the variances. He found a rule that did explain the frequency of suicide in most groups, namely, the rate of suicide varies inversely with the solidarity of the group.

A higher rate of suicide seems to be the price we pay for the increasing individualism of modern times. Thus, the normality of suicide increases in modern times. In recent decades it certainly has among some groups, especially teenagers and young adults. But the statistical normality of twenty-year-old men committing suicide does not lessen the abnormality of individuals committing suicide. The fact that something is a normal part of human experience is neither an explanation nor an approval of individual cases of suicide.

Suicide as Developmental?

For a person to think about suicide is both natural and normal, that is, part of human development. The commission of suicide, however, except as a possible culmination of human development, is unnatural and abnormal. The process of human development is endlessly mysterious and varied. I suggested that Kübler-Ross' stages of dying may throw light on stages of living. The stages of dying consist in a dialectic of yes and no: yes to life, no to death; no to life, yes to death; yes to life inclusive of dying. From earliest infancy, the process of affirming life through both the partial denial and the partial acceptance of death is at work.

The possibility of suicide is a developmental moment that people may reach quite early in life, as soon as choice is possible. There are recorded cases of children as young as six-years-old committing suicide. The thought of such a possibility may frighten adults, but trying to block out a child's awareness of suicide will not work. "Until we can choose death, we cannot choose life. Until we can say no to life, we have not really said yes to it, but only have been carried along by its collective stream."[115]

A parallel can be found in the child's ability to tell lies as the precondition of a moral commitment to the truth. Until he or she has an interior life that makes dissimulation possible, the child cannot sort out truth from falsehood. Fanciful stories by a small child are not lies; they are a necessary part of learning how to tell the truth. A person who could not tell a lie would be humanly under developed.

As soon as an interior life leads to playing with images and language, the thought of suicide provides a limit case for experimentation. "Suicide fantasies provide freedom from the actual and usual view of things."[116] Most children and teenagers have at some time entertained the question: "I wonder how they would feel if I killed myself?" Only a tiny minority of these young people move from vague fantasy to actually planning their own deaths. Some of them go so far as to put the plan into practice.

We do not know what percentage of attempted suicides are desperate attempts to get help. No doubt there is ambivalence in many cases, which is often indicated by the means that are chosen. An overdose of pills may or may not be an accident; it may be either an attempt to end one's life or else a cry for attention. More girls than boys attempt (or seem to attempt) suicide, but more boys succeed. Girls often do not know how much of an overdose is needed to cause death, but that ignorance may be part of their ambivalence about whether they really want finality. The estimate of half a million people a year in the United States who need treatment for attempted suicide suggests the confusion and mixed feelings that are usually present in the attempt to end one's life.

The mixed feeling about whether one wishes to live or die is related to the phenomenon of people trying to slowly kill themselves or acting in a way that makes death quite likely. Karl Menninger coined the term "chronic suicide" for this kind of activity; Edwin Shneidman's "sub-intentional death" seems to cover the same phenomenon.[117] In some respects this is a more puzzling issue than the 30,000 plus who are officially listed as suicides. Why do hundreds of thousands of people seem to be intent on dying by reason of automobile accidents, alcohol, or daredevil sports?

For the teenager, life-threatening risks are less likely to be a case of chronic suicide than a case of the illusion of invulnerability. The assumption is that death is for the sick and aged, not the nineteen-year-old motorcyclist. However, when a forty-year-old man is constantly acting in ways that are obviously dangerous to his health and safety, one has to wonder whether the drive for death has overtaken the wish to live.

Every individual takes calculated risks every day. Every time an individual gets into an automobile in the United States he or she risks being one of the hundred that day who do not get out alive. Crossing the street in New York or London is certainly life-threatening. Smoking can kill you, then again it might not. How far should one go in avoiding danger? An outsider may think someone has calculated the odds very poorly in regard to smoking, climbing mountains, or working on the bomb squad, but some risk-taking is not proof of chronic suicide. Only when the individual lives by a pattern in which the odds are terrible and no good purpose seems to be served by the risk has a line been crossed. Exactly where that line is may be unclear to the individual or to friends who would like to help.

One of the things that seems to be at work in chronic suicide is that the calculation of a balance between partial denial and partial acceptance of death has not been consciously worked out and integrated into one's adult development. Death has been banished from consciousness only to become encysted in the soul. While a clear choice to commit suicide could not be further from the person=s mind, a hastening of death is at the center of a person's life. The person may seem to act with fearless bravado and an exaggerated lust for life, but the seductive lure of dying actually underlies each activity.

The problem here is not the failure to recognize one's mortality but, rather, doing it in a duplicitous way that distorts the cycle that says yes and no to death. Many people who commit suicide are manic-depressive. This disease is a startling exaggeration of the yes and no stages. In the manic stage, the person overflows with life, often displaying extraordinary talent and creativity. In the depressive stage, life withdraws to the point of a paralysis of activity. Each cycle can increase the distortion of up and down, until the organism cannot sustain such jolts, and suicide then results. There is nothing romantic about this form of suicide. The control of manic-depression by drugs has been one of the welcome developments of modern medicine. Successful treatment means having the "normal" mood swings that people have, including sometimes feeling elated and at other times feeling depressed.

Carrying out suicide is not what anyone expects of a middle-aged, healthy person. When it happens, there is shock and the feeling that life has been aborted prematurely. The relatives and close friends of the deceased person feel conflicted about how this could have happened. As for the person who attempts suicide, it is noteworthy that in Raymond Moody's study of near-death experiences, the one group that did not have a pleasant experience were the attempted suicides.[118] The organism seems to be saying: Not yet; you still have work to do.

James Hillman makes the paradoxical claim that suicide is delayed death rather than premature death; suicide is "the late reaction of a delayed life which did not transform as it went along."[119] The person has failed to go through some of life's small dyings and renewals. Suicide is an urge for transformation but the means taken are too literal, too hasty, and too violent. The treatment to prevent suicide would have to include going through the death experience – for example, feelings of despair – to arrive at a newness of life.

"Until modern times," writes Robert Neale, "what every Tom, Dick and Harry has known is that you come to an end in order to come to a new beginning"[120] In trying to prevent suicide one has to move with the rhythm of yes and no, and be willing to wait for new life instead of trying to return to the old. "In the keeping of a kind of death vigil together, the panic reaction diminishes and with it the hasty assault on death."[121]

Such delicate counseling, when a person's life hangs in the balance, requires great skill. Sometimes a professional counselor is not available and a close friend may be the last link to life for the person who is suicidal. But the care and concern of one or a few friends sometimes makes all the difference on the side of life. A friend once recounted to me how, while sitting on a bridge and ready to jump, he was dissuaded by the fact that a couple of people would feel bad.

The urge to suicide does not usually increase as one ages. There has been some increase in the suicide rate among the very old but most of that refers to people who think that their dying is being over extended by medical technology. Healthy, old people are mainly concerned with living each day, not planning their deaths. Even people who have been diagnosed with a fatal illness are not prime candidates for suicide. Those who have learned to wait throughout life are content to wait for death. The process of yes and no may have been telescoped into six months or a year but the dying person is not inclined to speed up the process further.

When the sick are properly cared for, suicide is not an overriding issue. The biggest demand for the legalization of physician-assisted suicide has come from the middle-aged who are worried about whether anyone will care for them when they are old. Suicide is not a common demand in hospices. If pain can be controlled and no external factors overwhelm them, the dying do not clamor for suicide. Kübler-Ross writes: "Within the last twenty years only one person asked me for an overdose. I didn't know why and I sat down and asked him: 'Why will you have it'?"[122] It turned out that he was concerned that his mother could not bear the situation.

Patients who have been told that they have only weeks or months to live often have a better sense of life as a rhythm of yes and no. The impulse is not to choose death but to accept that there is a greater power than one's choice. A near-death experience or an attempted suicide can make one sensitive to death as a constant companion who does not have to be invited into one's life. After having attempted suicide, Gloucester, in *King Lear*, says: "You ever-gentle gods, take my breath from me/Let not my worser spirits tempt me once again/To die before you please."

## Is Suicide Dignified?

I have pointed out that the fundamental question about dying with dignity is whether we are referring to the dying patient or to the community of care givers. Is dignity something one tries to hold on to as life ebbs away or is dignity what is deserved by the dying person whatever his or her condition?

Advocates of legalized suicide are very much concerned with the first meaning of dignity. A person's dignity, they assume, consists in retaining rational control of one's faculties. Rather than become dependent on others for performing ordinary bodily functions, a person should have the right to end his or her life. While he or she still has some dignity left, suicide should be an available option. Few people would deny that this argument has some merit. Unless one believes in an absolute prohibition of suicide by God, it is difficult to see why suicide should not be acceptable in some circumstances. Who better to decide than the individual whose life is in question?

There is, nonetheless, a troubling aspect about the contemporary push to make suicide acceptable. It can miss the main point of dying – and living – with dignity. A widespread adoption of "rational suicide" could be dangerous for groups of people whose lives are disabled or who are in any way outside the "normal." At the least, the human race should go slowly in changing the legal and ethical status of suicide.

Some controlled experiments lasting years or decades should be studied before changing wider social policies. As noted in the previous chapter, the Dutch have been carrying out a useful experiment since the 1980s; it was not until the year 2002 that suicide was completely legalized. A physician is allowed to help a person commit suicide but only under strict conditions. The Netherlands is a small country with a population that is unusually independent and well-educated. Most people die at home rather than as in the United States where eighty percent die in hospitals. The Dutch provide a good testing ground for legalizing suicide but the results are not easily generalized to countries such as the United States.[123]

Within the United States the state of Oregon made sense as the first place for experimenting with physician-assisted suicide. It is a relatively small state with a long tradition of independent-minded people. Some important lessons can be taken from Oregon's experience without either immediate application to the country as a whole or interference by Congress which tried to reverse the law.[124]

When Australia initiated legalized suicide, it did so in the Northern Territory. As politicians quickly found out, that was the wrong place to start. The fact that the Northern Territory is twenty-five percent Aboriginal raised special fears. A government report concluded: "It has been expressed to us by a number of individuals that euthanasia is seen by some as a further method of genocide of Aboriginal people."[125] The law was revoked after bitter denunciations. The episode was unfortunate, particularly because Australia, with its relatively small population of independent-minded people, seems a good place to experiment with controlled suicide.

Advocates of "dignity promoting suicide" draw the picture of a candidate for suicide as a man who has been diagnosed with a fatal disease and who has nothing to look forward to except complete loss of everything that he values in life. The only reasonable thing seems to be to end his life on his own terms, avoiding the indignities of a failed body and the burden he would place on his relatives. Sherwin Nuland cites the example of Percy Bridgman, a brilliant Harvard professor, who shot himself on August 20, 1961. Nuland calls this suicide "close to being irreproachable."[126] Bridgman left a detailed explanation of why he was ending his life. Here was the case of a man facing his death with his dignity intact. Yet even here, more than a cool, rational choice was involved. He wrote: "It is not decent for society to make a man do this to himself. Probably this is the last day I will be able to do it to myself."

Most suicides do not resemble Percy Bridgman's. They run the gamut from murderers who kill themselves after killing others, to the despairing and the sick who are beside themselves with pain. In most of these cases, suicide is a failure of dignity but it may be difficult to say who is at fault.

The suicide/murderer has, for whatever combination of reasons, failed to find a dignity in life or in death. The violent end may be his or her own fault but usually there are environmental factors as well. The desperate wish not to feel the sting of disrespect destroys the very basis of respect and dignity.[127] The suicide may be hailed as a hero by other desperate people but such suicide should not be dignified as admirable.

People who are physically dependent on others for ordinary human actions (eating, dressing and cleaning themselves, going to the bathroom) are in a very different situation. Although they are not at fault for whatever they lack, they might be treated with something less than dignity by callous professionals or exhausted family members. The "temporarily abled" have to strive not to be short-sighted.[128] As death approaches, nearly everyone moves in the direction of a greater dependence on the surrounding community. If a caring community is absent, then the resulting isolation can pressure the individual toward suicide. Alvarez says that "total loneliness is the precondition of suicidal depression."[129]

It seems inevitable that suicide will find widespread legalization. But I think that the Hemlock Society should be restrained in celebrating a victory. At most, the success seems a sad necessity for some people. If considered to be a widespread solution to the increasing cost of health care in the United States – a motive that would never be admitted – the national acceptance of suicide would put great pressure on the elderly, the poor and the sick. A right to commit suicide could quickly become almost a duty to commit suicide. Not only the ninety-year-old who has multiple serious health problems but millions of young and middle-aged adults, who are a net loss to the nation's economic productivity, may feel a pressure to do the noble thing and stop being a drain on their relatives' resources. Their suicides would not be a net gain for "death with dignity." In the coming decades the policies concerning suicide and the practice of suicide may reveal what kind of society we are.

# CHAPTER SEVEN: SHOULD MOURNING HAVE AN END

Mourning is to survivors what stages of dying are to the terminally ill. One difference is that we know more, or at least we can know more, about mourning than about dying. The dead are not available to tell us about their experience of dying. But everyone past a fairly young age knows the experience of mourning for someone they loved. A second big difference is that the end of dying is clear and inevitable. Mourning, however, may go on indefinitely with seemingly no direction.

If, as it is often said, death is hidden in our culture, then one should not be surprised that mourning is, too. The dying cannot help what is happening to them. They stir up sympathy for their plight. The mourner is more likely to generate impatience and resentment. "Get on with your life" is the frequent advice given to the mourner. When mourning is hidden or suppressed, it does not go away; it operates quietly but endlessly. Similar to a patient who is on life-support seemingly without end, millions of people can mourn with no end in sight.

A few distinctions in the use of terms would help in setting out the problem and getting some bearings in the use of resources. Grief, mourning, and bereavement are the terms most often used in referring to a response to death in the lives of survivors. "Grief" is a feeling of sorrow that follows a loss; most commonly the word is used as a noun. Grief connotes a burden that a person carries when someone who had shared the burdens of life is now gone. Grief is the territory for psychologists and "grief counselors" who try to unlock the feelings of the griever.

"Mourning" might be helpfully distinguished from grief as its outward expression. Most commonly, mourning is used as a verb; to mourn is the activity of expressing grief. An individual mourns as a community member, that is, the main actor is a community or a group, while the individual both gives and receives as part of the process of mourning. This community of mourning can be a whole nation, at a time when the nation has lost a leader and occasionally when a nation has lost its soul. Psychologists know much about mourning but they are not the final experts. Every community has wise adults who have learned both to comfort and to mourn.

"Bereavement" is a state or condition in which mourners exist. The adjective "bereft" is not used much in English but it still carries the powerful image of feeling deprived and desolate. The noun "bereavement" is also not very common because a set period for mourning is no longer in vogue. People are supposedly freer to express their grief as they wish and for as long as they need to do so. But a bereavement having form and length survives among some religious groups and might be more supportive of personal freedom. Bereavement involves both senses of end: a fixed purpose and a termination point. Thus, the good thing about bereavement is that it actually ends.

Freud has a helpful essay on the difference between mourning and melancholy.[130] Both are feelings of loss but melancholy is without end. The sad person who is afflicted with melancholy, says Freud, loses his or her own life and becomes impoverished emotionally. In contrast, the mourner "bit by bit, under great expense of time and ...energy returns to reality." The existence of the lost "object" remains in mind. In the grip of mourning, the world becomes poor and empty; in melancholy it is the ego itself that is emptied. The absence of joy in one's life may paradoxically be due to an inability to mourn.

## Public Mourning

The main contention of this chapter is that mourning is a personal and communal act that can only be understood as a relational response. If there is no community with rituals for mourning, then feelings of grief cannot be accepted and dealt with in a healthy way. What we increasingly have is a dichotomy: on the one hand, intense private mourning that saps bodily and spiritual strength, and on the other hand, an ostentatious public mourning that promises what it cannot deliver. Public displays of mourning, such as the new practice of victims confronting criminals at a court sentencing, supposedly bring "closure," but more often they interfere with people coming to terms with their grief. Similarly, each time the nation relives some national calamity we simply repeat the grief.

Once again there is a comparison to be made between sex and death. Geoffrey Gorer in his 1960's study compared mourning in the twentieth century to sex in the nineteenth century.[131] Everyone is known to do it in private but one should not speak about it in public. Things have changed in the decades since Gorer's study but perhaps not as much as the surface would suggest. The place of sex was changed by adding public displays to the main activities that remain intensely private. Mourning, too, has acquired splashy public displays but feelings of grief are likely to remain bottled up in a private sphere.

Public mourning lacks a form of "public" that is not entirely cut off from the private. The bridge between private and public spheres is rituals of community life that sustain interpersonal relations. Rituals of their nature are conservative; they connect us to the past. They are always vulnerable to being attacked as outdated and irrelevant. But at the most intense moments of life humans need to be buoyed by routine gestures that hold the world together until new and reasonable actions can function again. Rituals have to grow organically; they cannot simply be invented. The best rituals are hundreds or thousands of years old. The funeral, with all its cultural variations, seems to have emerged at the very beginning of humanity.

Rituals can change without losing their effectiveness provided the change slowly emerges out of past experience. What can be especially corruptive of rituals surrounding death is the exploitation of tender feelings for the sake of profit. The "commodification of grief," including books, workshops, and chat rooms has been booming.

The beginnings of this grief industry were in the 1840s when the profession of undertaker or funeral director was born. The casket, a word taken from the jewel industry, replaced the plain, wooden coffin. Embalming became a standard practice to keep the corpse "natural" when clearly it is not. The funeral parlor gradually replaced the home as the setting for the mourners to gather. Reformers have periodically attacked the funeral industry for its callousness, pretentiousness and greed. Jessica Mitford's book, *The American Way of Death*, is perhaps the best known of these books.[132] But practices around death change very slowly. Until recently, most people trusted their local undertaker whose family had been in the business for generations.

A significant change occurred in the 1990s. For a long while, the big corporations had not seemed to notice how profitable the funeral business could be. When bad economic times come, many businesses suffer. Funerals provide steady and predictable income. Several corporations began buying up all the little, family-owned funeral parlors. The biggest entrepreneurs, Service Corporation International (SCI) and the Loewen Group, bought up one-fifth of the market. They expected to make millions of dollars. Surprisingly, a combination of greed and ignorance led instead to financial disaster. Between 1998 and 1999 both of these empires collapsed. SCI stock lost ninety-four percent of its value; Loewen filed for bankruptcy.

What has since been emerging is a new funeral industry which one can hope has learned from mistakes made by the big corporations. What should have been learned is that there is a limit to how far business can go in making grief just one more impersonal object that can be subjected to "economies of scale" for maximum profit. The profession to be successful has to reacquire some of the better characteristics it had in the past as a family-owned business. The mourner was dealing with a neighbor who had deep roots in the community and had other interests besides making money.

The students in today's fifty-two mortuary schools are generally interested in providing a service to a community rather than being a sales manager in a big company. About half the students in these schools are women (as opposed to five percent in 1971); almost a third are African-American. George Connick, executive director of the American Board of Funeral Services Education, has said: "The business has opened up. It's brought people into the field who have stronger academic backgrounds and stronger backgrounds in working with people. I think the quality of service will improve over time."[133]

The Jessica Mitfords of the country will remain suspicious of such lofty rhetoric but there does seem to be an opportunity for improvement. Nevertheless, one cannot expect a funeral industry to reflect better attitudes toward death than does the culture as a whole. Death education is not primarily a matter for mortuary schools, or even for schools. It starts with the way parents provide an example of mourning to their children, and the education continues by way of the many groups and organizations in which people participate. This education can include civic rituals that sometimes connect with genuine personal grief.

Television, now joined with the Internet, is one of the great variables in the modern expression of grief. Television is now old enough to have its own rituals. It can be an unsurpassable bond at moments of great sorrow. It can also be an instrument for the manipulation of mostly manufactured emotions.

When John Kennedy was killed in 1963, rituals on television and the ritual of television itself were relatively new. The assassination of a president, who had projected youth and vigorous action, came as a genuine shock to the nation and the world. Television provided a calming effect. The funeral was elegantly designed with admirable restraint in its form. For four days the nation stopped its business and felt the reality of death.

The event of Kennedy's death and funeral quickly became part of the national memory "Where were you when...?" The Kennedy image became inflated into a legend. A brief and not so successful presidency was turned into a glorious achievement. Airports, highways and schools were named for the fallen leader, a way to keep the memory alive. The grave site of Kennedy became a chief attraction for Washington tourists. Less helpfully, Dealey Plaza in Dallas became a kind of shrine where one could relive the horror of Nov. 22, 1963. Still, when one looks back at the event, John Kennedy's funeral provides a fairly good standard for how national tragedies might be handled.

It probably was not possible that television could ever repeat this simple and restrained approach to the need for national mourning. Just five years later, the deaths of Robert Kennedy and Martin Luther King, Jr. evoked some of the same feelings as did the assassination of John Kennedy. But the country's mood was much different and television could not heal the divisions that these deaths embodied. The artificiality of television's grief was evident. Since then, the deaths of famous people – rock stars, movie actresses, athletes – sets the grief machine in motion.

The death of Princess Diana in 1997 offers comparison to both the Kennedy proceedings and to the treatment of the glamorous celebrities in recent decades. Diana's funeral did create a bond of feeling in England, where she was not quite a national leader. The reaction was so intense and so widespread that many people predicted that the event would change the English character. England would now wear its emotions, especially grief, on its sleeve.

By the first anniversary of Diana's death, when the crowds failed to show up at the burial site, the predictions appeared exaggerated if not embarrassing. National character does not change drastically with one outpouring of emotion. In this case, as in many others since the 1990s, international television and twenty-four hour news channels have created mass outpourings of feelings.

In the United States, the event that bears closest comparison to John Kennedy's death is the bombings on Sept. 11, 2001. The date itself became an immediate marker of anger, grief, self-pity and insecurity. The spontaneous shrines that appeared in Union Square Park and Washington Square Park in Manhattan represented genuine grief and the need to mourn in an appropriately public way. Television's part was a mixture of the best and the worst. For the first few days, a cadre of television reporters who were close to the scene delivered graphic and calming reports. But television's voracious appetite for news has no built-in restraints.

Some of the memorials at political, athletic and educational gatherings during subsequent weeks were appropriate. The well-attended funerals of fire fighters and police officers gave mourning a visible and solemn form. However, the attempt to make Sept. 11, 2002 the greatest memorial ceremony in history reflected the nation's tendency to overdo its self-absorption. After listening to a thousand renditions of "God Bless America," many nations that had shared in the immediate grief reached the limit of their sympathy. It was time for the United States to put its grief in world perspective, which is not to forget the event but to situate it in a way that is helpful for itself and for other nations.

Washington D.C., which Philippe Aries described as a city of monuments to the dead, has one memorial that is different.[134] The Vietnam memorial, a plain dark wall with 58,235 names on it, has done as much as any one thing to heal the division caused by that disastrous war in Southeast Asia.[135] The young designer, Maya Lin, accomplished a near miracle in getting the monument built. "I had an impulse to cut open the earth," wrote Lin, then a twenty-one year old student at Yale. "The grass would grow back, but the cut would remain."[136]

Any doubts about the memorial's effectiveness were quickly erased not just by the size of the crowds but by the genuine emotion that the memorial elicited. A Veterans Day editorial aptly describes the usual scene: "They walk as if on hallowed ground. They touch the stone and speak with the dead. They come to mourn and to remember – an old ritual made new, creating in this time another timeless moment....As the long polished panels reflect those that move before them, the names of the past become etched on the faces of the present and, for a moment, the living and the dead are one."[137]

National monuments seldom carry such power because mourning (in contrast to grief) requires interaction. People rather than stones are the ordinary basis for interacting. The genius of Maya Lin's design is that, unlike so many recent memorials that merely relive the past horror, the Vietnam memorial has a narrative, a powerful story that begins with the grim facts but then moves the visitor beyond the grave. One walks down until one is literally overwhelmed by the dead but then one walks up and out.[138] Perhaps the only comparable memorial in Washington is the Holocaust museum, filled as it is with the ordinary stuff of life and the extraordinary means of death. The museum is most powerful for Jewish people but, as the crowds of visitors indicate, its stark simplicity crosses both ethnic and generational lines.

### Personal/Communal Mourning

For most people most of the time, mourning is possible because there are a few people who are physically present to share the grief. The correlative term of "to mourn" is "to comfort," a word that means to bring strength. The comforter brings strength mainly by being there. To comfort and to mourn are reciprocal actions; they can move back and forth in exchanges between mourner and comforter. Often the mourner ends up comforting the one who has come to offer support. No matter; the comforter and the mourner share the burden of grief and also share the healing that comes from genuine human encounter in dark times.

Words are important in such moments, although exactly what words are spoken is not so important. Religious rituals contain formulas that everyone in the community knows well. Such fixed formulas can be criticized as clichés or empty formalism. But in the midst of profound grief, few people are able to come up with fresh and brilliant insights that fit the situation. It is the strength of ritual sayings that they carry people through their sorrow. The standard Roman Catholic practice at wakes was to say the rosary ("a decade of the beads"), the repetition of a prayer formula without much thought to the words. Jewish religion probably has the most precisely specified gestures and words from the moment of death to the departure from the cemetery and for the week that follows.[139]

For people attending a funeral service, the uppermost question often is: What do I say? However, once they have suffered the loss of someone close to them they usually realize that one need not worry about what to say. In the United States the funeral service still has enough ritual about it to provide help in what to say and do.

The same is seldom true of the mourning period that follows. Widows complain that their friends and associates shun them for months and then pretend that nothing has happened. Writing a letter of condolence is something of a lost art but cards and letters are still an important form of comforting during the weeks and months after a death. Whether the card comes three days or six months later it is always welcome. Today's e-mail lacks some of the desired formality but it does have the advantage of providing easy access to world-wide communication. Harold Kushner's book, *When Bad Things Happen to Good People*, emerged from the author's own experience of mourning and the book offered helpful advice to comforters. When one tries to comfort it is difficult to know what to say. It is easier to list what not to say, such as anything critical of the mourner, anything that tries to minimize the mourner's pain, or anything that asks the mourner to disguise his or her feelings.[140] It is particularly important not to say to children: "Don't feel bad. God took your mother because he needed her more than you did."

Commenting on the Book of Job, Kushner says that Job's comforters did two things right: they came and they listened for several days. After Job was finished ranting, they should have said: "Yes, it's really awful." Their mistake was in thinking that when Job said "Why is God doing this to me," Job was asking a question and that they should try to explain God's ways to him.[141]

The words at funerals and in periods of mourning come close to what Bronislaw Malinowski called "phatic speech." This is 'a type of speech in which ties of union are created by a mere exchange of words."[142] We need this form of "social cement" when the community is bereft with sorrow and when whatever can be said is hopelessly inadequate to the sufferer's agony. Poetry and art are to be cherished if they are available. Most of us are stuck with saying "I"m sorry" or some other inane-sounding phrase. But the mourner who has tried to comfort in other situations readily understands the words that come with the presence of the person.

## The Process of Bereavement

Contemporary culture finds it difficult to accept that there is no substitute for time when it comes to mourning. The saying that "time heals all wounds" is demonstrably false but nonetheless time is an indispensable factor if wounds are to heal. "Every cell of the body has to be informed of what has been lost." (Proust). The closer the person was, the more intense is the body's reaction. This closeness includes someone who was not necessarily loved but who nonetheless had an intimate bond with the survivor. A son or daughter, who has been estranged from a parent or who constantly fought with a parent, will often be surprised at how intensely they feel the loss.

Confucius said "if a man ever reveals his true self, it is when he is mourning his parents."[143] What is unusual about the death of parents today is that we are among the first generations who are likely to have one or both parents alive when we are middle-aged. That is certainly better than losing one's parents when one is a child – a situation that has returned in much of southern Africa.

Having one's parents alive until one's forties or fifties might seem to make it easier to let go, but that is not what happens. Middle-aged people whose parents die are inevitably surprised that the word which comes forcefully to mind is "orphan." It is embarrassing to admit feeling like an orphan at the age of fifty-five. Always there had been a generation in front. The death of the parents means moving to the front pew at funerals.

The novelist Saul Bellow wrote to his biographer: "When my father died I was for a long time sunk."[144] One tries to come up for air and then coast along with the current. Many people insist after a few days that they have their feet back on the ground. The truth may be that they have postponed the reaction which is sure to be more severe a month, six months, or a year later. Most of the policies that allow leave from work provide three days to mourn one's parents. Then one is expected to "get on with your life."[145]

In some work settings, co-workers can be very helpful in providing a stable environment, but returning to work immediately after the death of a parent, spouse, or close relative can be an evasion of the time needed for mourning. The arrival of insurance agents, real estate brokers, and tax accountants the day after the funeral is not the kind of interaction that one needs.

The death of one's child is almost a different species of grief.[146] The sense of loss at a parent's death is balanced by the recognition that life has its natural cycles; after fullness of life there is inevitable decline and death. The death of a child is a screaming denial of what we assume are the ways of God or nature. Unless the parents can find a way to mourn together, the child's death will put a terrible strain upon the marriage. The parents need to talk and to talk to each other, something that the situation makes nearly impossible. The sudden death of a child raises the mortality rate of the bereaved parents five times above the average.[147]

Can one draw up any fixed rules about the process of bereavement? Does everyone go through "predictable stages of development"? There is strong resistance to the idea that the nature and length of a process of mourning can be universally charted. Certainly, anthropology has made us aware of the cultural variations surrounding death, disposal of the body, and mourning. More important, however, is anthropology's finding that every culture does have rituals for the funeral and a period of mourning. We are the odd ones in dissolving almost all the trappings of a bereavement process. Perhaps that represents progress but the medical and psychiatric toll suggests otherwise.

The claim in contemporary culture is that each of us is unique and must therefore deal with mourning in our own unique way. But human uniqueness is not about having nothing in common with others. On the contrary, it refers to an openness to learn from all sources, human and nonhuman. Human beings throughout the centuries have mourned their dead; some other animals also appear to mourn. What is uniquely human for an individual bears resemblance and comparison to the other mourners on earth. It would be rash to reject help from any source, even though "predictable stages" contain a nearly limitless range of particular details.

It is surprising that stages of mourning have not been studied more extensively. People often refer to Kübler-Ross' stages as stages of grief. But her study was entirely focused on stages of dying. The assumption that the two processes can be equated makes some sense, but there are some obvious differences. Mourning starts where dying leaves off (or possibly a little earlier). The end of the two processes also differs. "Acceptance" might apply to mourning as well as to dying but the connotations of the word in the two situations are not the same.

Mourning has been studied as one example of what are called "rites of passage." Arnold van Gennep coined the phrase in the early twentieth century to describe puberty rites and experiences that have a similar structure.[148] Birth, marriage ceremonies, and funeral rituals are characterized by a journey of withdrawal, seclusion and re-entry. The boy dies to being a child and, after a period of testing and transition, re-emerges as an adult. The engaged couple enter the ritual of the marriage ceremony and after a honeymoon transition take up life as a married couple.

The funeral ceremony is integral to the mourning process but it can be examined as a rite of passage on its own. There can be confusion here as to whether the funeral is designed for the dead person or for the survivors. The confusion is covered over by assuming that a parallel exists between the transitions undergone by the living and by the dead.[149] Someone who has died is thought to need time before coming to a final rest. No one can be certain of that transition, but the relatives and friends of the deceased clearly need time before returning to ordinary life.

In many cultures there are two funerals or a funeral in two parts.[150] The first funeral directly signifies the dying of the individual and the disintegration of the community. After some weeks or months, a second funeral is held; it moves the remains to a final resting place. Order has thereby been reestablished both for the community and for the dead person who has been reintegrated into life.

In the second funeral, men and women traditionally have distinctly different roles and the ceremony includes sexual imagery. There is nothing shocking in the close association of sex and death. The struggle of life to overcome death is represented by the mixing of young men and young women. From ancient Greece down to the modern Irish wake and African burial rites, funerals have always been a choice time for finding a sexual partner.

Modern cultures do not have two funerals. Sometimes, however, the body is quickly disposed of and a memorial service is held later. Friends and relatives, for whom travel to the funeral was impossible, can plan ahead for the memorial service. The mood of the second gathering is still somber but the life of the dead person is now celebrated along with his or her death being mourned. Favorite stories about the dead person are recalled by each of the living participants. Speaking appreciatively of the dead person is the meaning of eulogy.

For many people, of course, this second part of the funeral follows immediately on the first. The sadness at the cemetery gives way to a robust meal and sometimes overly robust drinking. The juxtaposition can seem incongruous, but, like sex, eating and drinking are the human challenge to death's finality. The drawback in the modern practice is the impatient attempt to settle everything in a few hours rather than letting time have its place.

Many communities are attentive to the widow having a prepared meal after the funeral. The test is whether there is concern for the eating patterns of the widow (and even more so, the widower) six months after the funeral. Failure to eat properly is a major problem during the time of mourning. "Why should I bother to cook for one" is a standard line among widows.

The funeral should be the beginning of the bereavement process. A dinner party after the burial can falsely imply that the mourning period is over. That is one reason why celebration and upbeat speeches would better be placed some time later. The funeral is mainly a time for absorbing a body blow. All the euphemisms for dying – passed away, expired, deceased – do not hide the absence. The person is gone; a gaping hole exists where there has always been a loved person.

I noted earlier, in reinterpreting Kübler-Ross' stages of dying, that she found a three part sequence: a no to death which is a yes to life, a yes to death which is a no to life, and then a yes to life which includes dying. The third is not really a stage so much as the synthesis of the two stages that have preceded. The two stages can be repeated any number of times. Kübler-Ross documented four stages plus acceptance, but she implies that there could be six, eight or any even number. The final synthesis, which is acceptance, can be reached only after the dialectic of yes and no has moved the elements toward each other.

The stages of mourning have this same structure. If anything, the stages are more obvious in the case of mourning than in that of dying. One criticism of Kübler-Ross' stages of dying was that not everyone has a lengthy period in which to think about their fatal disease. Kübler-Ross acknowledged the point in granting that people reach acceptance only if they have sufficient time.[151] For the experience of mourning, a lack of time is not the problem. Indeed, the problem here is finding a place to stop. Some people are still mourning the death of a child fifty years later.

For many people today the period of mourning begins before death. When a patient is on a life-support system for years, the family is likely to mourn the loss long before the system is discontinued. The experience of the survivors is that the organism is still living but the person has departed. A similar and sometimes more agonizing experience occurs with dementia, such as Alzheimer's disease. The person is still there but living in a different world. African tribal religions have a time between life and death where the person is "living-dead"; modern medicine seems to have created this state in the nursing home or the intensive care unit of the hospital.[152]

Kübler-Ross called the immediate preparation for death "anticipatory depression." So also, survivors who begin mourning before a death can experience "anticipatory grief." By anticipating grief, the blow is softened and a protective attitude is called forth. Occasionally, people start this process when they fear the death of a loved one. If the person does not die, a great strain is placed upon the reunion.

Erich Lindemann, who did one of the first systematic studies of grief and mourning, coined the phrase "anticipatory grief." Part of his study included soldiers who returned from war and found their wives no longer loved them and wanted a divorce. "The grief work had been done so effectively that the patient has emancipated herself and the readjustment must now be directed towards new interaction."[153]

Stages of dying are most evident in long, drawn-out instances of dying. It is difficult to imagine anything called phases or stages occurring in automobile crashes or shootings. Stages of mourning, in contrast, are most evident in sudden and unexpected deaths. The survivor is plunged into one emotion and sometime quickly reacts in an opposite direction. In such cases, when someone is informed that his or her spouse or child or close friend has died, the person reacts in the same way that a person does when informed that he or she has a terminal illness: "This cannot be true; there must be some mistake; I don't believe it."

Such denial is likely to persist until the dead body is seen. It is amazing what extraordinary efforts are made to recover dead bodies. It may seem pointless to search at length for the bodies of people killed by drowning, in plane crashes, or in collapsed buildings. Recovery of the body is followed by disposal of the body; the drowning victim may be buried at sea or the victim of a building collapse may be buried in the earth.

Part of the reason for the search is the respect and reverence that humans usually have toward the human remains. Part of the reason is that the survivor can begin the slow process of acceptance. One horrible aspect of the World Trade Center bombing was that survivors were deprived of both the life and the death of the loved one. The ash that covered southern Manhattan was composed in part of human bodies; the buildings had become crematoria.

Funerals are peculiar mixtures of denial and acceptance. The "viewing of the body" is customary among some groups. At the same time the dead body is made up to look as close to alive as possible. The whole production may seem ridiculous or worse to outsiders.[154] The funeral industry has undoubtedly exploited people's grief, selling the mourner unnecessary products. But one should hesitate to judge how people cope with death. If mourners really wish to spend their money in elaborate funeral practices, who can say it is not a good investment in their sanity. Everyone begins by denying what has happened. The greater concern should be for people who seem to act reasonably and appear to go on as if nothing has happened.

As in stages of dying, denial is a healthy first reaction at the beginning of mourning. Mark Twain's daughter, Sally, was killed at the age of twenty-four. Twain described his reaction this way: "The intellect is stunned by the shock and but gropingly gathers the meaning of the words. The power to realize their full import is mercifully wanting. The mind has a dumb sense of loss – that is all."[155] The mind's inability to quickly comprehend what has happened is a blessing of human nature.

As with the denial of dying, denial in grieving is a good thing that can go bad if persisted in too long. When the dead body has not been seen, the denial might go on for years despite overwhelming evidence of the death. Each time the door opens, the unrealistic expectation of the dead person's appearance is renewed. Children who have been lied to about a parent's death, which often happens in cases of suicide, are especially prone to living in denial for years. Mommy is away on a trip but she will come home some day.

There is one form of denial that applies to mourning though not to grief. When people have a relation that lacks social approval, the death of one of the partners is liable to cause "disenfranchised grief." The mistress of a married man or the partner in a homosexual union may not be able to express their grief. Colleagues at work will be puzzled by any display of emotion. "He was only a friend; it is not as if it was family." The grief is not denied but it does not have a healthy outlet in a ritual of mourning or a period of bereavement.

The attempt to deny mourning indefinitely is likely to have repercussions. Grief is a burden that the body carries; the grief needs to be shared so as to be lightened. Erich Lindemann was among the first to document that some diseases commonly occur when either mourning is delayed or when denial is followed by an exaggerated reaction of grief.

Lindemann's essay is somewhat confusing because he describes the reactions of "normal," but acute grief and then he lists the physical and mental problems of "morbid grief." Some of the same symptoms, such as respiratory problems, lack of strength, and digestive problems, appear in both parts of the study. The normal but acute reactions to grief are relatively mild and can be readily treated. What he describes as morbid grief can have life-threatening effects. He mentions as typical diseases ulcerative colitis, rheumatoid arthritis, and asthma, as well as complete disruption of the social order in one's life.

The danger in studies of mourning is that mourning itself may be seen as a sickness whereas mourning is actually the cure, to the extent that cure is possible. More than sixty years after Lindemann's study the American Psychiatric Association still seems uneasy about how to relate mourning and "normality." A proposed change in the *Diagnostic and Statistical Manual of Mental Disorders* for 2013 is to remove the "bereavement exclusion" from "major depressive disorder." The change would go perilously close to making all mourning a depressive disorder.[156]

The experience of being somewhat depressed for a period of time is not a sickness. Whereas denial is a no to death, withdrawal is a yes to death, or at least a partial acceptance of death. Denial insists on affirming life. In contrast, withdrawal is a refusal of life, an unwillingness or an incapacity to take part in the affairs of ordinary life. Withdrawal is for healing, for letting the land lie fallow.

All of the major religions recognize bereavement as an essential element in human life. Details for the observance of bereavement vary but they typically refer to how people dress, how they are addressed, what they eat, where they travel, who visits. Weeping is a usual way to express sorrow but religions provide a framework lest the wailing be excessive.[157] It may seem silly or even cruel that the widow had to wear black and did not go out in public for months. However, the practices did provide space in which the mourner quite literally learned to breathe again.

If one has stepped out of ordinary life there is a risk of not returning. To mourn permanently is to be one of the dead among the living. Religious traditions avoid this result by supplying a series of markers, at the third day, the seventh day, a month, a year. A period of bereavement is not a wandering in the desert; it is territory charted by hundreds of thousands of ancestors. At each marker along the way, a cloud of witnesses, a gathering of the community past and present, encourages a cherishing of memory in the context of a renewal of life.[158]

The final step in mourning is not a stage but a reintegration of the mourner into ordinary life. The mourner comes to a place where life wins out over depression and despair. One does not return to the same old things; instead one finds a new life with a new dimension. One will never again see life with the same eyes. The mourner now becomes capable of giving comfort to other mourners.

One paradoxical way of reintegration happens with the death of the mourner. There are numerous cases where the death of one spouse is soon followed by the death of the other.[159] Sometimes the second death seems to come from depression; the widow or widower dies of a broken heart. Sometimes widows or widowers go through a period of mourning, after which they show that they are capable of resuming ordinary life, but then they die shortly afterward. Reintegration in such cases is with the departed spouse. The bond with the dead is stronger than any bond with the living.

How long should the period of bereavement be? People vary in their needs but that does not mean some markers should not exist.[160] Religious traditions give weight to a year's anniversary. That is a longer period than secular culture's observance of mourning but secular culture has taken over the idea of observing anniversary remembrances. The practice of observing a year's passing has its arbitrary side but the sense of anniversary is deeply rooted in human nature.[161]

Six months to a year would seem an appropriate time of bereavement for most people in most situations, presuming that the mourning was not delayed. The objection raised these days might be that a year is not enough time. While allowing that that may indeed be true, I think the objection is due to blurring two realities that need distinguishing. The end of a period of mourning – bereavement – is not the end of sorrow and grief. For parents of a dead child or for a surviving spouse in a long-term marriage, the sorrow is unlikely to ever go away. Life will never return to what it was before the death.

"Acceptance," if the term belongs here, does not mean reaching an end point where a death is acknowledged as a fact. It means accepting that the death of someone who was loved has become a permanent part of life. Not a yes to life and a no to death, but a yes to life that includes the death of someone who will be forever loved.

# CHAPTER EIGHT: A CASE STUDY IN THE PHILOSOPHY OF DEATH: CHRISTIANITY

A question in modern times is whether Christian beliefs about death and an afterlife are credible. Secular thinkers today tend to dismiss the question as not worth pursuing. It is simply assumed that Christian belief has been outgrown by an enlightened world. This chapter is not an attempt to establish the truth of these Christian beliefs. Rather, it starts from the premise that something cannot be rejected unless it is understood. The Christian outlook on death is a complicated story that employs its own logic and a wealth of metaphors. It invites intellectual inquiry. At the least, Christianity should be recognized as continuing to shape much of the present world. The beliefs of hundreds of millions of people deserve some respect.

The Christian religion emerged from ancient Jewish religion and can never sever its connection to the original plant. In a different metaphor, Christianity and Judaism have rightly been called siblings, two developments from the mother religion embodied in the Hebrew Bible or what Christians call the Old Testament.[162] But, as the impossibility of even having the same name for their originating scriptures suggests, Christianity and Judaism are siblings that have had a stormy relation from the beginning. The conflict has sometimes been not only verbal but bloody.

Jews and Christians share many of the same words but the words often have different meanings. This confusing relation is not so unusual in the history of religions. Reformers who attempt to give a new direction to the religion use the terms that are familiar to both speaker and listener. The words continue while their meanings shift. Most religious reforms aim at two related results: an interiorized, simpler practice of the religion that in turn can lead to a wider practice of the religion.

A widespread religious reform is, if not anti-ritual, skeptical of complicated codes and rites. The highly developed rituals surrounding death and mourning are a primary target for religious reformers. Not surprisingly, the

Protestant Reformation set off from the issue of selling indulgences that were supposed to release souls from purgatory. One major division in Christianity is between Catholic and Protestant branches; but one must also distinguish Eastern and Western Catholic Churches, as well as a great variety of Protestant denominations. A claim to present the Christian view of death must therefore be a little suspect.

The invention of the term "Judeo-Christian tradition" in the 1890s has been mostly an obstacle to understanding Jewish tradition(s), Christian tradition(s) and the relation between Jews and Christians. The inventors of the term Judeo-Christian were not seeking understanding of the two religions. Arthur Cohen, who tracked the rise of the term, writes: "European intellectuals came to regard Judaism and Christianity as essentially similar – similar not with respect to truth, but rather with respect to untruth which they shared."[163]

The one element for which the "Judeo-Christian tradition" received some credit was for emphasizing the individual. Ironically, late twentieth-century writers attacked the "Judeo-Christian tradition" precisely on this point. Contemporary attacks of environmentalists on the "Judeo-Christian tradition" may be accurate insofar as they refer to a nineteenth century ideology, but they do not have much to say about the actual histories of either Jewish or Christian religions.

On some points of history and tradition, Jews and Christians do agree. But the term "Judeo-Christian tradition" hides the difference of approach that each religion takes. Judaism is a religion of ritual, law and tradition; it is for the most part closer to Islam than to Christianity. Christianity did not totally reject ritual, law, and tradition, but it is suspicious of ritual, critical of law, and rebellious against tradition. Christianity stakes its claim on belief in the Savior, on a proclamation that history has been fulfilled by the appearance of the God-man. The Jesus movement that evolved into the Christian religion radically shifted the emphasis from commandments given by God to a faith in God that is centered on the death-resurrection of Jesus.

The death of Jesus plays such a central role in Christianity that Christians have often been accused of glorifying suffering and being obsessed with death.[164] The Jesus movement did not begin with death but with the announcement "He is risen." However, Christianity has found it difficult to keep death and resurrection together. Historically, the figure of the risen Christ on the cross gave way to the crucifix with its portrayal of Jesus' agony. Extreme practices of asceticism sprang from the belief that "Christ died for your sins." Modern critics of Christianity accuse it of promising a reward in the next life as a way of justifying oppression and suffering in this life. Nietzsche was not praising Christianity when he wrote, "He who has a why to life can bear almost any how."[165]

One thing that Christians and non-Christians might agree upon is that Christianity has produced intricate and comprehensive systems of thought (theology). From Origen and Augustine in the early church to Karl Barth and Karl Rahner in the twentieth century, Christians have elaborated world views of impressive complexity and depth. Arising within the philosophical context of Hellenistic culture, Christian writers could not avoid developing their own philosophy, opposing but at the same time absorbing, the currents of thought that were present at one of the world's busiest crossroads. The tireless disciple, Paul, made disparaging comments about philosophy and its "unknown God." (Acts 17:23). Paul would probably be surprised to know that the "Pauline philosophy" has been endlessly discussed for two millennia.

Both the Gospels and Epistles of the New Testament are centered on the death and resurrection of Jesus. The account of Jesus' life is in the synoptic gospels of Matthew, Mark and Luke. The Letters of Paul theorize on Jesus as the second Adam and the one who redeems the whole cosmos. The fourth Gospel, attributed to John, presents a Jesus with divine qualities. Attempts to separate the history and theology in the New Testament can never be fully successful. The writings are testimonies, faith-based reports of historical events. Christianity spread across much of Asia, Africa and Europe, able to appeal both to the simple folk who could grasp the "good news" that Jesus saves, and to sophisticated thinkers, who were looking for a system of profound ideas.

On one side, the Christian church was thought to be a burial society, one of many associations in Rome that provided a social unit more inclusive than the family yet smaller than the city.[166] Christianity got much of its power by appealing to the dispossessed and by taking care of the widows and the orphans. At the same time, Christianity could present itself as an alternative to the world views of Stoicism, Epicureanism, Neo-platonism and every other school of thought. Although Tertullian in the West saw no connection between Athens and Jerusalem, the Greek Fathers of the Church showed that the Christian message was more than compatible with philosophical concepts.

In Christianity, as in Judaism, there is a dialectical relation between belief and ritual. Jewish religion moves from ritual to implied beliefs. In contrast,

Christianity largely moves from beliefs to ritual. Rather than examine in this chapter the rituals surrounding death, mourning and afterlife, it makes more sense to follow the doctrinal beliefs, noticing their effect upon ritual. Vincent of Lerins, one of the Latin Fathers of the Church, stated the principle, which is still repeated in Catholic liturgical writing today: “The rule of prayer is the rule of what is to be believed.” Nevertheless, throughout most of Christian history the beliefs have had the primacy.

Christian beliefs offer great comfort to many people. The way of salvation is clear. One’s sufferings can be “offered up” and can be borne with as participation in the sufferings of Christ. (Col. 1:24). On the other side of death is the stern judgment of God but also the intercession of the company of saints. What awaits the Christian who has faith in God and Christ is eternal happiness. Other religions have tried to give some explanation of death; Christianity is different. “The gospel of the Cross preaches salvation in death. Here complete impotence becomes the utmost development of power: absolute disaster becomes salvation; and thus what the mystery religions dare not speak of, nor mourn, is changed to highest bliss. Death annihilates death.”[167]

This startling paradox – complete impotence as power – has had earth-shaking consequences for individuals and societies. Christian doctrine can be a strong force for good, liberating the aspirations of people who have been dismissed as powerless. Unfortunately, the same ideas can be repressive when used as elaborate justifications for suffering. Elisabeth Kübler-Ross said that in her experience with the dying, she found that ninety-five percent of Christians seemed to be wracked with fear and guilt rather than finding hope and support. (She said the other five percent seemed to die with an attitude similar to that of atheists).[168] Anyone can dispute her unscientific findings but it is likely that she is pinpointing the inadequacies of Christian education and a Christian discipline of life. That is, the complicated beliefs of Christianity need to be connected to the experiences of ordinary life. Otherwise, when death is imminent, the Christian may know only enough theology to feel guilty and fearful.

## Death in the Christian Worldview

The Christian is asked to put his or her death into a cosmic perspective. Death is said to be a punishment for sin. Either death was not part of the original plan or else it would not have been experienced as painful and fear-inducing. Sin came into the world through the first parents who were banished from the Garden of Eden. Ever since then, the human race has been in search of a new paradise and is burdened by the faults and failures of its ancestors. The doctrine of "original sin" is strongly criticized by non-Christians; it can be the source of a negative and pessimistic attitude to bodily life. It can also be a realistic acknowledgment that each person's freedom is constrained by the limits that are present from the time of his or her birth. In the Christian belief system, this sinful condition is overcome by the death of Jesus which provides the grace of redemption.

What complicates Christian belief is that the death of the Christ, God's anointed, was to be the end of history. The earliest stratum of the New Testament indicates an expectation that the world is very soon coming to an end. The resurrection of Jesus is the beginning of the restitution of the whole cosmos. In the first and second centuries, the community prayed, "Come, Lord Jesus," with the expectation of the final appearance of the Christ as judge of the whole world. But by the end of the second century, if not earlier, it was apparent that the end was not arriving. Tertullian, writing at the end of the second century, cites a prayer that includes a petition for the *delay* of the end.[169] Like Rabbinic Judaism, Christianity had to settle into the flow of ordinary history. Unlike Judaism, Christianity has had a more severe tension between a world redeemed by the death-resurrection of Jesus and a world that clearly has a long way to go before peace reigns and justice is secure.

The unresolved tension in Christianity is manifest in its use of the term revelation (apocalypse). The term is Greek in origin; it means the unveiling of something that has been secret. The term made its way into Christianity through apocalyptic writing at a time when Jewish religion was deeply affected by Hellenistic culture. In this apocalyptic literature, there are sharp divisions between good and evil, this world and another world, body and spirit. Within the literature of the New Testament apocalyptic elements are present in the Gospels of Mark and Matthew. Paul occasionally uses the term apocalypse but without any special emphasis.

The energy behind the use of the term revelation or apocalypse came from the last book of the New Testament. Called the Revelation of John or simply Revelation, the book uses the word revelation only once at its beginning, but the whole book is a vision of the end and the final destruction of evil forces by the Christ. The inclusion of this book in the Christian canon was at first disputed but the book gave consolation to Christians of the first three centuries during times of persecution. While intellectual leaders, including Origen,

Jerome, and Augustine, interpreted the book allegorically, playing down its predictive character, the book continues to be central for many Christians.

Liberal theology and church officials eventually adopted the term revelation for what has been deposited in the past by God and handed on by authoritative officials to the Christian faithful. But the more marginal Christian sects continue to use "revelation" as predictive of the future. This deep gap has remained throughout Christian history and shows no signs of being overcome. The result is that Christians look to the past for the truth and they may also look to the future in hope, but the present remains a problem. How does the "word of God" speak to the experience of ordinary Christians today?

In the Catholic tradition, the answer is largely to be found in the sacramental rites. The sacraments, as delineated in the Roman Catholic Church, include Baptism and Confirmation to enter the community, confession of personal sin, and a final anointing of the sick and dying. The central act is the Eucharist (the Mass) which looks to the Last Supper of Jesus and looks forward to the Second Coming of the Christ and is celebrated as a daily prayer of thanksgiving. In the Protestant tradition, the sacraments are not generally so prominent or numerous. The word of God comes mainly through preaching. The ancient texts of the Bible are to come alive in the preached message of today.

Catholics and Protestants differ in their rituals surrounding death. For Catholics the burial Mass is central, along with music and prayers which are largely medieval in origin. The priest usually leads the prayer at the wake, the funeral mass, and the burial site. These days a family member may give the eulogy but that speech is usually relegated to the end of the service. The priest is still likely to deliver the main talk (homily) after the liturgical readings.[170]

Protestant services are usually simpler ceremonies. More attention is given to the eulogy and the reading of the scriptures. At the time of the Reformation, the anointing of the dying was one of the sacramental practices that were criticized as an inauthentic development. It is not a practice sanctioned by the Christian Bible. It found its way into Christian practice from the Jewish religion and other religions present at the birth of Christianity. When the Puritans came to seventeenth-century Massachusetts, it was to set up a society free of priests and sacraments. However, they quickly adopted ritual practices surrounding death, a tendency that made them vulnerable to the charge of Catholicizing or Judaizing the pure Christian faith.[171]

Christianity demands faith but in practice faith slides into beliefs. The two terms are often used interchangeably but "faith" as it emerged in the Hebrew Bible refers to openness and to trust. Faith means to "believe in" God as Creator and Redeemer of all. The act of "believing in" finds expression in formulated beliefs. A complex system of these beliefs, derived from the Bible and church teachings, may overwhelm rather than express the attitude of trust in and openness to God. Perhaps when many Christians come to die, they suddenly realize that they have a whole system of beliefs but it may not give much support to what or to whom they believe in.

Christianity has been the source of profound speculation that has produced works of complexity and insight. But the mystical side of the religion arose from quiet contemplation and can be startling close to agnosticism. For the mystics, God is not found along the route of the rational faculty. Faith, hope and love are the main ways of attachment to the divine. Karl Rahner was the most profound thinker and prolific theologian in the Roman Catholic Church of the twentieth century. Yet, in his works on prayer, Rahner is often shocking in his stark description of the Christian's lack of knowledge of God's ways. Christianity is, according to Rahner, "a religion which sets man face to face with the Incomprehensible which pervades and encompasses his existence...."[172] "The Christian has fewer ultimate answers which he could throw off with a 'now the matter's clear' than anyone else."[173]

Christian beliefs offer a partial and changeable picture of what Christianity is. Some beliefs are more central and fixed than others but even the most important beliefs (Trinity, Incarnation) are subject to development, that is, reform. Protestant tradition keeps close to the scriptural sources but interpretations will always vary. Catholic tradition defines certain doctrines as necessary and true, but at most these doctrines are a fence around faith, "protocols against idolatry."[174]

Most often the doctrines are formulated as negatives or, where the doctrines are intended to be positive, they are stated as double negatives. On the question of whether God is alive, Thomas Aquinas agrees with Maimonides that God is not dead.[175] Thomas begins the *Summa Theologia* by saying that "since we cannot know what God is but only what God is not, let us proceed to examine the ways that God does not exist."[176] The vast treatise that follows, instead of being an explanation of God, is an exploration of all that is not God. Thomas is not far from the fourteenth-century mystic, Meister Eckhart, who noted that while a doctrine may be true it is likely to leave out as much truth as it includes.[177]

From the beginning of Christianity there have been intense debates and disputes over matters of doctrine. The defining of doctrines regarding Jesus in relation to God provided a stable basis for the Church's survival. But insistence on formulas could obscure recognition that other views might include the truth. Unlike Judaism, minority reports were not recorded at Christian councils. The term heresy, which had begun by simply meaning a sect, came to mean error. The condemnation of heretics might drive their views out of official belief but often the ideas lived on because they had a partial truth not included in official teaching. For example, in trying to reconcile divine power and human freedom, no formula is completely successful. What is called heretical may be a valid representation of an aspect of human experience.

In 553 C.E., the Second Council of Constantinople said that "whosoever shall support the mythical doctrine of the pre-existence of the soul and consequent wonderful opinion of its return, let him be anathema."[178] It is understandable why the Council condemned belief in the reincarnation of the soul. The belief seems to run directly contrary to belief in the resurrection of Jesus and those redeemed by him. Nevertheless, belief in reincarnation among Christians has never entirely disappeared and is probably stronger today than it has ever been. Perhaps reincarnation needs to be looked at again in official circles – at least as a possibility for some people. If people are judged on how well they have lived their lives, what can one say of the millions who die as infants?[179] Is it possible that Christian belief would be more intelligible if reincarnation were left open as a possibility for lives prematurely aborted? Humans can only guess at what deaths are premature but that there are such cases seems plausible.

Christian doctrines are not a series of truths handed down from heaven. They are a kaleidoscope of interrelated statements interpretive of Christian experience. They make the case for living and dying according to a pattern of activities that praise God and serve one's neighbor. The lynchpin, at least in official teaching, is the death-resurrection of Jesus. Belief in the last things, that is, judgment, heaven and hell, follows upon belief that Jesus' death-resurrection is the center of human history and the revelation of its meaning.

The term Christ is what gives Christianity its unity and Christian theology its conceptual strength. From the later Pauline writings to the mysticism/science of Teilhard de Chardin, Christ is a term that comprehends all time and place, the basis on which the world was created and the judge of the world on its last day. At the same time, the term refers to an indelible image of an itinerant preacher put to death on a hill outside Jerusalem near the year 30 C.E. Not surprisingly, Christianity has a difficult time holding together such a complex belief.

Insofar as Jesus was a Jew, he unites Jews and Christians. Insofar as he was proclaimed the Christ, he divides Judaism and Christianity. The Greek term, Christ, was a translation of the Hebrew term, Messiah. From the beginning, however, the two terms diverged in meaning. The Christ was said to fulfill the Jewish hopes for a Messiah – but not in the way that Jews had expected. "Christ" quickly acquired a philosophical meaning associated with God's Son in a way that was unknown to the Hebrew scripture.

The danger, already present in the New Testament, was that Jesus, who died and was raised from the dead, could almost disappear, absorbed into the meaning that "Christ" took on. The not entirely successful resolution of this problem was to use the liturgical formula "Jesus Christ" as a name. Although the term Jesus retained a sure reference to an historical person, "Christ" became used as a surname, instead of as a term that would connect the story of Jesus to his Jewish ancestry and to present and future Christian experience. In Christian speech, "Christ" is most often the name of someone, and, when used alone, a name often interchanged with God.

The Christian doctrine of resurrection is difficult to make sense of when it is seen as a spectacular feat by one man, but it would not be so surprising if the man is God. The Christian apologetic quickly jumps into trying to prove the divinity of Jesus Christ. If instead, the Christian wishes to get intelligible connections to the past and the future, the resurrection would be understood as Jesus becoming the Christ, a process that continues until the last day. "For the Catholic tradition the resurrection is a cosmic event, it means that Christ is present to the whole world whether believers are present or not. The resurrection meant not just that a church was founded, it meant that the world was different."[180]

"Resurrection is an assertion about God before it is a puzzling reported fact about Jesus."[181] The Christian who is to die with the hope of resurrection needs more support than belief in a puzzling fact about the past. Resurrection, or some sign of the beginning of resurrection, has to be experienced in the present, particularly in the communal effort to resist injustice. "No community can credibly speak of the resurrection unless it has placed itself in the situations of the struggle for justice and truth in human affairs."[182]

Here is where Christianity badly needs to re-conceive its relation to Judaism, a change that has begun but has a long way to go. Resurrection could be a bridge to unite Jews and Christians, instead of the dividing line it has been. Jews sometimes joke that it is the newspaper that separates them from Christianity. The Jew reads the newspaper and asks, "Is this a redeemed world?"[183] It is possible, however, that with some moves on both sides, Jews and Christians could give the same answer to the question, "Is the world redeemed?" Both Jews and Christians could reply: "Partly." For both religions, God's grace, forgiveness, and transformation are present in the world but the world is not (fully) redeemed until the messianic age arrives, or in the Christian formulation, until the entire body of Christ is formed.

For Christians to keep their exalted meaning of "Christ" concretized and realistic, they need to situate Jesus in his Jewish milieu and the Jewish beliefs of the time. Gerard Sloyan, referring to Jesus' resurrection, writes: "He was for the Jews who first believed in him, the 'first fruits' of a harvest of all the dead. If you had the faith of the Pharisees, his appearance would have startled you, but it would not have surprised you. You would have been stunned chiefly that he was alone. That he was risen in the body was something that ultimately you could cope with."[184]

Despite the terrible portrait of the Pharisees in the New Testament, it is the pharisaic doctrine of resurrection that Christians borrowed and still use. And the Pharisees would have had good reason to be surprised that Jesus was alone. Resurrection is ultimately about community, history, and the cosmos. To be consistent with itself Christianity has to articulate an answer to what the Pharisees expected.

For the individual Christian, the doctrine of resurrection is, as it is in Judaism, an affirmation of bodily life. Of course, it is impossible to imagine life beyond death with fleshly desires and pleasures. Nevertheless, resurrection is a powerful symbol of trust in the body, community, history, and earthly life. As a doctrine, it can only be cast as a negation, or more exactly a double negative, that is, a denial of those who deny the value of bodily life. Karl Rahner writes that resurrection tells us two things that death is not. The doctrine denies that "we change horses and ride on." It also denies that "with death everything is over."[185]

In the history of Christianity, a belief in the immortality of the soul has been more dominant than belief in the resurrection of the body (or person). Similar to Jewish history, the two appeared at almost the same time, although the resurrection of Jesus gave a single, clear focus at the start of Christianity. Nonetheless, Greek ideas of the soul were in the air and were quickly absorbed into Christian belief.[186]

By the Middle Ages, belief in the soul seems to have become the heart of Christian hope for an afterlife. As was true of Jewish thought, Christian thinkers found support in philosophy for the immortality of the soul; a similar philosophical support could not be mustered for resurrection. Popular piety gave support to the soul's survival, even as the corpse was lowered into the ground. The immortality of the soul and the doctrine of resurrection are often thought to be equivalent but they represent opposing views of the body, history and community. Are the pleasures as well as the pains of the body to be included in a good, moral, and Christian life?

The belief in resurrection had the same problem in Christianity as it did in Judaism, namely, the status of the deceased between death and resurrection. With belief in the immortality of the soul, the problem shifted to the status of the soul before the last day. Thomas Aquinas argued that the soul continues to exist but is not a person until the restoration of the body. In recent times, Oscar Cullman argued that only resurrection was authentically Christian and should replace immortality.[187] While many other authors have argued for re-establishing the centrality of belief in resurrection, belief in an immortal soul will likely continue to have a major place in Christian belief and prayer.

## Last Things

According to Christian belief, what follows death is judgment and then either heaven or hell. More precisely, death is followed by the particular judgment of the soul, a possible stint in purgatory, a final judgment on the last day, and eternity in heaven or hell. The idea of two judgments was a theological development that was needed to explain what happens immediately after death and at the same time to maintain belief in a resurrection on the last day.[188] The New Testament pictures a final accounting when the good and the evil are separated. In subsequent centuries, as the focus shifted from the final resurrection to the individual soul, the judgment at death emerged as a frightful occasion. People prayed to be saved from sudden death (the opposite of what many would pray for today) in order to get themselves ready for the great trial.

In the thirteenth century, judgment was thought to take place before a stern divine judge. One's deeds were placed in a scale. The hymn sung at the Catholic Mass warned: "Lo, the book exactly worded, Wherein all hath been recorded, Then shall judgment be awarded."[189] No one could hope to survive the scrutiny without help from the Virgin Mary and the saints who might be able to temper divine justice.[190] Later in the Middle Ages, there developed belief in a final temptation at the moment of dying. The individual would see his or her whole life in review and be tempted either by despair over one's sins or vainglory over one's good deeds.[191] The belief gave support to deathbed conversions and the last act of contrition to gain forgiveness of sins.

An echo of this belief is found in a modern theological theory that each person has a final option at death. One can choose to die alone or one can die in communion with Christ.[192] The intention here is positive, a last chance for those who have messed up their lives. But this dramatic, all-important choice can also be a source of terrible anxiety and unrealistic expectation. William Lynch wisely notes that "Christianity must always remain realistic, even about death, and should refuse to increase its burdens. Therefore, it will not demand a surcharge of fantasy at the very moment when that is least possible."[193]

*Purgatory.* The theological development of purgatory came largely from Augustine, while the imagery is especially from Dante.[194] Purgatory was needed to explain a final readying for heaven of the souls not yet perfect. The fires of purgatory were said to be as bad as those of hell but arrival in purgatory meant ultimate success. The doctrine of purgatory created a link between the living and the dead. The Christians on earth prayed and performed good works for the "poor souls in purgatory," who could no longer help themselves. The calculations of time to be served and the efficacy of certain prayers, especially the Mass, created a complicated system. By the time of the Protestant Reformation, the system had been corrupted by money and power-brokers. Protestant Christianity tried to eliminate purgatory but was never entirely successful. By the nineteenth century, there were references to an "intermediate state" or "progressive sanctification after death."[195] Given the remainder of Christian doctrine, something like purgatory is probably unavoidable.

Other religions also have an ambiguous condition following death. Jewish religion needed an intermediate state for the saved but imperfect soul. Reincarnation in Buddhism and Hinduism plays a similar role. In Catholic tradition, even up to the present time, purgatory is the glue for a grand cosmic design called the "communion of saints." The saints in heaven and the faithful on earth are linked by their working to liberate the souls in purgatory.

*Hell.* The final destination for the dead is believed to be either hell or heaven. Of the two, hell has received the greater attention. The description of hell has been carried out in detail, often to lurid excess. One might guess that the horror of hell was too well described for the doctrine's own good. At some point, the doctrine becomes so truly awful that it strains belief. A decline in belief in hell may paradoxically be tied to the success of preachers, poets, and playwrights in describing what a terrible place it is.

That line of thought, surprisingly, was raised by one of the most famous preachers of hell fire. Jonathan Edwards, a brilliant and learned man, is most remembered for his sermon on God holding the soul over the fires of hell. At the conclusion of one sermon on hell, Edwards says: "I suppose some of you have heard all that I have said with ease and quietness....You have been too much used to the roaring of heaven's cannon to be frighted at it. It will therefore probably be in vain for me to say anything further to you."[196] It must be wondered how accurate are the polls that show a decline of belief in hell during the twentieth century. In the distant past, many people said they believed in hell but their life's activity casts doubt on the belief as more than notional assent.

The Christian belief in hell emerged from the Jewish understanding of Sheol that had developed over the centuries. That hell of the Jews was a place where the just were awaiting redemption, along with the wicked who were being punished. Christians say in their Creed that "He (Jesus) descended into hell." In the imagery of the fourth Gospel, Jesus begins his resurrection from the center of the earth, carrying space and time with him. Having been "lifted up" on the cross, he is able to lift up the souls waiting in hell.

In the early centuries of Christianity; hell became a much worse place. The second-century Apocalypse of Peter described hell in obscene detail (for example, blasphemers hanging by their tongues).[197] Later centuries continued to add frightful details. Some of the imagery goes back to Jesus who did refer to the wicked being cast into everlasting fire.

A statement of Jesus that has been the basis of fiery sermons was Mk 9:48: "Hell, where their worm never dies and the fire is never quenched."[198] Jesus, as he often did, was adapting a text from the prophets (Is.66:24) and applying it to the afterlife. Hell understood as a place of fire has always been a part of popular piety and was affirmed by church teaching. Fire is a powerful image but one that is difficult to take literally. John Hick, a contemporary theologian, writes that "bodies burning forever without being consumed or losing consciousness is as scientifically fantastic as it is morally revolting."[199]

Earlier commentators did not put the case that strongly but they looked for a meaning of hell that went beyond torture by fire. Augustine, while insisting that hell is real fire, identified the greatest suffering as spiritual, the fruitless repentance of the damned.[200] The same path was followed by Thomas Aquinas, that the souls in hell are tortured by what they have lost.[201] Even Dante, who had so much to do with the popular images of purgatory and hell, places the ultimate punishment in spiritual misery. Dante has Virgil say to the blasphemer, Capaneus, "only your own rage could be fit torment for your sullen pride."[202] And Milton's Satan says: "Which way I fly is Hell, myself am Hell."[203]

Christian poets, mystics and philosophers have thus been able to interpret the fantastic idea of hell fire as a psychologically profound metaphor. If a human being is to share his or her life with others, then love becomes the highest Christian virtue. Conversely, the ultimate failure in life is the absence of love. Although pride is said to be the first of the capital sins, it is so because it blocks the capacity for love. "The sorrow, the unutterable loss of those charred stones which once were men, is that they have nothing more to be shared."[204] Jean-Paul Sartre's *No Exit* nearly reverses the meaning of hell by saying that it is other people, but the lack of true love continues to underlie the Christian understanding of hell.

Whatever images of hell are used, Christian writers insist that "the misery of hell is not so much a penalty imposed by God to make the sinner pay for his sins, as it is the necessary outcome of living a sinful life."[205] Heaven is God accepted, purgatory is God purifying, hell is God rejected. "The flames of hell," said Catherine of Genoa, "are the rejected flames of God's love."[206] Following this logic, hell could be understood as invented and imagined by the sinner. The Tibetan Book of the Dead describes the soul on its journey in the "intermediate state" as it meets a series of frightening figures. Relief is found in the realization that these terrifying encounters are a product of the soul's own imagining. There is also offered the comforting thought that since you are already dead they cannot kill you.[207] In a contrasting logic, Dante's despairing description of hell is that there is "no longer even a hope of death."

At the heart of this despair is the fact that hell is eternal. That has always been a feature of the Christian hell, one defined as a doctrine by the Catholic

Church. This belief in eternal punishment separates Christianity from Judaism which has the wicked suffering for at most one year. Many people who can understand the logic of a final judgment that corrects the injustices suffered in this life are still appalled by the seeming lack of proportionality in the idea of an eternity of punishment. Perhaps the most appalling aspect of the doctrine of hell was the belief commonly held – even by Thomas Aquinas – that one of the joys of heaven would be watching the punishment of the damned in hell. Contemporary people, including most Christians, are repelled by that idea. But for some other Christians, an unwillingness to believe in an eternal hell is a sign that Christianity has been corrupted by modern sentimentality.

The belief in a "universal salvation" is not an entirely new doctrine. Origen is the best known writer in the early church to posit that eventually all of creation is saved.[208] Many writers, without directly taking on the doctrine of hell, suggest that God's ways are unknown to us.[209] Hell may exist as a possibility but there is no proof that anyone (including Judas Iscariot) fails totally. Juliana of Norwich's saying that "the Lord shall make well all that is not well" undermines the doctrine of an eternal hell without attacking it. John Hick uses the interesting analogy of God as a therapist. The number of sessions it may take to restore psychic health is unpredictable, but the divine therapist will not simply reject the patient as unsalvageable (an image that suggests a belief in reincarnation).[210] The seriousness of human choice, the outrage of injustice, and the need for retribution are not undercut by a non-eternal hell.

*Heaven.* As for heaven, the idea is easy to understand: the fulfillment of all human dreams and desires. But working out the details of that idea presents a challenge. Christians feel that they have inside information on heaven, but they still have to work within the range of images and metaphors that human history offers. The recounting of Jesus' resurrection and his ascent into heaven are central to any Christian version of heaven but that report needs considerable filling out.

The New Testament is skimpier in details about afterlife than the Qur'an and many other religious traditions. The task has been left to poets, philosophers, and mystics to exercise their imaginations and conceptual skills. Christian writing over the centuries has been more concerned with describing hell than with describing heaven. Perhaps that is just the nature of the human imagination. But the somewhat pale versions of heaven offered as a lure to the faithful might not stir up an eager enthusiasm for the good. Many Christians might want to go to heaven simply because they are intensely aware of the only alternative.

Christian speculation on heaven is based on the New Testament but here, as elsewhere, Christian imagery is drawn from the Old Testament. One tension in the Bible is between heaven imagined either as a garden or as a city. Those who prefer the latter are quick to note that the Christian Bible starts in a garden and ends in a city. The movement from garden to city is what human history shows. However, people who think that the contemporary urban scene is a nightmare are tuned into biblical and post-biblical suggestions that the end of history is a return to the garden. Paradise is a restored but better garden, according to Augustine.[211]

The images of both garden and city require some reference to ordinary human experience. Heaven is conceived of as better than what is already very good. The garden is an obviously attractive image, especially for people who are used to the desert. Abundance of food, rest from oppressive surroundings, and the fertility of the earth make up the image of an earthly paradise, which is a prefiguring of a heavenly paradise. Humans were excluded from the garden at the beginning of time but they have never lost their hope of return to harmony and peace.

The image of heaven as a city has a more distinct historical track. The first glimmer in the Bible is in the Book of Ezekiel which dates from the sixth century B.C.E. The center of Jewish life, the city of Jerusalem, becomes the model for a greater city in the world-to-come. The earliest Christians took over the language of a new and heavenly Jerusalem. The last book of the New Testament, the Revelation of John, was especially influential in permanently fixing the "new Jerusalem" as a Christian, as well as a Jewish symbol.

The most dominant image of the endtime that Christianity adopted from Judaism was kingdom or reign of God. Here, too, the image of heaven is based on a particular earthly experience. The Hebrews had tried having a king ruling over a kingdom. Although David is thought of as a great king, the whole experience worked out rather poorly. Thus, God's kingdom is thought not to be a projection of a human kingdom but its correction. The sharply different ways that one can interpret this image have played a role in Catholic-Protestant differences on the role of church.

Catholics and Protestants do agree that the image of kingdom underwent radical transformation in the preaching of Jesus and his death-resurrection. In the nineteenth century, one of the most quoted texts of the New Testament was Luke 17:21: "The kingdom of God is within you."[212] This metaphor of an interior kingdom does not seem logical. Jesus describes the kingdom as having gates, seats and rivers. The "reign of God," which many Christian exegetes prefer to kingdom, largely overcomes the logical problem but offers a thinner image. Jesus seems to have applied the idea to his own body so that kingdom or reign of God take their meaning from Jesus' resurrection.

This re-centering of kingdom or reign in the person of Jesus, the Christ, gave rise to the Christian ways of imagining heaven. On one side of the tradition is the vision of God, on the other side is union with the divine. The two symbols are shared with Jewish and Muslim traditions but Christianity worked its own distinctive twists around the Christ figure. The philosophical-minded have sought for a vision of truth and reality "in Christ." The mystics have sought a final unity, when "all things will be Christ's and Christ will be God's." The great figures in Christian history, such as Augustine, Aquinas and Dante, tried to hold on to both images.

The image of heaven as a "beatific vision" was almost a foregone conclusion once the language of revelation was adopted. Revelation is a visual metaphor, the unveiling of the truth which comes out of the darkness into the light. Although the New Testament says that "no man has ever seen or can see God (1Tim. 6:16), it also says "now we see in a mirror, dimly, but then we will see face to face." (1Cor.13:12).

As Christian theology developed, emphasis was placed on the understanding of a complex belief system. Aristotle and Plato played a large part in the forming of Christian doctrine and theology. Christianity absorbed the premise that the highest human power is intellect and that intellectual knowing is a kind of seeing. Early Christianity struggled mightily with Gnosticism, the claim to a secret knowledge of the divine held by a superior class. For Christians, the unveiling of the truth can only come at the end. "We shall see him as he is" (1Jn 3:2).

Even Augustine, with his insistence that love (*caritas*) is the heart of Christian life, gave support to heaven as a kind of vision. A more erotic form of love was excluded by Augustine in his controversies with those who expected a thousand years of earthly delights.[213] Thomas Aquinas devotes two sections of his *Summa* to the beatific vision.[214] Human intelligence when strengthened by the "light of glory" will be flooded with joy at the sight of God. Aquinas has other more mystical and affective possibilities for imagining heaven but they are only hinted at. Aquinas had a vision a few weeks before his death that made him wish to destroy all he had written. Perhaps his having a vision confirms his metaphor of vision or it could suggest that the vision was of something greater than vision.

The more affective side of Christianity was left to the mystics. Bernard of Clairvaux in the twelfth century was at the beginning of a tradition that used sexual and marital imagery to describe the relation of human and divine. Vision is superseded by the tactile and the inter-subjective.[215] These writings often veered close to a monistic or pantheistic philosophy in which the human is finally absorbed by the divine. The great mystic, Meister Eckhart, has often been treated as a misplaced Buddhist.[216] Eckhart certainly used dazzling phrases that confounded church officials. However, all Christian mystics, including Eckhart, hold to the Christ. What may sound like pantheism is the exaggerations of love poetry. The paradox of the Christ as both divine and human provides a distinctive characteristic for Christian mysticism.

For many Eastern writers, Christian mysticism is necessarily flawed; it can never get beyond a duality. For Christian writers, mystical union in Christ is not a final obstacle to be overcome. As Kierkegaard put it: "Never anywhere has any doctrine on earth brought God and man so near together as Christianity.... Neither has any doctrine so carefully defended itself against the most shocking of all blasphemies, that after God had taken the step, it then should be taken in vain"[217]

What ordinary Christians have believed about heaven may have only a faint connection to either beatific vision or mystical union. The believers have been sure that heaven is where their recently deceased loved ones are gathered around Christ, the Savior. Some believe in heaven because they hate their lives; some believe in heaven as the fulfilling of what is best in their experience. Neither scripture nor church doctrine gives a clear picture of what heaven is supposed to be. The Christian is free to let his or her imagination roam. The fact that Christian believers usually can only come up with stereotypical banalities, which Hollywood movies employ, does not prove that the belief in heaven is unreal. It is not beyond human hope even if it is beyond human imagination.

# CHAPTER NINE: HEAVEN, HELL AND BEYOND

As the previous chapter described, the last things, according to traditional Christian belief, are heaven and hell. After the individual judgment and the final judgment, after the repairs of purgatory, all that then remains is the eternal happiness of heaven or the eternal punishment of hell. The previous chapter viewed Christianity almost entirely from the inside. Its ideas and language also need to be looked at in comparison to other religions. Can a modern person make any sense of a life beyond life or a world-to-come? Christianity shares a concern with other religions and philosophies about the meaning of human life and what constitutes a fulfilled life.

Some people wonder whether dismissing the concern for an afterlife is itself realistic and whether that attitude could bring us frightful substitutes. George Steiner, meditating on the Holocaust that happened in the midst of an enlightened age and an enlightened country, writes: "To have neither Heaven nor Hell is to be intolerably deprived and alone in a world gone flat. Of the two, Hell proved the easier to re-create."[218]

Is it possible that the only way to get free of heaven and hell is to go beyond them? Is it possible that heaven and hell are symbols of something deeper and greater that calls for exploration? Any attempt to shut down individual life at death threatens to make death into the final god of life. Human beings throughout the centuries have seen their lives connected to some larger purpose and meaning.

A modern individualism which proclaims "tears of joy, alleluia, I am setting us free; no more heaven, no more hell, only the earth,"[219] is certainly attractive to some people at some times. Whether a thorough individualism can be sustained without being parasitic on assumptions from past centuries is still being weighed in the balance. The individual's death is a test of the meaning that unites past and present, person and community, humanity and the cosmos. Tolstoy's question, "Is there in my life a meaning which would not be destroyed by inevitable, imminent death?" has to be answered implicitly or explicitly by every individual.[220]

The Christian answer of heaven or hell provided a simple, clear answer to the question of life's meaning. But as the previous chapter suggested, any extensive reflection on traditional images of heaven and hell reveals their vulnerability. Hell was overdeveloped in imagery to the point where its horrors became ludicrous and for most people unbelievable. Heaven has been underdeveloped and remains a less than compelling attraction for many people, a place of white gowns, billowing clouds, and harp playing. The idea of infinite joy and unending happiness overwhelms the imagination and can leave the Christian with a blank mind. Other religions, such as Islam, supply some concrete details for heaven, but there is a problem in finding nourishing images of heaven that can withstand the bite of modern criticism.

Despite the relentless intellectual attack on religion in recent centuries, it shows no signs of disappearing. Some secular thinkers may believe that the recent resurgence of religion is a last gasp before its final demise. What seems more likely is that, while all traditional religion is under severe challenge, new forces in the world are pushing toward a radical rethinking of religion. The worldwide environmental movement is one of the most obvious factors. But any new religion will almost certainly have to emerge from attempts to reform ancient religions. A single religion for the world is highly unlikely but some converging of the world's great religions is quite possible.

Religion very likely started with the funeral ritual, an affirming of life in the face of death. Religion is a confidence that the "ultimate environment of our lives is trustworthy and fulfilling rather than indifferent or hostile toward us." If that belief is to be sustained, religion has to speak candidly about death and the meaning of a life that leads to death. Death has to be a prospect for life not simply an end to life.

Human corpses deserve respect and usually get it because they are understood to be transitional to another reality. "The gorilla, the chimpanzee, the orang-outang and their kind must look upon man as a feeble and infirm animal whose strange custom it is to store up his dead."[221] Samuel Beckett painted a picture of twentieth-century life as one of barren suffering. There are numerous cries of protest against the absurdities of life. But the most despairing line in all of Beckett is from *Endgame*: "There are no more coffins." In a world where war, famine or disease make impossible a respectful treatment of the dead, human society would reach the edge of disintegration.

Throughout the centuries humans have believed that the dead do not stay dead; they go on to another existence, either on this earth or somewhere else. Religious traditions demand that the living recognize a bond between the unborn, the living, and the dead. If individuals ask only "what's in it for me?" and "what has the future ever done for me?" then the human project is near collapse. "Tradition refuses to submit to the oligarchy of those who happen to be walking around."[222]

Although it is impossible to imagine eternal life, religions make a legitimate protest against seeing time as merely a series of moments ending in death. Modern science, economic systems, and management theory subscribe to an image of time as a sequence of points with before and after. That image of time threatens to exhaust human life of any depth. If the past is gone, the future has not arrived and the present is a disappearing point, where is serious life to be found? "Do you believe in the life to come?" Clov asks Hamm in *Endgame*. Hamm answers: "Mine was always that.... Moment upon moment, pattering down, like the millet grains... all life long you wait for that to mount up to a life."[223]

The past does not disappear; it remains in the depths of the present and is the material out which the future is fashioned. Similarly, it can be imagined that the death of an individual does not annihilate what has been his or her participation in the temporal process. "The most general formulation of the religious problem is the question whether the process of the temporal world passes into the formation of other actualities, bound together in an order in which novelty does not mean loss."[224] The religious hope is that what has emerged as novelty, including human lives, is present not merely evanescently in our lives but enduringly in the universe itself.[225]

The religious believer who professes belief in eternal life may perhaps be saying, "I believe in earthly historical life that is so truly life that it is stronger than death."[226] Religion is sometimes accused of being a higher form of selfishness, a sacrifice of goods in this world to get a greater return in the next. Undoubtedly, religion works that way in the lives of some people; the individual is out to protect his or her investment in eternal life. What they expect as a payoff is difficult to imagine. Some people talk about eternal life, wrote G.K.

Chesterton, who don't know what to do with themselves on a rainy Sunday afternoon.[227]

Belief in eternal life is not always a product of selfish desire. In the lives of ordinary people, as well as religious mystics, belief in eternal life arises from an outgoing love. The most common reason why people believe in some form of survival is that someone they have loved is dead. Although it is difficult to imagine that the dead person is alive, it is more difficult to believe that the person is simply no more. The question of life everlasting, John Baillie wrote, is not "Do I want it for myself." Even if I say that I am reconciled to the finality of my own death, can I say that is all I want for people I love. "The man who can see his beloved die, believing that it is forever, and say 'I don't care,' is a traitor to his beloved and to all their love has brought them. He has no right not to care."[228]

Many people have beliefs about an afterlife that involve communication with the dead. In today's culture, these beliefs are usually considered loony, and, indeed, specific examples are often revealed to be fraudulent.[229] Nonetheless, we are all thrown back on basic human experiences for shaping our attitudes and beliefs concerning death. No experience is more powerful than mourning the death of a close friend or a family member. Until someone has that experience, the basis of his or her belief may be thin. The death of a loved one can transform a belief system in a flash. Reflecting on the death of his close friend, Charles Williams, C.S. Lewis wrote: "When the idea of death and the idea of Williams thus met in my mind, it was the idea of death that was changed."[230]

Although it is impossible to demonstrate that the intuitions of love are valid, it is possible to invalidate one charge against the religious belief in afterlife survival. The claim has been made, especially by Marxists, that belief in an afterlife arose from a vain hope held out to oppressed people. The "opium of the people" was a promise of "pie in the sky." From archeology and anthropology we now know that ancient people believed in a better world for those who had the best things in this world. For the majority of people, the next life did not promise a social and economic reversal.[231]

The rise of the great world religions did signal a new concern for every individual's destiny, not just the king's or the hero's. The pharisaic image of God as a loving father suggested that the individual would not be abandoned. In all three of the Abrahamic traditions – Judaism, Christianity, Islam – the fate of the individual became central. In these three religions, a person has one chance to get it right, and what is right is specified in sacred texts. Eastern religions include scriptures as guides to experience but not as the word of God. Because of their more flexible outlook, which allows several religions to overlap in individual lives, the religions of the East are thought to be more tolerant of differences.

Any suggestion that the Jewish, Christian and Muslim views of an afterlife might need serious comparison with Eastern views runs up against deeply entrenched beliefs. Any tampering with beliefs in Christianity or Islam is likely to be called heretical. Judaism does not enumerate beliefs in the same way but it too has its own distinct boundaries.

There may be an ultimate and impassable gap between the Abrahamic religions of revelation and the spiritual disciplines of the East. But before we can even ask that question, the world needs a dialogue among Christian, Muslim and Jewish religionists. All three religions seem to present an obstacle to worldwide dialogue. They need to address each other and examine their respective languages which strike many other people as highly intolerant.

The question in the following section is not whether Jewish, Christian and Muslim religions have always acted tolerantly. The question is whether there is any room for interpreting these religions in a tolerant way. Can a Jew, a Christian, or a Muslim be open about the salvation of others and still be a faithful Jew, Christian or Muslim? Asking about a religion's belief in the salvation of "the other" is one of the best ways to understand each religion in its relation to other religions.

## Ultimate Intolerance?

Jewish writers do not charge Christianity with the belief that Jews go to hell; instead, they presume it is obvious that Christians do and must hold this belief. Herman Cohen, for example, cites Maimonides' teaching that "the righteous of the gentile nations have a portion in the world to come." This position is in stark contrast with Christianity in all its forms. "In Christianity," writes Cohen, "Christ is the indispensable condition of redemption."[232]

Milton Steinberg cites the same passage from Maimonides. And Steinberg makes the same contrast of Jewish universalism and Christian particularism: "Paul's universalism applies to professing Christians only, and of them only to those who profess correctly, that is, in harmony with Paul's ideas. All other men, no matter how truth-loving, devout, and good are irretrievably damned."[233] Even more surprising is to find this contrast bluntly stated by Emil Fackenheim: "Judaism is 'universalistic' for it teaches that the righteous of all nations enter the Kingdom of Heaven. Christianity is 'particularistic' for it bars from the Kingdom all unsaved, non-Christians, no matter how great their righteousness."[234]

The irony of this contrast – universal Judaism versus Christian particularism – is that it perpetuates in reverse the unfair accusation that Christians have often made against Jews. It has seemed self-evident to some Christians that the Jewish religion is for one particular group while Christianity is catholic or universal. If there is to be understanding between Christians and Jews, this claim that one's own religion is universal and the other's is particularistic must stop.

What has to be realized is that Jews and Christians (and Muslims) use the same logic. Each of these religions points toward the universal by affirming their particular language of belief. While Christians, Jews and Muslims have traded charges of narrow-mindedness among themselves, these three religions can seem to the rest of the world to be remarkably similar in the intolerance of their claims.

Secular outsiders and believers in other religious traditions have plenty of evidence for intolerance by Christians, Jews and Muslims. But the beliefs of Jews, Christians and Muslims may be more complex than many people assume. As Abraham Heschel says, religions are forced to use a language "the terms of which do not pretend to describe, but to indicate; to point to rather than to capture. These terms are often paradoxical, radical, negative."[235]

The logic of the three religions is closer to the artistic than to the scientific. That is, it is based upon looking for the universal by going more deeply into the particular. Its literary form is the narrative, the poem, or the play. It looks for the deeper truth in the lives of a community and the experience of persons. In contrast, scientific logic moves from individual cases to general statements; it deals with controlled experiments and statistical surveys. On the basis of scientific logic, Jewish, Christian and Muslim statements of who gets saved certainly sound arrogant.

Christianity may have a bigger problem than does Judaism of explaining this logic. Christian missionary activity in the past was often accompanied by political and military force. Islam, too, has a bad reputation, at least in the West, for failing to live according to the principle in the Qur'an that there can be no compulsion in religion (2:256). Whether Christianity or Islam has more often failed in practice does not have to be decided here. I am interested in the logic or grammar that is inherent to Jewish, Christian and Muslim religions.

### A Parallel Logic

All three religions believe that there is one God, creator of all, who is good and just. Each religion also believes that this God of the universe spoke to their particular group at particular times and at particular places. The paradox here is obvious to everyone in the world who is neither Jewish, nor Christian, nor Muslim. How can a just and benevolent God condemn people who through no fault of their own do not accept and practice the Jewish or the Christian or the Muslim religion?

The solution to that question is found in the way that each religion uses several of its key terms that refer to something very particular but also point to a universal ideal. The major documents in each religion, using the inner language of the group, are addressed to the believers. Little is said about outsiders. The doctrines are warnings to the believers in each group not to be smug.

The statements about people inside a religious group can sound offensive when they reach the ears of anyone outside the group. Each of the three religions has a new task in the present world because intramural doctrines are now readily accessible outside the group. When the Vatican makes a statement about Judaism, Jewish leaders are more likely to pay attention to it than most ordinary Catholics. But unless one devotes a lot of time to understanding the history of Vatican documents, the statements may be unintelligible or offensive.

The problem is not peculiar to Vatican documents; the problem is inherent to religious statements. In the case of a particular religion, writes George Lindbeck, "one must have some skill in *how* to use its language and practice its way of life before the propositional meaning of its affirmations become determinate enough to be rejected."[236] A religion cannot abandon the only logic it has; nonetheless, each of the three religions has a major educational task in trying to improve its intelligibility. That does not mean converting people to the religion. It means changing some formulas that may have once made sense but no longer do; more often, it is trying to explain the context and the limits of statements that sound intolerant of other religions.

*Christian Logic.* Christianity uses several key terms that are particular but they are also pointers to the universal. The most important of these terms are Christ, church, and baptism. From its earliest centuries, Christianity has maintained that "Christ is the one savior," that "outside the church there is no salvation," and that one needs to be baptized in order to be saved. Salvation appears to be limited to the Christian.

From the earliest centuries, however, Christian thinkers have wrestled with the question of the salvation of the non-Christian. Tertullian said that the soul by nature is Christian. Clement of Alexandria thought that Christ saves souls even if they do not realize it.[237] Augustine developed a place called Limbo for the unbaptized; God would not damn those who died without baptism.[238]

Alexander of Hales in the twelfth century did not see a problem with Jews finding salvation by following the revelation in the Torah; for other people, God must provide a special revelation.[239] Thomas Aquinas asks what happens to the unbeliever in Africa who has never heard the gospel preached. Aquinas' answer is that perhaps God sends an angel to deliver the gospel to such a person. The solutions were often clumsy but at least they were tried. The official doctrine makers did not directly address the question; they concentrated on practical guides for Christians rather than speculative questions about non-Christians. The assumption was that the Christian Church was the "ordinary way of salvation." Today based on sheer numbers, the church would have to call itself the extraordinary way of salvation and therefore rethink its role in history.

The logic of Christianity can be seen in the double meanings of Christ, church and baptism. The term "Christ" has always been a title attributed to Jesus of Nazareth. But in the later Pauline literature, in the fourth Gospel, and in the philosophical thrusts of Justin Martyr or Clement of Alexandria, "Christ" became the name of a universal ideal. Thus, in Christian terms the path of all righteous men and women leads to "Christ" whether they have ever heard of Jesus, Pope or sacraments.[240] In Christian terms one must be a follower of Christ to attain salvation.

The continuation of this logic is found in the outrageous-sounding doctrine that outside the church there is no salvation. The doctrine has been especially insisted upon in the Roman Catholic Church. To people outside this institution, the meaning of the doctrine seems obvious. Yet, Pope Pius XII excommunicated Leonard Feeney, a priest in Boston, who wanted to be more Catholic than the Pope. Feeney took the doctrine literalistically. By insisting on the need to be within the church, he ironically found himself outside the church.

"Church" has a different meaning for Protestants and Catholics. The typical Protestant usage of church is to refer to the local congregation. Catholics usually mean the world-wide institution. In both cases, however, church refers to the assembly of Christian believers. But church can also be used as a pointer to the gathering of the elect, a meaning that was quite common until the twelfth century and reappeared during the Reformation. In this meaning, there is no salvation outside the church – by definition. Even if one is Jew, Muslim, Buddhist or atheist, one is saved because of the church.

Karl Rahner's phrase "anonymous Christian" has often been attacked, sometimes ridiculed. But it is simply an attempt to state in Christian language that salvation is not restricted to card-carrying members of the Christian Church. In Rahner's words, "it is a profound admission of the fact that God is greater than man and the church." The phrase, anonymous Christian, would be better understood as "follower of the path of goodness that Christians see summed up by the term Christ" rather than meaning an unwitting member of the institution called the Christian Church.[241]

Paul did not say that Jews would come into the church or accept Jesus as the Christ. Paul never denies the validity of the Torah path for those Jews who cannot accept Jesus as messiah. Paul's main problem was not "how do I find a gracious God" but "how can Jew and Christian live in one community."[242] Salvation was from the Jews, according to Paul, while the Christians were to be grafted into the tree of salvation.

With the term "baptism" there was a more contrived distinction. In addition to baptism of water there was baptism of desire. The "good pagan" was said to receive baptism of desire if he or she was seeking God with a pure heart. The same path of salvation was possible for those who are baptized by water and for people who had never heard of baptism.

The Catholic Church's teaching is stated by the Second Vatican Council: "Those who, through no fault of their own, do not know the gospel of Christ or his church, but who nevertheless seek God with a sincere heart, and moved by grace, try in their actions to do his will as they know it through the dictates of their conscience – these too may attain salvation."

This Vatican II language is admittedly more positive than was the teaching in the past, but it is not the invention of a new doctrine. The Catholic Church is now much more aware that it has to relate its statements to other religions. A Joint Commission for Catholic-Jewish Dialogue" declared in 2002: "While the Catholic Church regards the saving act of Christ as central to the process of salvation for all, it also acknowledges that Jews already dwell in a saving covenant with God." [243] There is no explanation given for what to many people might seem incompatible claims. The "ambiguities" in the statement led to a Vatican document in 2009 that upset many Jewish leaders. The journey along the rocky road of trying to find compatible language continues.[244]

The Christian who says to the non-Christian "you are saved because you are unknowingly a follower of Christ" may be offering the highest compliment that the Christian can offer. However, Christians have to realize that what is offered as a compliment may be received as an insult. This is especially the case in Christian-Jewish relations because of past conflicts. A Buddhist might not be offended by being told he is Christ-like, just as the Buddhist may offer the Christian the compliment that he or she has a true Buddha-nature. But Christians had better refrain from complementing a Jew as a follower of Christ – at least for another millennium or two.

*Jewish Logic.* Christianity's historical aggressiveness presents a more obvious problem than the one that Jewish religion has. Nonetheless, the logic of Judaism is similar. The misunderstanding of that logic in the gentile world is widespread. Three key terms that Jewish religion uses to link particular and universal are chosen, Torah, and covenant. Each term is an obviously particular word with specific references in Jewish history. Nevertheless, each term also points, in a Jewish way of speaking, to an all-embracing universality.

The Jewish claim to be the chosen people sounds outrageously arrogant to many gentiles. Some modern Jewish writers try to soften the claim or avoid the claim to be the chosen, but it is the central Jewish claim. God chose "his people." The prayer book, *Gates of Prayer*, says: "We must praise the Lord of all, the Maker of heaven and earth, who has set us apart from the other families of earth, giving us a destiny unique among the nations."[245]

If chosenness were an achievement and a possession of the Jewish people, it would be a claim to moral superiority. But chosenness is said to be a burden, the place where responsibility lies. In the Bible the burden is usually Israel's but it can suddenly shift. "Blessed be Egypt my people and Assyria the work of my hands and Israel my heritage."(Isa. 19:25).[246] When the Egyptian soldiers who were chasing the Israelites drowned in the Red Sea, the angels in heaven began to sing. God stopped them and said: "My children lie drowned in the sea and you would sing"?[247]

This occasional reversal is a reminder to the Jewish people that the real chosen people are people; that Israel is a stand-in for the vulnerable creature that God placed in the middle of the garden. The unique destiny cited in the above prayer is not an exclusion of gentiles but openness to all humanity. Jewish thought at its best has always recognized this vocation: "The election of Israel constitutes in no sense an exception; it is rather the symbolic confirmation of the love of God for the whole race of man".[248]

The term Torah involves the same logic. "When Torah came into the world, freedom came into the world." Torah is a term that starts out as the instruction of a parent to a child. It becomes the name for God's revelation to Moses and thereby the center of Jewish life. Although Torah is a term unknown to most non-Jews, the Talmud premises the salvation of the gentile on the fact that he or she "engages in Torah."[249] How can someone engage in Torah who either has never heard of it or wishes no part in Jewish life?

Torah is structurally parallel to Christ in Christianity. It is a Jewish way of affirming the universal in the particular. The Torah, which was offered to all other nations before Israel, is meant for all peoples.[250] The righteous of all nations who are following their best lights are – in Jewish language – following the way of Torah.

A similar connection is made with the word covenant. It starts as a secular word but it is taken over to refer to God's relation to his chosen few at Sinai. Over time "covenant" comes to have a more universal meaning. In Jewish terms, God made a covenant with all peoples through Noah. According to the Talmud, salvation for the gentiles depends on following the prescriptions of the covenant with Noah. How can gentiles follow the commands to Noah if they have never read the Bible and do not accept Jewish doctrines?

Once more the covenant with Noah provides a Jewish way of affirming the universal in the particular. All of the children of Adam and the descendants of Noah are part of the covenant relation. From a Jewish perspective, those non-Jews who avoid murder, idolatry, incest (the three absolute commands) are living according to the covenant.[251]

In summary, the righteous man or woman is someone who is chosen by God, engages in Torah, and lives according to the covenant. The Jew becomes the demonstration project of God's care for the human race, the chosen people of God. When a rabbi friend refers to me as an amateur Jew, I take the phrase as it was intended, namely, as a compliment. To someone who does not appreciate the logic, such language could be offensive.

*Muslim Logic.* Islam has the same problem as do Christianity and Judaism in the way that its logic or grammar sounds intolerant. It speaks of Islam,

Muslim, and Qur'an in ways that limit salvation to those believers. The Qur'an seems to praise Muslims to the exclusion of everyone else. "You are the best people that has been brought forth for mankind." (3:110)

The Qur'an is parallel not to the Bible but to Jesus as the Christ; it is the "word of God." The Qur'an was given to Muhammad at particular times and places. It has been cherished by Muslims ever since. The Qur'an is also said to be not a book but (as its name indicates) a recitation from a book which exists nowhere but in heaven, it is a text for all peoples. The Qur'an itself says that every nation has its own messenger.(10:48)[252] Thus, the Qur'an, in the Muslim way of speaking, is the affirming of a universal revelation.

Similarly, Islam is not only the name of a religious institution founded in the seventh century C.E. It is an attitude that every person must have toward God in order to be saved. "Verily, the religion in the eyes of God is Islam." (3:19). Outside of Islam – that is, submission to God – there is no salvation. "There is only one doctrine of unity which every religion has asserted and Islam came only to reaffirm what has always existed and thus to return to the primordial religion."[253]

For Islam, "Muslim" refers to a believer. "Every child is born a Muslim" is a Muslim doctrine that may sound outrageous. It merely indicates the universal meaning of the term Muslim. The strictures about being a true Muslim are meant for those who have professed to be Muslim. In Muslim language, only a "true Muslim" can be saved. "Whoever believes in Allah and the last day and does good, they shall have their reward from their Lord." (2:62)

Similar to the saying that someone is an anonymous Christian or an amateur Jew, a true Muslim refers to all those who live by their birthright and follow the path to the one God of all. Some of those who call themselves Muslim turn out to be false Muslims. Some of the "true Muslims" turn out to be Christian, Jewish or Buddhist. When I have been called a true Muslim I am grateful for the compliment.[254]

Why do these three religions use a logic and grammar so easily misunderstood? Why don't they just say "anyone who is good goes to heaven"? I think it is because that kind of generalization does not help anyone and it would undermine the power of religious doctrine. It would obscure the fact that people live particular lives and speak different languages. For any religion to try to speak directly about the salvation of everyone would dissolve the religion into philosophy.

However, each of the religions finds it difficult to remember that its particular way of pointing to the universal does not itself create a universal language. It has to leave open the possibility that there are other ways to point toward the universal. There is no universal or catholic religion. The fact that one group intends to include another is not necessarily experienced as a compliment by the other; no one wants to be part of someone else's system. Religion lives on the basis of passionate commitment to particular events, persons, beliefs, causes. If the three Abrahamic religions were to disappear, religious passions would find expression elsewhere. Movements that can generate passionate commitment will always pose some danger.

Neither Jews, nor Christians nor Muslims have done a very good job educating their own people or explaining themselves to outsiders. Still, I would prefer to struggle for improvement with these profoundly human traditions rather than turn over religious passion to the -isms that have tried to replace traditional religion. Fascism, Communism and Nazism have probably been the worst -isms but every movement that has a name ending with -ism threatens to coerce the rest of us with its ideology while not necessarily having the play of ritual, humor and paradox that have been the salvation of Jewish, Christian and Muslim religions.

Jews, Christians and Muslims have been divided in the modern world, each trying to defend its own revelation. But if there is only one God, one creation, one redemption, then there is urgent need for a conversation that would open a better way of affirming one's own religion without insulting the other two. Admittedly, it is difficult enough to learn one's own religious tradition so that trying to master three is impossible. But believers in any one religion have to be aware that, when using terms such as chosen, covenant, grace, faith, revelation, redemption, there are other religions that have a legitimate share in those term. At the least, there must be an unambiguous affirmation of salvation beyond one's own religion even if one's theology cannot explain just how that works.

In the Christian New Testament, the clearest standard of judgment for one's life is found in Matthew 25:31-46. The judge will say: "I was hungry and you gave me food; I was thirsty and you gave me something to drink; I was a stranger and you welcomed me...." No test of denominational membership or orthodox doctrine is demanded. Christians have been warned that who turns out to be God's people will be a surprise. Jews and Muslims have similar warnings from their prophets past and present. Only God is judge.

Gabriel Moran

## Human Uniqueness

Whatever human beings believe about life beyond death is based upon human experience. Even religions such as Christianity, Judaism and Islam that claim a divine revelation have to rely on the human experience of responding to such a divine initiative. Those who are certain that there is simply nothing beyond death are likewise basing their certainty on the experiences of this life. No conclusive evidence has appeared in the last five years or the last five hundred years to seal the case for something or nothing.

The best insight would be based on the widest and deepest experiences that humans have. Human life is a peculiar tension between two contrasting forms of uniqueness: differentiation that goes in the direction of exclusion by means of secure boundaries and differentiation that is open to an ever increasing inclusiveness. The process of dying only heightens that tension; no outsider is final judge of how the tension is resolved in a particular life and death.

Insofar as humans share space and time with other objects on earth, they are concerned with the vulnerability of their bodies. But insofar as humans are intellectual and spiritual beings, they know no inherent limits to thinking, willing and receptiveness. This latter form of uniqueness involves all that human beings highly value, including love and beauty. Religious people do not see why they should believe that the things that they value most are at the mercy of the things they value least. Does disease or the decay of bodily organs simply erase the human drive for beauty and meaning?

If one takes the uniqueness of increasing inclusion to be the more important form, as the uniqueness that is specifically human, then the trajectory of a human life is toward the possibility of greater openness to all humanity and the whole cosmos. Human experience would support the belief that death is a transition to further inclusiveness. As Karl Rahner suggests, death does not make the human being a-cosmic but rather pan-cosmic.[255] Freed from the limitations of this life's space and time, the human drive toward further inclusiveness is radically accelerated.

Religions maintain that practically all human beings get it wrong, or more exactly, that humans get it only partially right. For a variety of reasons, humans lead imperfect lives, their intellects and wills caught up in illusion. They need the discipline of a spiritual wisdom to extricate themselves from the individual and social obstructions that prevent them from realizing their immense potential. Here or elsewhere they will eventually have to open their minds, hearts, and souls to a purifying truth that strips away pretense and hatred.

In the conditions of earthly life, truth and goodness in all their splendor are never available. We can make statements that are neither false nor empty but *the* truth, the whole truth, and nothing but the truth, is beyond human grasp. We can know the good not only as the object of our desires but as life that overflows itself, yet we cannot grasp the source of being, life, and intelligibility. Religions at their best give intimations of a source beyond our power to comprehend. It is also unfortunately true that religions, insofar as they are subjected to the pressures of historical existence, can also be one of the obstacles that they claim to transcend.

Consider the claim to divine revelation in the Abrahamic religions. The unveiling of the divine makes sense only if the boundaries of perception are constantly being stretched. Whatever is claimed to re-present the divine reality is not identical with it. The credibility of the revelatory symbol does not depend upon its length, breadth, or coercive power. In fact, if human uniqueness is the guide, the enormous size of an object or the world-shaking character of an event is less likely to be revelatory than receptiveness to diversity and beauty.

The religious person cherishes a small community or a series of events that historians may see as marginal. In some religions, one event in one person's life is believed to hold the key to all history. This belief is unintelligible if it does not lead in the direction of greater inclusiveness. But such prophetic openness to all humanity and to the future as well as the past, is difficult to sustain when there is a threat to the community's existence. In Christian history, the claim to interpret a divine revelation gave way to a claim to possess "the Christian revelation." The language became fixed in the late sixteenth century as the Christian Church was hampered by internal wars as it was fending off the attacks of the new sciences.[256]

If Christianity is to throw light on life and death today, it needs a dialogue with other religions that speak of divine revelation, as well as dialogue with secular culture and its revelations. The Christian religion, with its peculiar story of death and resurrection, is credible only if it is embedded in ordinary experience. "Only if God is revealed in the rising of the sun in the sky can he be revealed in the rising of a son of man from the dead."[257]

Jewish religion has been tempted by the same split that has affected Christianity in modern times: either defense of the symbol as if it were a Jewish possession or else abandonment of symbols for pure reason. But under duress, the tradition can become revivified. Victor Frankl tells of an interview he had with a survivor of the death camp. She said that her only friend was the branch of a chestnut tree that she could see from her cell. She said that she often spoke with the tree. Frankl asked her the tree's response. She said it replied: "I am life, eternal life." Eliezer Berkovits comments on her story: "Such are, of course, the unique expressions of unique people."[258]

The quality of the uniqueness depends on the tradition in which it is embedded. The tree spoke and it spoke of life because of the attitude toward life and toward God's speaking that were the context of the woman's listening. In a world in which everything can speak of God, it is not illogical that the tree said "I am life, eternal life." A tree is a tree to be appreciated for its own beauty and usefulness. It is also a manifestation of the nature of life. "Either all occurrences are in some degree a revelation of God, or else there is no such revelation at all."[259]

One can, of course, view the uniqueness of human life according to the first meaning of uniqueness in which life only narrows down to the final moment. At that end point, dying is a uniquely isolating event. But human life can also be seen in the second meaning of uniqueness as a journey of the deepening relation to one's ancestors and to the cosmos. In this framework, dying is unique acceptance into the matrix of relations which have always been there.

The concluding paragraph of Kübler-Ross' *On Death and Dying* uses two metaphors for human uniqueness. The first refers to the uniqueness of separation and extinction. "Watching a peaceful death of a human being reminds us of a falling star, one of the million lights in the vast sky that flares up for a brief moment only to disappear into the endless night forever. To be a therapist to a dying patient makes us aware of the uniqueness of each individual in the vast sea of humanity." The picture of a bright star extinguished forever is romantic but ultimately despairing.

Kübler-Ross' second metaphor in the same paragraph uses a different meaning of uniqueness, a movement toward inclusiveness. This meaning of uniqueness is better suited to the story that the book has told. "Few of us live beyond our three score and ten years and yet in that brief time most of us create and live a unique biography and weave ourselves into the fabric of human history."[260] This unique biography extends from person to humanity to the whole cosmos. The contribution of human uniqueness is never extinguished.

The ultimate truth of the human condition resists all attempts to jump beyond the particular existent. "Whatever is actual is contaminated by its actuality. For the universal can never lend its full sanction to any particular."[261] When the human mind is scandalized by time and it grasps for a universal truth, it comes up with abstract generalities. The universal is available, to whatever extent it is, in the depths of the particular and as the result of a particular journey.

Faith is expressed by a religious commitment that is particular and seemingly exclusive. But if faith, hope and love are genuine, the seeming exclusivity opens out into relations that have no preordained limits. To love someone, as Thomas Aquinas said, is to love his or her relatives, which potentially includes the whole universe. Someone who says "you are the one and only one" can mean I am fully committed to you rather than no one else is worthy of commitment.[262] Religions would not be improved by trying to create an eclectic unity. The most profound truths of religion will emerge only from dialogue which respects the differences between traditions. This dialogue has barely begun so that at present what happens at death can only be glimpsed from within the differences of religious images and language.

## Unity With Some Difference

The most fundamental divide among religions would appear to be whether in the end human individuality is preserved. The divide may be unbridgeable although it is possible that an alternative formulation of the question might narrow the difference. What is affirmed in one tradition may only seem to be negated in another tradition. Traditions might agree on what they are opposed to while not (yet) finding a way to express what they do agree upon. For example, all religions would agree that life is *not* a set of points with the last point called death. There is, however no agreement on how death is to be situated in relation to the time of a human life.

For speculating on the ultimate state toward which human life goes, it is helpful to think of the human being as constituted by three elements or aspects. The three-foldness of human life is suggested in both Eastern and Western thought. The human mind is always tempted to imagine that the individual's life is a conflict between two parts, called by such names as body and soul, or matter and spirit. In a dichotomous picture of the human being, one part is thought to be good, the other part imagined to be evil. Liberation is then imagined as escape from the evil part which threatens to imprison or infect the good part.

Popular forms of Platonism assume an opposition between an unchanging form or soul and a body whose senses and desires are a hindrance to the intellectual pursuit of truth. There are passages in Plato's dialogues that support this view, for example, Socrates' confidence that his soul would survive his body.[263] However, Plato has a more complex picture of the human being as threefold. In one of his well-known images, two horses are pulling in opposite directions. One should note that the rider is a third element holding together the other two.

In the *Republic,* Plato has intellect and appetites at odds; but a swing vote lies with *thymos,* a word sometimes translated as 'spiritedness'. This spiritedness or courage is a different kind of appetite than one seeking a sensual object. It can either work to unify intellect and emotion or cause a worse split. Plato has a striking allegory near the end of the book comparing the human being to a man, a lion and a hydra. If the lion is lazy, the hydra with its irrational appetites takes over. If the lion is untamed, it takes over the man. The man has to train the lion which can control the hydra; in that way a unity and harmony are achieved.[264]

A three-foldness is also suggested by some of the biblical literature. The spirit of God has been breathed into the human being. From the beginning, however, there has been a conflict of desires that lead to bloodshed and to trust in idols. The mortal flesh weighs down the spirit but it is never condemned as evil.[265] A resolution of the inner conflict depends upon coming into a transformed life, a third party beyond spirit and flesh. The belief in resurrection that eventually emerged carried the transformation beyond death.

In the New Testament, Paul articulates an anthropology in which flesh and spirit are in conflict. "If you live according to the flesh, you will die; but if by the Spirit you put to death the deeds of the body you will live" (Rom. 8:13). Paul's words, taken out of context, can feed the dangerous temptation to view the world as one in which the good spirit is imprisoned in evil matter. But Paul's context is that "the whole creation has been groaning in labor pains," while we wait for "the redemption of our bodies." Not just souls but the "mortal bodies" are to be transformed and saved. "It is sown a physical body, it is raised a spiritual body. If there is a physical body, there is also a spiritual body."(1Cor. 15:44)

The phrase spiritual body would be an oxymoron in many linguistic contexts. Paul, like the Bible as a whole, does not work from metaphysical concepts of matter and spirit but from a pattern of development. The spiritual is achieved only by the transformation of bodily experience. The final result is a condition which can only be described by a paradoxical phrase, such as spiritual body.

Working within a very different history, Hindu religion also reflects a conflict of desires. The individual has to discover that one's attachments are to illusions, to transitory goods that prevent humans from perceiving a deeper truth. The true spirit in the human is hidden from us and we may need more than one lifetime to realize the final truth. According to Hindu tradition, we need a discipline of life to help us break free at death from the cycle of birth and rebirth. We have to be liberated from petty desires and attachments. Only when we have emerged from these illusions do we realize that the human spirit (*atman*) is identical with the divine spirit (*Brahman*).

Buddhism arose as a moral critique of Hinduism and the Hindu explanation of the individual's position in the world. While Hinduism begins with the perfecting of the self, Buddhism boldly declares that there is "no self." The Buddhist interest, however, is not metaphysical debate but a criticism of selfishness and a rebellion against complacent acceptance of injustice. Buddhism is interested in "selfless" activity rather than a negation of the philosophical concept of self.

With its persistent refusal to accept any entities, Buddhism could be taken to be nihilistic. It is more accurately described as concerned with liberation from suffering and the interrelation of all experience. It refuses to speculate beyond the cycle of birth, death and rebirth. It speaks in double negatives about the "not born, not become, not made, not compounded" to push language to the limit and to remind us that the most important things cannot be said. Its last word is not "void" but "the void is void, also of voidness." The religions that claim to possess the "word of God" might experience a healthy chastening effect in an encounter with Buddhism.

What might be indicated from a more detailed comparison of religions is that heaven, hell and similar pictures of an afterlife are necessary images for orienting human lives. Such images, however, can become idolatrous, feeding human selfishness instead of inspiring loyalty, love and an increasing openness to others. As even the most fervent believers surely recognize, any image of heaven or hell is a projection from earthly experience to a realm beyond our power to imagine. The mystical strands in each of the religions, while retaining cultural differences, agree that there is no way beyond the double negatives in trying to speak of ultimate reality.

If one starts from a three-foldness in human beings, the terms body, soul, and spirit are perhaps as good as one can find. Body and soul are not metaphysical elements so much as aspects of our experience. Body is not simply matter but the human immersion in the flux of earthly desires, delights, and sufferings. Soul is not Aristotelian form but the experience of reflection, willing and the contemplation of beauty. Spirit is a highly ambiguous term but ambiguity can be useful here. For a long while it had seemed that the spiritual was in decline in Western religions but it has vigorously reappeared in recent decades. The acceptance of the spiritual is the most likely meeting place for diverse religions and also for people who may reject what religion connotes but who are open to a great beyond.

The key question when people use the term spiritual is whether it is a negation of bodily life or its fulfillment. If the spiritual is not to negate the body, it cannot be reached by grabbing hold of it. One has to respect the historical journey with its slow development of a unified self. The body can become a "spiritual body" only when life, including death, is fully accepted.

Thus, two distinct paths lie open for journeying to the spiritual. On the first path, emphasis is placed upon a spiritual discipline that aims to purify the individual ego of self-centered desires. The journey is mainly a withdrawal from those distractions that would hold the individual captive to desires that enslave. The most fundamental drives of the body for food, drink and sex, along with the means to acquire them, can so dominate a life that human desire is shut down at a primitive level.

The spiritual seeker discovers that there are more subtle attachments than to bodily pleasures; these desires can form a stronger chain of bondage. Attachment to one's knowledge, to one's reputation, or to performing good works is a worse danger because the objects of attachment seem to be spiritual. The saying that "the corruption of the best is the worst," was a mainstay of medieval piety. This first path attempts to take a direct route to the spiritual. It is intent on one goal which is never lost sight of, namely, release from the "ego" and contemplation of what is ultimately important. Even people who are skeptical of this journey as a lifetime project may recognize the value of many of the practices in it. A child or an adolescent who has not learned any "self-control" is headed for a life in disarray.

The second path to the spiritual does not reject the first but sees it as incomplete, and as making a dangerous jump from the individual to the final good. Along this second path of personal development, soul and body must slowly work through their tensions on the way to the spiritual. Instead of withdrawal from "the world," there is emphasis upon the joint development of person and community. The experience of brotherhood or sisterhood provides the main disciplining of the affections. A greater community is sought which can only emerge out of a struggle for justice. Thus, the spiritual is sought in roundabout fashion with excursions along side paths and immersion in the delights and the sufferings of this world.

The danger in this second way is that the goal can simply disappear from the map. One is so intent on doing good, on improving organizations, and producing new ideas, that the spiritual purpose is submerged. As one's energy flags and death approaches, the activist for good causes may wonder if that's all there is. Nonetheless, if a life is truly devoted to love and justice, then religions would call that a spiritual journey, even if God, heaven and salvation are not invoked.

Each of the world's great religions incorporates both paths, emphasizing one or the other in particular contexts. The mystical strand in each religion comes closest to uniting the two paths. Mysticism is intent on transcending all the divisions which wrack individuals and societies. Mysticism includes a withdrawal from ordinary politics but it is not apolitical. A disciplined life devoted to mystical union can have political repercussions.

Mysticism has dangers on either side. Its stark quest for "non-duality," or being "oned with God," can end in the despair of a dark night. Its refusal to play politics can go askew into violence. The mystic needs a community to remind him or her of ordinary concerns that no human can entirely neglect. The mystic needs patience of soul. Instead of grasping for the end, one must quietly wait for the end.

Mysticism suggests that the final state of the humans is an overcoming of the dichotomy of subject and object. Mysticism can misleadingly be called "atheistic" in that it denies a theism that pictures God and humans as separate beings. A god who is looked upon would not be god, a point that Meister Eckhart tried in vain to convey to his prosecutors.[266]

The alternative to the dichotomy of subject and object need not be either an undifferentiated unity or a void. The richest human experience is an interpersonal and communal unity in which the opposition of personal differences nearly disappears. A subject/subject relation is not the opposition of two things but a unity that preserves enriching differences. If love is our ultimate intimation of reality, then beyond heaven and hell is a unity that has been enriched by what we experience as personal love. Each of the religions provides a glimpse but only a glimpse of that possibility

# Endnotes

1 Chapter Three
Plato, *Phaedo*, 64.

2 Baruch Spinoza, *Ethics* (London: Dent, 1986), IV, 67.

3 Martin Heidegger, *Being and Time*, (Albany: State University of New York Press, 1996), 228.

4 Heidegger, *Being and Time,* 236-46.

5 Sigmund Freud, *Beyond the Pleasure Principle* (New York: W.W. Norton, 1920).

6 The HBO film "9/11," first shown on May 26, 2002.

7 Elisabeth Kübler-Ross, *On Death and Dying* (New York: Macmillan, 1969).

8 Ariès' book on the history of childhood is *Centuries of Childhood* (New York: Vintage Books, 1972).

9 Philippe Ariès, *Western Attitudes to Death* (Baltimore: Johns Hopkins University Press, 1974).

10 The program was broadcast on Sept. 21, 1994.

11 Kübler-Ross, *On Death and Dying*, Preface.

12 Sherwin Nuland, *How We Die*, (New York: Knopf, 1994), Acknowledgments.

13 Erasmus, as quoted in Philippe Ariès, *The Hour of Our Death* (New York: Oxford University Press, 1998), 346.

14 Sogyal Rinpoche, *The Tibetan Book of Living and Dying* (San Francisco: Harper, 1992).

15 Philippe Ariès, *The Hour of Our Death*, 536-38.

16 James Quackenbush and Lawrence Glickman, "Helping Adjust to the Death of a Pet," *Health and Social Work*, 9(1984), 42-48.

17 On this question, see Daniel Schaefer, *How Do We Tell the Children* (New York: New Market Press, 1988).

18 Jeffrey Moran, *Teaching Sex* (Cambridge: Harvard University Press, 2000).

19 William James, *Varieties of Religious Experience* (New York: New American Library, 1958).

20 Chapter Four
Elisabeth Kübler-Ross, *On Life after Death* (New York: Celestial Arts, 1991), 25.

21 Elisabeth Kübler-Ross, *Questions and Answers on Death and Dying* (New York: Collier Books, 1974), 3.

22 Elisabeth Kübler-Ross, *On Death and Dying* (New York: Macmillan, 1969), Preface.

23 For example, in Lorrie Moore, *Birds of America* (New York: Picador, 1999), a character who is mourning the death of her cat refers to going through the stages of anger, denial, rage, Hagen-Dass. Perhaps the most spectacular use of Kübler-Ross' five stages is the structure of the movie *All That Jazz*.

24 I refer here to the collections *On Life after Death* and *Death is of Vital Importance* (Barrytown, NY: Station Hill Press, 1995) and her memoir *The Wheel of Life* (New York: Bantam Press, 1997).

25 For example, Dr. Samuel Klagsbrun, a psychiatrist well known for his work with the dying, said: "She is actively destroying the work she has done, which I think will long live after her attempts to destroy it....She's killing her own work by denying death." Quoted in Jonathan Rosen, "Rewriting the End: Elisabeth Kübler-Ross," *New York Times Magazine*, Jan. 22, 1995, 24.

26 Kübler-Ross, *On Death and Dying*, Preface.

27 Kübler-Ross, *Questions and Answers on Death and Dying*, 25-6.

28 Kübler-Ross, *Questions and Answers on Death and Dying*, 26.

29 Jean Piaget, *Illusions and Insights of Philosophy* (New York: New American Library, 1971).

30 James Hillman, *The Dream and the Underworld* (New York: Harper and Row, 1979).

31 Gail Sheehy, *Pathfinders* (New York: Morrow, 1981), 9.

32 Kübler-Ross, *The Wheel of Life*, 280.

33 Sigmund Freud, *Beyond the Pleasure Principle* (New York: Norton, 1920).

34 Erik Erikson, *Insight and Responsibility* (New York: Norton, 1964), 133.

35 Robert Jay Lifton, *The Broken Connection: On Death and the Continuity of Life* (New York: Basic Books, 1983).

36 David Kuhl, *What Dying People Want: Practical Wisdom for the End of Life* (New York: Public Affairs, 2002). In one of his exchanges with the dying, the

author asks the patient if he is afraid of dying. "No," the patient said, "It's different from anything I have experienced before. I have a calmness within me, and a quiet confidence that my life on earth is complete." (253)

37 Gail Sheehy, *Passages* (New York: Dutton, 1976), 252.

38 Kübler-Ross, *Questions and Answers on Death and Dying*, 36.

39 39 Joan Acocella, "The English Wars," *New Yorker*, May 14, 2012, 115-20, which reviews Henry Hitchings, *The Language Wars: A History of Proper English* (New York: Farrar, Straus &Giroux, 2012).

40 Kübler-Ross, *On Death and Dying, 40.*

41 Kübler-Ross, *On Death and Dying.*, 39.

42 Kübler-Ross, *On Death and Dying.*, 49.

43 Kübler-Ross, *Questions and Answers on Death and Dying*, 36.

44 *The Dhammapada*, ed. Gil Fronsdal (New York: Schambhala, 2006), ch. 17; Thich Nhat Hanh, *Anger: Wisdom for Cooling the Flames* (New York: Riverhead, 2002).

45 Thomas Keating, in *Spiritual Silence*, ed. Susan Walker (New York: Paulist Press, 1987), 285.

46 Kübler-Ross, *Questions and Answers on Death and Dying*, 24.

47 Kübler-Ross, *On Death and Dying*, 86.

48 Kübler-Ross, *On Death and Dying*, 112.

49 Kübler-Ross, *On Death and Dying*, 120.

50 William James, *The Varieties of Religious Experience* (New American Library, 1958), 49.

51 William May, *Testing the Medical Covenant* (Grand Rapids: Eerdmans, 1996), 72-73, has a criticism that is almost the opposite of mine. He says that Kübler-Ross "overlooked this element of distancing that occurs in all authentic relationships." Instead, she "wrongly urges a kind of intimacy between the healer and the dying, a mystical merging of the two, that does not fully honor the complicated transparency/opaqueness of all human encounters, from the most intimate to the most crisis-laden." Perhaps she is vulnerable to that criticism in general but it is hardly a description of what she advocates at the time of the actual dying.

52 Dylan Thomas, *The Collected Poems of Dylan Thomas* (New York: New Directions, 1957), 128.

53 Kübler-Ross, *On Death and Dying*, 120;

54 Kübler-Ross, *On Life after Death*, 30, 36, 37.

55 Kübler-Ross, *On Life after Death*, 30.

56 Kübler-Ross, *On Life after Death.*, 138.

57 Kübler-Ross, *On Life after Death*, 139.

58 Thomas Aquinas, *Summa Theologia*, IIa, IIae, 40, 1, ad 3.

59 Gabriel Marcel, *Philosophy of Existence* (New York: Citadel, 1944), 32.

60 Simone Weil, "Human Personality," in *The Weil Reader* (Mt. Kisco, NY: Moyer Bell, 1977), 315.

## Chapter Five

61 William May, *The Physician's Covenant* (Philadelphia: Westminster Press, 1993), 16, accepts the language of active and passive euthanasia but then argues that "the moral justification in each case depends upon the motive and intent of the agent and the wishes of the patient rather than on the act defined as an omission or a commission." I think James Rachels, "Active

and Passive Euthanasia," *New England Journal of Medicine,* 29(1975) is logically on stronger grounds in dismissing any significant difference between active and passive euthanasia. If motive and intent are crucial to May, he should not accept Rachels' language in the first place.

62 *Oxford English Dictionary*, 904.

63 "The Physician and the Dying Patient," in James Rachels, *The End of Life: Euthanasia and Morality* (New York: Oxford University Press, 1986), 88.

64 Robert Burt, *Death is that Man Taking Names (*Berkeley: University of California Press, 2004), 181.

65 Betty Rollin, *Last Wish* (New York: Simon and Shuster, 1985).

66 Anonymous, "It's Over Debbie," *Journal of the American Medical Association* 259(Jan. 8, 1988).

67 Timothy Quill, "A Case of Individualized Decision Making," *New England Journal of Medicine,* 324(March 7, 1991), 691-94.

68 Herbert Hendin, *Seduced by Death* (New York: W.W. Norton, 1998), 26-7; Richard Fenigsen, "The Report of the Dutch Governmental Committee on Euthanasia," *Issues in Law and Medicine*, 7(No. 3, 1991), 330-44.

69 Joanna Groenewoud and others, "Clinical Problems with the Performance of Physician-Assisted Suicide," *New England Journal of Medicine*, 342(No. 8: 2000), 551-56.

70 *American Journal of Public Health,* cited in the *New York Times*, Jan. 14, 1993.

71 Carol Tauer, "Philosophical Debate and Public Policy on Physician-Assisted Suicide," in *Must We Suffer Our Way to Death,* ed. Ronald Hamel and Edwin DeBose (Dallas: Southern Methodist University Press, 1996), 60.

72 President's Commission for the Study of Ethical Problems in Medicine and Biomedical and Behavioral Research, "Deciding to Forego Life-Sustaining Treatments: A Report on the Medical and Legal Issues in Treatment (Washington: U.S. Government Printing Office, 1983).

73 Congregation for the Doctrine of the Faith, *Declaration on Euthanasia* (May, 1980).

74 May, *The Physician's Covenant*, 76.

75 Pope Pius XII, "The Prolongation of Life," *The Pope Speaks*, 4(No. 4: Spring, 1958), 395-96.

76 Peter Singer, *Rethinking Life and Death* (New York: St. Martin's Press, 1994), 70

77 Daniel Callahan, *The Troubled Dream of Life* (New York: Simon and Schuster, 1993), 81.

78 Mildred Solomon and Others, "Decisions Near the End of Life: Professional Views of Life-Sustaining Treatment," *American Journal of Public Health* 83(1993), 14-17.

79 Cathy Siebold, *The Hospice Movement* (New York: Twayne Publishers, 1992), 48.

80 Solomon and Others, "Decisions Near the End of Life: Professional Views of Life-Sustaining Treatment," 33: "Eighty percent of physicians agreed that "all competent patients have the right to refuse life-support, even if that refusal may lead to death. However, the wishes of patients often go unrecognized."

81 *New York Times,* Oct. 18, 1994.

82 Interview on the ABC Television program 20/20, Dec. 5, 1985.

83 Stephen Carter, *The Culture of Disbelief* (New York: Basic Books, 1993), 242-43.

84 Ronald Dworkin, "What the Court Really Said," *New York Review of Books*, Aug. 8, 1996.

85 Jonathan Glover, *Causing Death and Saving Lives* (New York: Viking, 1990), 166.

86 Burt, *Death Is That Man Taking Names*, 163, 167.

87 *Washington v. Glucksberg*, 1997, 117 S. Ct 2258; *Vacco v. Quill*, 1997, S. Court, 2258.

88 Dworkin, "What the Court Really Said."

89 Burt, *Death Is That Man Taking Names*, 116.

90 *New York Times,* June 27, 1997, A 18.

91 Thomas Lynch, *The Undertaking: Life Studies from the Dismal Trade* (New York: W. W. Norton, 1999), 170-71, asks the ironic question: "Why not a pearl-handled, silver-bulleted, hair-triggered, 22 caliber Smith & Wesson? Pressed under the right earlobe, the entrance wound is tiny, the severance of the spinal cord is immediate and humane, and the exit wound, if there is any, leaves no mess at all."

92 *New York Times*, Dec. 9, 1990.

93 William May in *Must We Suffer Our Way to Death*, 105.

94 Chapter Six

Albert Camus, *The Myth of Sisyphus* (New York:Vintage Books, 1955), 3.

95 *The Surgeon General's Call to Action to Prevent Suicide* (Washington: U.S. Public Health Service, 1999), 3.

96 *Oxford English Dictionary,* 3145.

97 John Donne, *Biathanatos* (Dover: University of Delaware Press, 1974).

98 Anthony Flew suggests that the use of "commit" with suicide signals the act as negative; Daniel Maguire, *Death by Choice* (Garden City: Doubleday, 1984), 183.

99 For historical studies, Alexander Murray, *Suicide in the Middle Ages* (New York: Oxford University Press, 1999); Georges Minois, *A History of Suicide* (Baltimore: Johns Hopkins University Press, 1998); for the medical side of suicide, Kay Redford Jamison, *Night Falls Fast* (New York: Knopf, 1999); for philosophical and psychological insight, James Hillman, *Suicide and the Soul* (New York: Harper, 1975).

100 G.K. Chesterton, *Orthodoxy* (Garden City: Image Books, 1959), 73.

101 Augustine of Hippo, *City of God* (Hyde Park: New City Press, 2001).

102 Alfred Alvarez, *The Savage God* (New York: Random House, 1970), 52.

103 M.T. Clancy, "Review of Alexander Murray, *Suicide in the Middle Ages*," in *Times Literary Supplement,* April 2, 1999, 14.

104 Minois, A History of Suicide.

105 Jamison, *Night Falls Fast*, 18.

106 Jamison, *Night Falls Fast.*, 17.

107 Jamison, *Night Falls Fast.*, 100.

108 Maurice Lamm, *The Jewish Way in Death and Mourning* (New York: Jonathan David, 1969), 217.

109 Hillman, *Suicide and the Soul*, 30.

110 Margaret Pabst Battin, *Ethical Issues in Suicide* (Englewood Cliffs: Prentice Hall, 1982), 55.

111 Battin, *Ethical Issues in Suicide*, 63

112 Hillman, Suicide and the Soul, 60.

113 Alexander Murray, *Suicide in the Middle Ages*.

114 Emile Durkheim, *Suicide* (New York: Free Press, 1951(1897)).

115 Hillman, *Suicide and the Soul*, 63.

116 Hillman, *Suicide and the Soul*, 70.

117 Karl Menninger, *Man Against Himself* (New York: Harcourt, Brace, 1938); Edwin Shneidman, *Definitions of Suicide* (New York: John Wiley, 1985), 21.

118 R. A. Moody, *Life after Life* (New York: Bantam, 1975), Afterword.

119 Hillman, *Suicide and the Soul*, 73.

120 Robert Neale, *The Art of Dying*, (New York: Harper and Row, 1973), 63.

121 Neale, *The Art of Dying,* 68.

122 Elisabeth Kübler-Ross, *On Life after Death* (New York: Celestial Arts, 1991), 18.

123 Carlos Gomez, *Regulating Death: Euthanasia and the Case of the Netherlands* (New York: Free Press, 1991); Johanna Groenewoud and others, "Clinical Problems with the Performance of Euthanasia and Physician-Assisted Suicide in the Netherlands," *New England Journal of Medicine,* 342, (No.8, 2000), 551-56.

124 "Meddling with Oregon's Law," *New York Times*, (Oct. 30, 1999), Editorial page.

125 "Aborigines Fear Euthanasia May Be Legal Suicide," *The Australian*, August 4, 1996.

126 Nuland, *How We Die*, 152.

127 D. J. West, *Murder Followed by Suicide* (London: Heinemann, 1965), 150.

128 The phrase "temporarily abled" is a useful reminder by the writer Reynolds Price. His book, *A Whole New Life: An Illness and a Healing* (New York: Scribner's, 2003), is his beautiful account of life as a paraplegic.

129 Quoted in Daniel Maguire, *Death by Choice*, 2nd ed. (Garden City: Doubleday, 1984), 3.

130 Chapter Seven
Sigmund Freud, "Mourning and Melancholy," *Standard Edition of the Complete Psychological Works of Sigmund Freud* (London: W.W. Norton, 1953-74), vol. XIV, 244.

131 Geoffrey Gorer, *Death Grief and Mourning* (New York: Ayer, 1979), 128.

132 Jessica Mitford, *The American Way of Death* (New York: Simon and Schuster, 1963); also, Jessica Mitford, *The American Way of Death Revisited* (New York: Knopf, 1998).

133 *New York Times*, Nov. 11, 2000.

134 Philippe Ariès, *The Hour of Our Death* (New York: Vintage Books, 1982), 550-51.

135 Robert Burt, *Death is That Man Taking Names* (Berkeley: University of California Press, 2002), 64, points out that the Civil War memorial at Yale University that inspired the Vietnam memorial took fifty years to be built and dedicated. There was controversy over whether its praise of devotion and unity should include Confederate as well as Union soldiers.

The Vietnam memorial could be constructed quickly because it does not ascribe any meaning to the deaths.

136 Laurie Kellman, "Vietnam Memorial Still Heals Wounds," Associated Press Online, July 19, 2002

137 *New York Times,* Nov. 11, 1987

138 Jack Hitt, "The American Way of Dealing with Death," *New York Times*, August 18, 2002, 4.

139 Samuel Heilman, *When a Jew Dies* (Berkeley: University of California Press, 2001).

140 Harold Kushner, *When Bad Things Happen to Good People* (New York: Avon Books, 1981), 89.

141 Kushner, *When Bad Things Happen*., 88-90

142 Bronislaw Malinowski, "The Problem of Meaning in Primitive Languages," in C.K. Ogden and I.A. Richards, *The Meaning of Meaning* (New York: Harcourt, Brace, Jovanovich, 1989, 315.

143 Simon Leys, *The Analects of Confucius* (New York: W.W. Norton, 1997),19:17.

144 James Atlas, *New Yorker,* Oct. 13, 1997

145 C.S. Lewis, *A Grief Observed* (New York: Bantam Books, 1976), 61: "To say that the patient is getting over it after an operation for appendicitis is one thing; after he's had his leg off quite another. After that operation, either the wounded stump heals or the man dies. If it heals, the fierce continuous pain will stop. Presently, he'll get back his strength and be able to stump about on his wooden leg. He has 'got over it'. But he will probably have recurrent pains in the stump all his life...and he will always be a one-legged man."

146 Judith Cook, "A Death in the Family: Parental Bereavement in the First Year," *Suicide and Life-Threatening Behavior*, 13 (1983), 42-61.

147 Sylvia Rees and Dewi Lutkins, "Mortality of Bereavement," *British Medical Journal*, October, 1967.

148 Arnold van Gennep, *Rites of Passage* (Chicago: University of Chicago Press, 1960), 146-65.

149 Robert Hertz, *Death and the Right Hand* (Aberdeen: Cohen and West, 1960), 86: "Mourning, at its origin, is the necessary participation of the living in the mortuary state of their relative."

150 Richard Huntington and Peter Metcalf, *Celebrations of Death* (Cambridge: Cambridge University Press, 1979), 93-118.

151 Kübler-Ross, *On Death and Dying,* 112.

152 John Mbiti, *African Religions and Philosophy* (Garden City: Anchor Books, 1970), 33.

153 Erich Lindemann, "Symptomatology and Management of Acute Grief," *American Journal of Psychiatry*, 101(1944), 148.

154 For a positive view of the whole process, see Thomas Lynch, *The Undertaking* (New York: W.W. Norton, 1997).

155 Mark Twain, *The Autobiography of Mark Twain*, ed. Charles Neider (New York: Harper, 2000).

156 For the proposed revisions of the "DSM," see www. dsm5.org.

157 Although Jewish tradition warns against excessive weeping, the Talmud also says that anyone who cries at the death of a good person is forgiven all his sins; *Shabbat 105b*. See also *The Tibetan Book of the Dead,* ed. W. Evans-Wentz (New York: Oxford University Press, 1960), 87, 195.

158 C .S. Lewis, *A Grief Observed*, 69: "Grief is like a long valley, a winding valley where any bend may reveal a totally new landscape....Sometimes the surprise is the opposite one; you are presented with exactly the same sort of country you thought you had left behind miles ago. That is when you wonder whether the valley isn't a circular trench. But it isn't. There are partial recurrences but the sequence doesn't repeat."

159 Rees and Lutkins, "Mortality of Bereavement."

160 Robert Kavanaugh, *Facing Death* (New York: Penguin Books, 1972).

161 Mircea Eliade, *The Myth of the Eternal Return* (Princeton: Princeton University Press, 1954), 51-92.

Chapter Eight

162 Hayim Perelmuter, *Siblings: Rabbinic Judaism and Early Christianity at their Beginnings* (New York: Paulist Press, 1989); on the close relation of early Christianity and Judaism, see Daniel Boyarin, *Dying for God: Martyrdom in the Making of Christianity and Judaism* (Stanford: Stanford University Press, 1999).

163 Arthur Cohen, *The Myth of the Judeo-Christian Tradition* (New York: Harper and Row, 1970), xviii.

164 Elie Wiesel, *Messengers of God* (New York: Simon and Schuster, 1976), 76.

165 Friedrich Nietzsche, *Genealogy of Morals* (Garden City: Doubleday, 1956).

166 Wayne Meeks, *The Moral World of the First Christians* (Philadelphia: Westminster Press, 1986), 40.

167 Gerard van der Leeuw, *Religion in Essence and Manifestation* (Gloucester: Peter Smith, 1967), 112.

168 Elisabeth Kübler-Ross, *Questions and Answers on Death and Dying* (New York: Collier Books, 1974), 162.

169 Tertullian, *Apology*, 39.2; 32.1.

170 In 2003, the Vatican's Order of Christian Funerals approved the U.S. guidelines that include a friend or family member speaking at the funeral mass after the communion; New York *Times*, January 23, 2003, 5.

171 David Stannard, *The Puritan Way of Death: A Study in Religion, Culture and Social Change* (New York: Oxford University Press, 1997).

172 Karl Rahner, *Belief Today* (New York: Sheed and Ward, 1967), 111.

173 Karl Rahner, *Christianity at the Crossroads* (London: Burns and Oates, 1999), 23.

174 Nicholas Lash, *Easter in Ordinary* (Charlottesville: University of Virginia Press, 1988), 265.

175 175 Maimonides, *Guide of the Perplexed*, cited in Gershom Scholem, *Major Trends in Jewish Mysticism* (New York: Schocken Books, 1941), 11.

176 Thomas Aquinas, *Summa Theologia*, 1.1.3.

177 Frank Tobin, *Meister Eckhart: Thought and Language* (Philadelphia: University of Pennsylvania Press, 1986), 86.

178 *The Nicene and Post-Nicene Fathers*, Series 2, Vol. 14 (Grand Rapids: Eerdmans, 1956), 318.

179 Christians who believe that abortion is the taking of human life would seem to need a doctrine of reincarnation.

180 Hebert McCabe, *What is Ethics All About?* (Washington: Corpus Books, 1969), 142.

181 Joseph Sittler, *Ecology of Faith* (Minneapolis: Muhlenberg, 1961), 40.

182 Peter Selby, *Look for the Living* (Philadelphia: Fortress Press, 1976), 179.

183 Lionel Blue, *To Heaven with Scribes and Pharisees* (New York: Oxford University Press, 1976).

184 Gerard Sloyan, *Jesus in Focus* (Mystic: Twenty-Third Publication, 1980), 146.

185 Karl Rahner, *Foundations of Christian Faith* (New York: Seabury Press), 436; see also Paul Tillich, *Systematic Theology* (Chicago: University of Chicago Press, 1963) III, 416.

186 Robert Wilken, "The Immortality of the Soul and Christian Hope," *Dialog* (Spring, 1976), 110-17. Jaroslav Pelikan, *The Christian Tradition: The Emergence of the Catholic Tradition* (Chicago: University of Chicago Press, 1971), 51: "The idea of the immortality of the soul came eventually to be identified with the Biblical doctrine of the resurrection of the body, a doctrine one of whose original targets was the immortality of the soul."

187 Oscar Cullman, "Immortality of the Soul or Resurrection of the Dead?" in *Immortality and Resurrection*, ed. Krister Stendahl (New York: Macmillan, 1965), 9-53; John Hick, *Death and Eternal Life* (San Francisco: Harper and Row, 1976), 180.

188 Tertullian seems to have been the first to refer to an interim state between individual death and the last day; see Jeffrey Russell, *A History of Heaven* (Princeton: Princeton University Press, 1997), 67.

189 The lines are from the medieval hymn, *Dies Irae*.

190 Philippe Ariès, *The Hour of Our Death* (New York: Vintage Books, 1982), 31.

191 Ariès, *The Hour of Our Death*, 36.

192 Ladislaus Boros, *The Mystery of Death* (New York: Herder and Herder, 1965); Karl Rahner, *Theology of Death* (New York: Herder and Herder, 1961).

193 William Lynch, *Images of Hope* (Baltimore: Helicon, 1965), 108.

194 Jacques Le Goff, *The Birth of Purgatory* (Chicago: University of Chicago Press, 1984).

195 Hick, *Death and Eternal Life,* 202.

196 Jerry Walls, *Hell: The Logic of Damnation* (Notre Dame: University of Notre Dame Press, 1992), 154; Jonathan Edwards, *The Works of Jonathan Edwards* (New Haven: Yale University Press, 1957), 7: 504-05.

197 Wayne Meeks, *The Origin of Christian Morality: The First Two Centuries* (New Haven: Yale University Press, 1993), 176.

198 Augustine, *Commentary on the Gospel of Mark*; John Wesley, *The Works of John Wesley* (Nashville: Abingdon Press, 1984), 3:37.

199 Hick, *Death and Eternal Life*, 199.

200 Augustine, *City of God* (Hyde Park: New City Press, 2001), 21:9.

201 Thomas Aquinas, *Summa Theologia,* Suppl. Part III, q.98, a.9.

202 Dante, *Inferno*, Canto 14: 60-63.

203 Milton, *Paradise Lost,* 4:75.

204 George Bernanos, *Diary of a Country Priest* (New York: Macmillan, 1962), 127; Fyodor Dostoevsky, *The Brothers Dostoyevsky* (New York: Signet, 1957), 297.

205 Walls, *Hell*, 150

206 Cited in Morton Kelsey, *Afterlife: The Other Side of Dying* (New York: Crossroad, 1982), 176.

207 *Tibetan Book of the Dead: The Great Book of Liberation through Understanding in the Between* (New York: Bantam Press, 1993).

208 Origen, *First Principles*, 3:1:7.

209 A text in the Qur'an speaks of eternal fire (23:105) but the Qur'an adds "unless God decides differently."(11:09)

210 Hick, *Death and Eternal Life*, 250.

211 Russell, *A History of Heaven*, 85.

212 The Revised Standard Version of the New Testament translates the text as "the kingdom of God is among you."

213 Augustine, *City of God*, 20:7, where he laments the millennialists who are awaiting "the most unrestrained material feasts."

214 *Summa Theologia*, II.II. 12.1-5.

215 Caroline Walker Bynum, *The Resurrection of the Body* (New York: Columbia University Press, 1994), 329.

216 D. T. Suzuki, *Mysticism: Buddhist and Christian* (Westport: Greenwood, 1975).

217 Soren Kierkegaard, *Fear and Trembling; Sickness Unto Death* (Garden City: Doubleday Anchor Books, 1954), 248.

218 Chapter Nine

George Steiner, In Bluebeard's Castle (New Haven: Yale University Press, 1971), 55.

219 Jean Paul Sartre, *The Flies* (New York: Vintage Books, 1989)

220 Leo Tolstoy, *A Confession, The Gospel in Brief and What I Believe* (London: Oxford University Press, 1958), 26.

221 Miguel de Unamuno, *The Tragic Sense of Life* (New York: Dover Publications, 1954), 20.

222 G.K. Chesterton, *Orthodoxy* (Garden City: Doubleday Image), 1959, 148.

223 Samuel Beckett, *Endgame* (New York: Grove Press, 1958), 49, 70.

224 Alfred North Whitehead, *Process and Reality* (New York: Free Press, 1978), 340.

225 W.P. Montague quoted in John Baillie, *And Life Everlasting* (New York: Scribner's, 1933), 192.

226 Edward Schillebeeckx, *Understanding of Faith* (New York: Sheed and Ward, 1974), 12.

227 Chesterton, *Orthodoxy*, 120.

228 Baillie, *And Life Everlasting*, 62.

229 Studies indicate that many well-educated people believe that they are in communication with the dead; see Andrew Greeley, *Death and Beyond* (Chicago: St. Thomas More, 1976).

230 C.S. Lewis, *Essays Presented to Charles Williams* (Grand Rapids: W.B. Eerdmans, 1947), Preface.

231 John Hick, *Death and Eternal Life* (Louisville: Westminster/John Knox, 1994), 62.

232 Cited in Raphael Loewe, *Studies in Rationalism, Judaism and Universalism* (London: Kegan Paul, 1966), 55; Maimonides' statement is in *Mishneh Torah*, XIV, 5,9,1.

233 Milton Steinberg, *Basic Judaism* (New York: Harcourt, Brace, Jovanovich, 1975), 99.

234 Emil Fackenheim, *To Mend the World* (New York: Schocken Books, 1982), 39.

235 Abraham Heschel, "Jewish Education," in *The Insecurity of Freedom* (Philadelphia: Jewish Publication Society, 1966), 119.

236 George Lindbeck, The Nature of Doctrine: Religion and Theology in a Postliberal Age

237 (Louisville: Westminster/John Knox), 2009.

Jeffrey Russell, *A History of Heaven* (Princeton: Princeton University Press, 1994), 128.

238 Augustine, *The Enchiridion on Faith, Hope and Love* (Chicago: Regnery, 1961).

239 Russell, *The History of Heaven,* 128.

240 Gerald O'Collins, *Salvation for God's Other Peoples* (New York: Oxford University Press, 2008), 215-16.

241 Karl Rahner, Christianity and Nonchristian Religions," *Theological Investigations* (Baltimore: Helicon, 1966), 115-34.

242 John Ziesler, *Pauline Christianity* (Oxford: Oxford University Press, 1983), 86.

243 Consultation of the National Council of Synagogues and the Bishops' Committee on Ecumenical and Interreligious Affairs; see *The Hebrew Catholic*, 77(Fall, 2002), 39-47.

244 J. J. Goldberg, "A Counter Revolution in Jewish-Catholic Ties," *The Jewish Daily Forward*, Sept. 4, 2009, 1.

245 *Gates of Prayer* (New York, CCAR Press, 1975), 615.

246 Michael Fishbane, "Torah and Tradition" in *Tradition and Theology in the Old Testament*, ed. Douglas Knight (Philadelphia: Fortress, 1977), 278 calls this "the most extreme transposition of a national historical memory conceivable."

247 C. G. Montifiore and H.Loewe, *The Rabbinic Anthology* (New York: Schocken Books, 1970), 52.

248 Cohen in *Studies in Rationalism, Judaism and Universalism*, 63.

249 Michael Rosenak, *Commandment and Concerns: Jewish Religious Education in Secular Society* (Philadelphia: Jewish Publication Society, 1987), 90.

250 Frank Crusemann, *The Torah: Theology and Social History of Old Testament Law* (Philadelphia: Fortress Press, 1996), 9; *Mekita Bahodesh,* 5.

251 Jonathan Bishop, *The Covenant: A Reading* (Springfield: Templegate, 1983), 40.

252 S.H. Nasr, *Ideals and Realities of Islam* (Boston: Beacon Press, 1972), 86.

253 Nasr, *Ideals and Realities of Islam,* 130.

254 Khaled Abou El Fadl, *The Place of Tolerance in Islam* (Boston: Beacon Press, 2002)

255 Karl Rahner, *The Theology of Death* (New York: Herder and Herder, 1961).

256 On the origin of "Christian revelation," see Gabriel Moran, *Both Sides: The Story of Revelation* (New York: Paulist Press, 2002), chapter 4.

257 William Temple, *Nature, Man and God* (London: Macmillan, 1951), 306.

258 Victor Frankl, *Man's Search for Meaning* (Boston: Beacon Press, 2006), 68-69; Eliezer Berkovitz, *With God in Hell* (New York: Sandhedrin, 1979), 69.

259 William Temple, *Nature, Man and God*, 306.

260 Kübler-Ross, *On Death and Dying*, 1969), 276.

261 William Ernest Hocking, *Living Religions and a World Faith* (New York: Macmillan, 1940), 57.

262 Paul Knitter, *No Other Name* (New York: Orbis Books, 1985), 186.

263 Plato, Apology, 38c-42a.

264 Plato, *The Republic,* 588c-590a.

265 Robert Herford, *The Pharisees* (Boston: Beacon Press, 1962), 155. There are two inclinations or impulses: *yetzer hara* and *yetzer hatob.* Sometimes *yetzer hara* is said to be the source of evil. More accurately, the two have to be held in tension, similar to Plato's lion and hydra.

266 C.F. Kelly, *Meister Eckhart on Divine Knowledge* (New Haven: Yale University Press, 1977).

3469243R00122

Made in the USA
San Bernardino, CA
04 August 2013